RECOVERING MY VOICE
A Memoir of Chaos, Spirituality, and Hope

RECOVERING MY VOICE

A Memoir of Chaos, Spirituality, and Hope

By ARUNI NAN FUTURONSKY

iUniverse, Inc.

New York   Bloomington

Recovering My Voice:

A Memoir of Chaos, Spirituality, and Hope

iUniverse books may be ordered through booksellers or by contacting:

iUniverse
1663 Liberty Drive
Bloomington, IN 47403
www.iuniverse.com
1-800-Authors (1-800-288-4677)

ISBN: 978-1-440-10988-1 (pbk)
ISBN: 978-1-440-10989-8 (ebk)

Printed in the United States of America

iUniverse rev. date: 12/4/2008

Contents

PART FOUR: OPENING

PART FIVE: SURRENDERING

Gratitudes

I am profoundly grateful for:

Dearest Audrey—friend, sister, advisor, coach, shiny mirror of my Self. Your wild belief in me and your committed willingness to hold me accountable are pillars of my growth. Without you this would not have happened. Beyond thank you.

Dearest Michael—perfect person, in the perfect place. Thank you.

Dearest Kavi—for support of all shapes and forms, forever. Thank you.

Dearest Derek—for your visual brilliance and your love of God. Thank you.

Dearest Adam—for decades of love and support, with decades up ahead. Thank you.

Dearest Bree—cheerleader, coach, therapist, advisor, muse, supporter, editor. Brilliance disguised as youth. I am forever grateful. You have allowed me to be me. Thank you, always and always, thank you.

Dearest Ras—for patience, for laughs, for growth, for warmth, for tears, for home. Finally, for home. For all the ways you allow me to be who I am and for all the ways you insist that I continue to grow, I thank you.

To all—I am blessed by your love and support.

Author's Note

This memoir is a work of creative non-fiction. The events described are remembered through the filters of time, memory, and my own recollections. Some timelines have been altered; some characters are composites. Together, they accurately reflect my experiences as I offer them to you.

PART ONE: STRUGGLING

1. Haven
1954

It seemed as if I had been traveling forever. The car trip between my childhood home in Scranton, Pennsylvania, and our yearly summer vacation in Beach Haven, New Jersey, was an endless unraveling ribbon of highway after yet another highway. Change in pavement sounds announced a shift in the road, each one weaving us closer to the prize: the ocean. Different sights appeared on the side of the road signaling geographic advancement—the dirt on the shoulder became more and more sandy, and the blueberry vendors, selling crates of plump, purpled berries out of their cars, their hand-painted signs reading "Jersey Berries," rendered me almost giddy. New Jersey! We were getting there.

Yet there was no marker of our progress so exciting as the smell of the ocean. It tickled my nose, smelling like nothing else on earth, a salt-heavy smell that translated into freedom, play, and open space. As we made our way across the causeway onto the island, my sister L. and I would play our ritualistic game: Did you smell it? Was that the ocean? Who smelled it first? I did, not you! Grasping it into me, gasping it into me, breathing it into my cells, the smell of the ocean was the key that magically clicked opened the doors of my barred heart to the heat and possibility of summer.

We stayed every summer for a week in the Sierra Motel, tucked on the quiet little corner of Ocean and Amber Streets. The two-room suite was musty and darkish, always a little sandy and gritty no matter how Mommy cleaned, and completely inconsequential to my experience. For me the experience was outside. To our right was the thrill of beach and ocean. Behind and all around us were my beloved dunes, sculpted mounds of sand shifting and changing in the wind, dotted with tall, skinny dune grasses that stung my legs as my six-year-old body ran through them on great adventure and magical exploration. The sand dunes were home of great and fantastic fantasy for me, land of pirates and sunken ships, of treasures and the forbidden kisses of ladies.

I came alive at the beach. Its scent, its movement of breezes, the call of the waves, the power of the sun, all released me from my childhood fears and numbness, springing me into aliveness.

The four of us, Daddy, Mommy, L., and I, would hike down to the beach in the morning, not wearing shoes—we didn't have to wear shoes very much on the island, a tantalizing part of the journey for me. We were a caravan of excitement and accoutrements: folding chairs that captured damp sand between their blue and red webbing, snacks mommy made safely stored in the red plastic cooler—peanut butter and jelly sandwiches without the crust, especially for me, plums purple with juicy ripeness, and sweating cans of diet soda—varieties of suntan lotion, water, my essential kite, toy buckets and my trusty shovel, the too-heavy blanket, and our beach umbrella, which fascinated me. The umbrella was made of green and white canvas panels with a heavy wooden pole. Daddy would have to wiggle it and wiggle it from side to side, urging its way into the sand. I occasionally appreciated the shade it offered out to us, a brief yet essential contrast from the unstoppable sun.

We would sit, play, nap, rest, and talk as the hours peeled away, as the power of the shore saturated me. And I would play in the ocean.

The ocean was always my friend, playing with me, mesmerizing me with its rhythms, its sounds. We played so many games together, the ocean and I. One game was jumping the waves (here it comes, it's a big one, can I get over it, spring up, jump!). Another more dangerous one was diving into waves (woosh, right into the center of the chaos of water I go, so bravely daring to be swirled by the churning, almost-dangerous movement). Even at night, lying in bed, still the ocean was my companion, duplicating the feelings of movement, of pull-push, of alive nature (I'm in bed, but I'm in the ocean! I feel the waves). I knew I was particularly skillful in regard to this ocean, my young body-blood and the ocean already in a synchronistic rhythm. This I knew to be true.

Finally my mommy would walk down to the shoreline, hands on her hips, her brunette hair swept back with a clip, and announce to me, "Nan, your lips are blue! That's enough for now. Come out now." And I would begrudgingly make my way back to the blanket, shivering inside the terry towel she wrapped around me, her hand on my back, guiding me. Eventually the noon siren would announce midday, and we would unhappily trek back to the room for an anticlimactic lunch, only to return later, savoring the games and rituals and all the ways of being together that this haven offered us.

I remember one particular morning walking along the shoreline with my mommy. The day was young, the hum of ocean already circulating inside my head. I knew having this time alone with her was an unusual gift. How odd it was that she wasn't doing something, making something happen, taking care of some problem. No, not on this day. On this day we just walked together, together yet apart, my mommy in her separateness, me in my six-year-old body. She was so close to me—right there—yet so strangely distant and unattainable. Like a fierce momma-bear at the mouth of her cave—that was my mommy. But a busy momma-bear, a distracted momma-bear, a bear whose heart looked elsewhere. What did she look for? For danger? For her mate? To protect those she loved?

We walked and walked, Mommy on my right, sun over her shoulder, ocean to my left, my always companion. The world stopped in this memory; there was nothing to distract us. There was no grocery store, where she and Daddy worked so hard (for me, it was always for me), none of Daddy's menacing and terrifying chest pains, no errands to run, always running errands was my mommy. Always moving, always doing, always thinking ahead and taking care of us all—that was my mommy, my beautiful, slim, dark-haired mommy, quiet and strong. No, not now. On this simple strand of beach, on this particular summer morning, on this journey of daughter/motherhood, there was only sand and salt and ocean and mother and daughter and sun. The ever present, ever powerful sun painted my body brown—"like a paint brush," Mommy used to say, for which I was always so secretly proud, my copper badge of summer.

As we walked, a game emerged for me, a game of heel-and-sand, a game of weight-and-balance, as my heel-print miraculously appeared on the damp sand beneath me. If I walked just right, with just the right weight of heel, of speed, in just the right spot of dampness, a circle magically materialized around my footstep, a circle of presence, a circle of me. My mark. Challenges appeared everywhere now: to keep up with my mommy's uncompromising gait, to keep my balance while walking on my heels, to find just the right spot of dampness. And most of all, to hide my game from her, for it was my game and somehow it might annoy her. All these challenges needed my attentive focus. It was a delicious game that called me to full liveliness.

Mommy kept on walking. Her offering was this silent presence that carried with it a strange absence, an emotional distance, a distracted focus that would chill my heart and drive me inside myself throughout my life. For how many years would I struggle to make her different? For how many years would I declare her wrong inside my head and will her to be a regular mommy, cooking and baking and caring for me, only me? For how many years did I decry her working, her rushing, her serving other kids' parents? For how many years did I resist her cool, loving attention? For how many years did I silently rail against her, to allow me to be the child, not him, not Daddy? I wanted the essence of her heart, never realizing it was right there for the taking.

And it will take what it will take. It will take my leaving, my sliding into my own darkness; it will take his dying, my growing up, her grieving, for us to know, to really know each other. And it will end on that exquisite and excruciating evening when I sit next to her, and witness her final breath, as she had witnessed my first; as I hold open the gates for her leaving, as she once welcomed my coming. It will take what it will take.

But for now we walk, me in my private game, her in her perfect stride. Heel-prints marked my presence and faded instantly, disappearing into the dryness of the magical sand. And then I noticed the miracle— my mommy's shadow, thrown over me, from right to left, covering my walking, bigger than and encompassing my body. My mommy's shadow swept over me, extending long and strong and big across the sand, touching into the ocean. And in that instant, I knew that I had her, always and now and forever, like I had the surge of waves inside of me. I had my mommy's presence to be drawn upon, here, now, always.

Back to our blanket and chairs we hiked, the moment evaporating, my six-year-old epiphany diving deep inside, to hibernate inside the corners of my heart.

The rest of the week unfolded in images of precious summer: walking barefoot to the drug store just as the light began to leave the day, to get drippy coffee ice cream cones—eat them fast before they melt!; swimming lessons with the lifeguard and his girlfriend, their wood-paneled car that took me and other faceless kids to the mosquito-y bay to swim; the lifeguard's girlfriend with the long willowy legs holding me afloat, one hand on my belly and one on my back, my heart lurching open to her presence, to her touch; watching daddy eat oysters at the greasy clam bar, sitting on the stool next to him cracking oyster crackers open with one clean and severing bite.

Endless memories of light and love and ease that ended, faded in a week's time.

Over the causeway we drove, quiet now in our leaving, our haven behind us, looking inside and not outside now. I was driving back to that city where I did not fit, back to that school where I could not talk, back to that life where I was not enough. These realizations were so confusingly painful that all I could do was close my eyes, huddled into the corner of the back seat, and listen to the roar of ocean that lived inside my head. Folded into the seat, with eyelids heavy, I napped, disguised to myself as a child.

"Like a fierce momma bear…"
Mom and me.

"The thrill of the beach and the ocean."

Precious Beach Haven with Mom and Dad

2. John Jay Audubon #42
1958

His name was Mr. Cafferty. His glasses were exaggerated coke-bottle lenses, making his eyes appear bug-like and somewhat terrifying—the frames were black and thick and appallingly uncool. Dandruff seemed to always speckle his suit jacket, a fact that grossed out us sixth graders. He reeked of an unfamiliar and nauseating odor—it was like a sour cheese, or something yucky. "It's Roquefort," suggests Terri Ziman, cool and popular Terri, my sometimes-but-not-really friend. I heartily agreed, even though I did not know that cheese, had never smelled or tasted it. We ate Kraft Swiss individually wrapped singles in our family, or maybe sometimes wedges of spongy and yellowed Munster.

The previous summer had just come to an end, a roasting summer, and I had loved playing in the attic by myself with Kraft Swiss single cheese slices and tiny Dixie cups of milk. I was pretending to be Heidi, lucky, lucky Heidi—to live in the Alps, to have such a grandfather. I lived in Scranton, Pennsylvania. There were no Alps, no chances for adventure, no loving grandfather with a white beard. My grandfather scared me. He smelled of old cigar smoke and his cheeks were rough with unshaven, darkened stubble. He teased me, chased me with his insulin needles around my grandmother's tiny linoleumed kitchen. No, no Alps here, no white-bearded grandfather. But my Heidi game was fun and, oh, such a secret. Slices of cheese, the waxy quart of milk container, the individual American cheese slices snuck up to the attic, under my *John Jay Audubon School #42* t-shirt, bulging under its blue-jay mascot. I nibbled cheese and contentedly drank my milk, my increasing dairy intake transporting me into the world of Heidi, a world of cool peaks and good outcome, just like in the beautiful large

9

picture book. Only fake-Heidi here, only play-Heidi, hide, don't let them know Heidi, never let them know Heidi. Somehow, even Heidi was wrong, relegated to the world of secrecy, where I, my entire ten-year-old self, most fully resided. A place where outcome could not be good.

John Jay Audubon #42. That was our school, a fortress resting high up on the hill at the intersection of Colfax Avenue and Mulberry Street. The halls were dark and cavernous and echo-y, the floors treacherously waxed, the classrooms pea green with a lingering scent of disinfectant and ancient fear and pee. I sat in Mr. Cafferty's class—on the second floor now that I was in sixth grade, now that I was older. I didn't feel older. My stomach hurt, my eyes burned. I wanted to run, to return to a silent and private fantasy somewhere, somewhere else—a game, a privately constructed world, somewhere alone. I wanted to go home, to be alone in the silence of our house—no mother, working, always working—no father, always working—no sister, off being social, off being cool. Only me and my fantasies: Heidi, the Alps, the stories I wrote in my head, the worlds I created. Off to the bike I rode ritualistically around and around the band-shell in the park, pretending to be a Canadian Mountie—my bike a trusty steed, off to get my woman, off to save the heroine, off to save the day. Off, to save.

The desk made my petticoat itch. It gathered around my waste and scratched at my emerging girl skin. There was a scab on my left ankle bone from falling off my bike the week before. I tried to itch it with my opposite saddle shoe, somehow intensifying the sensation. The flat part of the desk hinged open, revealing a cavernous space for storing books—did anybody ever really use it? My books sat next to me, safely ensconced in my red plaid bookbag, of which I was secretly proud. It was dank in that desk thingy, hinting of hidden and sticky prehistoric candies. The inkwell was an ancient thing too, obsolete in the world of Bic pens. I loved my cartridge pen, not Bic, never Bic. I used only clear cartridge pens with dark black ink, a "bold" point, thicker and bolder, better to write my stories with. I always picked black ink and bold point. Around this inkwell words, names, and echoes of the past were carved. "Fred Sat Here," and some ancient initials. I ran my finger around its rim, hoping to stir, like a crystal ball, an opening, an escape, an exit from this moment.

Mr. Cafferty's monotone voice droned on. My level of attention and alertness was in low-gear—I could tell from his rhythm that I was safe for now, no class participation. He was teaching, talking and talking. My attention faded and, although my antenna was always up, sleepiness nevertheless entered my eyes. It was warm, I was sticky and alone and deeply, deeply bored. Back in school after a summer at camp—back in school after a summer of green, a summer of kind, attentive counselors, of waterfront, of sports. A summer of connection and possibility, of the healing and all-encompassing love of women.

In an instant shimmer, like a flash of the heat lightning my daddy and I watched this summer, I knew it had all changed around me. I bolted upright in my chair, startled back into the humid moment. We were going around the room, reading from the English book, each student in turn reading a verse of the poem. Adrenalin like electricity surged through me. My breath caught, slowed, almost stopped, then sped up, like a speedboat, like Kenny my cousin's speedboat—sweat beaded my neck, my hairline, my hands. I fumbled with the book, searching for the right page. There it was, page 57—*The Highwayman*, by Alfred Noyes. Oh, God, oh, no, oh, which verse will be mine? Which words will I have to say?

The words hovered in the air threateningly:

> *"….a torrent of darkness…amongst the gusty trees…*
> *….ribbon of moonlight…over the purple moor….."*

I privately and frantically counted—how many kids between me and the reading, how many kids per row, how many rows? If everyone read one stanza, where did that leave me? Eight. I counted eight kids between me and doom, sweaty, embarrassed doom. Eight verses. Let me see:

> *"….spurred….like a madman…shrieking a curse to the sky…"*

Oh! I couldn't say that *s* sound. I knew I couldn't. *S* sounds were my death knell, the nails of my public coffin. I couldn't, I couldn't, I knew I couldn't. It was coming closer.

My row now, oh no! Ohno. Maybe the earth would open up, maybe the desk would swallow me, maybe there would be an air raid and we would have to hide under the desks in case of nuclear attack. Maybe... two now, and now, one, only one, the girl in front of me, Caroline with the pig tails and the red silly ribbons, red with white blobby dots. I stared and stared at the ribbons, willing myself to speech, willing myself to death, willing myself to oblivion, to invisibility.

It didn't work. My turn now. Deep silence swallowed the classroom, a gurgle arose in my throat, a bubble of sound wanting to explode. It came out too loud, explosive, meaningless, wordless sounds—sounds of deep and dark shame, sounds of stuttering, sounds of a stupidness and difference. No words, just babble. I tried again, like that speedboat, revving the engine fruitlessly and hopelessly alone, shrouded in sweat. I sat, and I died. I died a thousand deaths in those few moments.

My memory blanks—I am lost again to myself. What happens? Do kids really laugh? Does the teacher intervene, with kindness and appropriate attention? No, not him, not then. Only one single teacher, from grades first to final, had the skillful kindness to respond to me appropriately in those inevitable intersections of terror and trauma and isolated shame. Mrs. Horger, my sophomore English teacher, who Mommy talked to—oh, such shame! In her cool distant detachment, she was a balm of comfort, guiding the reading students over me, mercifully skipping me. I became an English teacher years later in the memory of her calm presence.

Somehow this moment ended. Somehow the poem continued, following the highwayman to his doom, too. Somehow I returned again to my self, my sweaty young girl self.

How many times did this moment reoccur? From the first to the final grade, from the kindergarten floor to the college classroom, from my tiny child's body to my coed self, I was confronted over and endlessly over again with the need to speak, to read, to perform on demand. To read the words as they were given, without the profound power of synonym-creating, at which I excelled—I knew how to speak around things, to hide safely in easier, more count-on-able words. I was forever confronted with the spotlight of attention, to speak. And I just could not. The words were stuck, the syllables frozen, the sentences blocked in my throat. Why? Too much too say? Too hard to say it? What was there to say, anyway, about all of this? This school, this building, these people who did not, could not, would never be able to know me. What is worth saying, anyway?

I left limp, freed at the 3:30 bell, eyes averted from others. I allowed myself to be pushed toward the door, book bag in hand, its heavy weight the only thing keeping me on the earth. Knees weak, legs stumbling, I walked, skipped, and fled down the block to the store, my daddy's store. There he stood, my hero, my friend, my all-loving heart, my daddy. Hands on hips, white full apron covering his khakis and his sleeveless sweater vest, soft smile welcoming me. But even with him I could not share this. Even with him I could not speak the shame. He had learned to ignore it. "Just ignore it," the doctor said to them, Dr. Coffin, the throat man, who smelled of bad cigars, too, and talked about me as if I were not even there. "Just ignore it."

So ignore it we did, while in every syllable there lived an explosive threat, every phone ring a confrontation, every teacher a potential enemy, every word a landmine, waiting to explode open my heart, to leave me bared, to leave me seared, to leave me: alone, in my shame.

"What is worth saying, anyway?"

3. The Colfax Market
1956

I remember my father's store with a surprising sharpness of vision. On a slide and a breath and an instant: I am eight years old. I walk the aisles, touch the cereal boxes, feel the chill of the neat stacks of frozen food with ghostly fingers of memory. This place lives as a home in my heart, a home so much more beckoning than our real house—this was the core, the center of my childhood.

On one special day, I walked from home the three blocks to the store where my parents were working. I played my favorite walking game: *step on a crack, break your mother's back.* I hummed its mantra, its intent. My high-top black sneakers agilely dodged the cracks—my form of hop scotch. Real hop scotch was too scary, too competitive, too girly for me. But alone I was a star. I was an athlete and a marathon runner, just like those runners we used to watch on television. I still lived within this body; I still moved and breathed a living animal. Trauma has not yet yanked me fully away from my own self. The cracks were beginning, the disconnect starting. But not now—now I hopped, I leaped, I jumped, I dared to play this game well.

The game faded as I crossed the sleepy intersection of Colfax Avenue and Linden Street. The store stood on the corner, as it had since my grandfather's day, as it would for so many more years ahead. It was an offering, a permanent fixture in this residential neighborhood. It was one-leveled and brick, with new glass windows in the front and block-lettered, stenciled signs announcing the specials of the week:

Ground Beef .69 Cents a Pound

Green Beans Three Cans for .62 Cents

Pulling the metal door handle open, the world unfolded unto me.

My mother stood at the register, my strong, beautiful, and quiet mother, so undemonstrative and so contained, ringing up an order. The customer's face before her was a blur. But my mother's posture—oh, her posture was unforgettable. Upright and focused she stood, almost overly determined, working, always working, framed by the cigarettes rowed in neat stacks above the register and the candy layered on shelves behind her. To all that she did she brought this focus, this intent. She saw me, nodded and acknowledged me, and offered some greeting. But the focus, ah, the focus. The focus was not on me.

I wandered aimlessly down the first aisle—produce case to my right, celery at attention, carrots wrapped like good soldiers in their plastic bags of freshness. I liked the large linoleum floor—red and green diamond patterns, also good for jumping and hopping, when people weren't here. There were customers now, interfering with my private fun. There was Mrs. Mandel from Arthur Avenue whose daughter was in the class above mine, and that woman with the noisy dog from Wheeler Avenue—I forgot her name and didn't like her at all, for no particular reason.

I saw my daddy and my heart jumped. He stood behind the meat counter, his apron lightly spattered with blood around mid-chest. He was wrapping hamburger, which he had just ground—I loved watching the striggley streams of red meat gush out of the grinder in weird patterns. He saw me and brightened; his words were gentle. "Hi, honey. Do you want lunch?"

It was a tender, special, and unusual invitation. It was rare that he was not busy with customers, not working hard to please them, not flirting with the student nurses from the hospital across the street who come in for Cokes and Newports on their break. He was going to make me lunch! I skipped behind the counter to witness the ritual.

He took a fresh hard roll out of the basket on the counter, held it up like a magician, and pretended to roll up his invisible sleeves with dramatic gusto. He presented me the roll from all angles. Then he reached into the vast meat display and came out with a long, oblong turkey roll—my favorite! He presented this to me with another flourish of exaggerated bravado. He flipped on the slicer and cut just the right combination of thin and thick slices of meat off the roll with effortless and almost amusing nonchalance, part of his magician's game. I giggled. And then, most importantly, he found and opened the Hellman's mayo and spread exactly the perfect amount across the bun. The completion: a perfect sprinkle of pepper, to garnish it all. This magical meal rested on one slice of waxy, square butcher paper—a more profoundly perfect place-setting I have never been offered. With the task complete, he scooped the sandwich up in his palm, paper holding it all neatly wrapped, and offered it to me, with a mock bow.

And the moment freezes, memory holds it close. As a child I somehow knew that I was being offered the ultimate eucharist, the holy of most holies. I knew I was being offered the blood, the body, the essence of this man's love for me. Disguised as a sandwich, my daddy has offered me the purity of his love, the depths of his caring. I was so, so fed by his tenderness, now and then and always.

Moments reconstruct themselves as I time-travel to a rare Sunday morning in the store. We were not busy at all. "Where are all the customers?" Daddy asked nobody in particular. I knew intrinsically this was a very bad thing, but I was secretly elated—because now my daddy and I could play catch in the milk aisle.

The ritual involved pitching (me), and catching and umpiring (him). It also involved the perfect ball, the search for which I dedicated much of my youthful energy. It could not be a hardball—way too stinging on the hands! It could not be too spongy and soft a ball—not effective. It had to be the perfect combination of bouncy hard ball. I had several of them stashed around my bedroom, and, of course, had one with me today, just in case. Just in case.

I, the pitcher, stood with my back to the milk case, my willing spectators. Daddy, the catcher, crouched down at the top of the aisle, near the canned vegetables. I wound up my pitch, just like he taught me to do. Leg in the air, arms above my head, I cupped the ball, looked at the target, two fingers spread in a V on the ball, and released. "Keep your eyes open," he instructed, "Watch the ball go through the air." The ball thumped into his cupped hands. He grinned and yelled, "Strike one!" I was elated, surprised and not. Still aware of this effective little body, I knew I could count on its fluid and full participation.

And the game continued, Daddy counting balls and strikes, as I, the mighty hero, struck out imaginary batter after imaginary batter. Certainly customers came in to buy their thick *Scranton Times* Sunday paper and sticky buns from Uncle Lou's bakery. Certainly we were interrupted. Yet this time with him lives whole, uninterrupted, precious and untouched in my heart, our time, only our time, while the world disappeared around us.

As an adult, I occasionally tested this arena of childhood mastery—I'd throw a pebble at a tree, a snowball at an unoffending fence post. *Strike one*, I would hear him say. Yep, my aim is good. He taught me well. He loved me well. Mommy made it all work, the container around us, while he attended, with such gentle focus, to my fragile, fragile heart.

"The store stands on the corner."

4. Zorro—Not
1958

It was the way he jumped on his horse from the balcony—the way his cape swished in the ink-black night. It was how he effortlessly saved the woman, always the beautiful, dark-eyed, and heartbroken woman. And his mask, oh, what a dashing mask. It was a clever way to hide, I thought, I who knew plenty about hiding. A nobleman, and then a bandit, working for the people, always for the good, always for the people—just like the Lone Ranger, a former hero of mine. But I truly did love Zorro. I was ten and I was Zorro, inside my head, making things right, kissing the beautiful woman and fleeing, always fleeing and escaping capture. Zorro made everything all right, kept good people safe, offered unconditional protection. I felt safer because of him. Every Wednesday night at 8 o'clock, I religiously watched the television show in deep rapture. I let nobody in the den where the TV was situated, especially not my bossy sister who would laugh at me. I needed to concentrate fully, memorizing his moves, his gestures, his attitude. I wore my Zorro hat and mask during the show and in my bedroom afterward—but never anywhere else, ever.

That day was an exciting and good one, even in school, because it was the day I had been waiting for—the day I would get my Zorro sword. My daddy promised me, when he went downtown that morning to get the big grocery order from the Banner, that he would stop in the Ten Cent Store and buy it. I was so elated—now, all would be safe and well. Now the costume would be complete, and I would be safely hidden, tucked away in another identity, fantasy absolute. The morning dragged by in school as Miss Gallagher's voice faded in and out, talking about William Penn and the Pennsylvania colony. I didn't care. Through force of focus I willed the big hand of the clock around and around, its tick startlingly loud, a bell of freedom waiting to be released. Noon was so far away, but it ticked, it climbed, it crawled its way, that big clock hand, through the airless and tiresome morning. And finally, the click of noon.

The lunch bell rang, kids jumped up, and I dashed, ahead of the throng, tumbling toward the door. The light of day caught me and I darted down the concrete steps, onto Colfax Avenue. The crossing guard, a pimply and stick-skinny eighth grade boy wearing a safety vest of day-glow orange and a badge sash that warned "Caution," guided me across the empty street. I skipped and ran down the block to my daddy's store where Zorro's power awaited me, soon to be my own.

As I flung open the oh-so-familiar door, that first breath of air told me it was different. It was all different now. My mommy, always at the register, was, unthinkably, not there. My daddy, always at the meat counter, was missing. In an instant I assessed these airless catastrophic changes, and cool doom seeped into the soles of my feet and began its long, slimy crawl up toward my awaiting belly. All logic faded, all images blurred, all memory washed over me, like a wave, floating me into a ghostly darkness.

The next image is a ghastly one, never to be uprooted from my being. I stood in my winter coat and hat next to my sister, she in hers, at the foot of my parents' bed, gathered in a little wooly vigil—my hat was itchy and I was terrified. It was lunchtime and my daddy was in bed—this incongruity was overwhelming and almost nauseating. He was white, stark white, and sick, starkly sick. My mother stood behind, her shaky voice disembodied and floating over us saying, "Sidney, you're as white as a sheet." I looked and yes—yes, it was true, sheet and face were one color. I had never heard this expression before, and it repeated itself rhythmically in my head, *white as a sheet, white as a sheet.* I looked outside and my blood stopped—an ambulance pulled itself up in front of our house. I knew all was lost now, never to be repaired, never again to be whole.

The plug of memory is pulled. The question of why we were taken there to witness this trauma has not been answered for me, over all these many years. But I remember the empty terror. I remember the cool, seeping doom. And I remember knowing that life would never be the same again.

My father had a heart attack. I was in fourth grade, ten years old. He was thirty-eight years old. And his life was over. The cosmic joke that life plays on us was this: my father lived to be eighty-four years old, dying an old man in 2000, slipping right over the millennium and floating away, bidding farewell to the new century that he sampled for merely six small days. But even then he was stuck in the old century, back in 1958, and he lived each day of those forty-two remaining years as a dying man would. He faced each day terrified of chest pains as he looked around the corner of each experience for danger. And he found plenty, plenty of illness, plenty of pain, plenty of physical suffering—he found disappointment, too, and debt, frightening and crushing old man debt. He was a dear, kind man, tainted by the fearful hypochondriac who manifested illness and anxiety.

And we, his family, we signed a silent and invisible contract that day, a contract deeper than blood, deeper than DNA, a contract that said: today is the day that daddy is going to die. And we lived out that contract, day after day, for the next forty-four years of his life. We waited, and we worried, and we fretted. And we never, never spoke a word of this to each other. Our contract called for silence, like Zorro's servant—sworn to silence, the silence of hiding, the silence of secrets, the silence of, shhh, don't speak it, don't speak it aloud. It never did stop, the worry and the fear. I never stopped being that child in winter coat and hat standing at the foot of his death bed. And when he did die, a tired and old man who lived a long life, watching his children and their children grow, I felt a light-headedness, a burden evaporating from my being, of which I was profoundly ashamed.

But not on that first day. Oh, not on that day. There was no evaporating of burdens then. On that day there was no Zorro sword for me—in my bed that night, all I wanted was a sword to make me invincible, my sword. I never asked for it again. It was out of reach. Even the wanting of it provoked my guilt and hot-faced shame.

Daddy didn't die that day. What died was my child-veil of belief in invincibility, in impermanence. It was torn from me. And now I knew the truth of life: something terrible really was going to happen at any moment.

"My daddy promised me…"

5. Applenook
1962

The tapping of the light evening rain on the tent was like soft fingers of grace. It pattered, it intensified, it softened—it beckoned wonders to come. I lay bundled, zipped in my sleeping bag, its flannel lining of cowboys and bucking broncos warming me. I was so tired from this day of Girl Scout camp's activities—free swim in the morning for thirty cold and exhilarating minutes, swim lessons in the afternoon practicing survival skills, camp craft class in which I learned to tie a bow hitch, cooking lunch out over the wood fire we built in the unit, canoeing—I was worn, gloriously and glowingly tired, yet I was elated, excited about tomorrow, about summer and its freedom. The five other girls in the cots spread about the tent (toes to head, never head to head—the Girl Scouts were smart in the ways of germ prevention) rested in different levels of repose. There was some tossing from Gladys, whom I knew was still awake, so familiar was I with her breathing. Bobbi Safire was lightly snoring, already asleep. The others were resting and floating off, their cots making different squeaking noises as they shifted their weight. The noises together formed a soft and assuring harmony of community and connection, and the rain, oh, the glorious evening rain, blessed us all.

This was the place of my soul's purpose, this camp of mine. For every summer since I was eight, I came here. I rushed, I ran, I counted days and months to return here, and I bloomed. The pressure of school faded, my feelings of deep inadequacy evaporated. Here I was beyond competent. I swam, strongly and with accurate Red Cross form, as they taught me so well—I was a white cap by now, the highest swimming level. It was a reason for quiet pride. I chopped wood well, I built fires quickly, I ran on strong and sure-footed legs. I came alive here, held by the country air, the gentle soft Pennsylvania hills, and the loving support of the kind counselors—college girls who snuck cigarettes on their break in the staff house, girls with tanned knees and life wisdom and enough patience to engage us with equanimity and kindness. I fell in love with one counselor, only one, each summer, and monogamously lived within that fantasy.

We sang grace in the dining hall; we learned respect, trust, and a quiet, unspoken faith, though I didn't realize it for many years. My favorite grace was Johnny Appleseed. The whole camp sang it together before meals, with impeccable harmony:

> *Oh, the Lord is good to me,*
> *And so I thank the Lord,*
> *For giving me the things I need,*
> *The sun, and the rain, and the appleseed.*
> *The Lord is good to me.*

That rainy night I faded into a deep and dreamless sleep.

I was a pioneer scout now, and so proud of it. I was spending the month in Applenook, the grouping of tents farthest from main camp. There was a rough wooden troop-house with windows that opened out onto a glorious open field, a wash stand with water facets for drinking and washing up, and our tents. The walk up to Applenook from main camp was a fifteen-minute uphill hike. At night I challenged myself to not use my flashlight, to be guided by the trees that lined the trail, trees I knew so intimately. I looked to the heavens and the sky to guide me, more effectively than any flashlight. It was a badge of coolness, this walking without a light. And I was cool here, easy, almost but not quite a leader. I was a strong and willing woman-child who could say whatever she wanted, not harnessed into specific words that had to be pronounced.

I woke to the early Applenook morning around dawn, light just beginning to seep into the new day. The stillness around me was broken by a cacophony of bird sounds—the perfect melody of harmonized chirping. I wiggled in my bedroll toward the open tent flap and looked out. We were surrounded, this tent and our neighbor tent, by an enormous number of birds. I wasn't sure what kind—swallows, maybe—but they hunkered down in the surrounding trees, on the tents, the washstand, all around us. There were hundreds of them, gracing us with an early morning serenade of indefinable beauty. My skin tingled in response as I dived into the oneness of the moment. Any division between human and animal, between young woman and bird were washed away in the beauty of this heavenly sounding. With nobody else awake, I shared in the birds' waking celebration. I never told a soul of this moment, yet it lives so powerfully in me today. It harkened the beginning of yet another perfect Camp Archbald day.

The day dawned with glorious August puffs of mist rising from the earth. I remember walking to the Dining Hall, my sneakers wet with delicious morning dew, my toes wiggling in cold dampness. After a rowdy breakfast in the Dining Hall, the sun rose a bit, drying up the dew on Schoonover Hall lawn where our morning flag ceremony was held. In a horseshoe formation around the flagpole we stood, campers of all sizes, counselors at the end line. With some seriousness, some snickering, we managed the Girl Scout pledge (*On my honor I will try…*), the Pledge of Allegiance, and a gruff yet efficient raising of the flag by a half-dozen younger campers. Then campers were dismissed, and we scattered to our individual units, bellies filled with over-syrupy soggy pancakes.

Our campcraft project for the week was an ambitious one—to create a shower of lashed saplings near our Applenook washstand. This was an idea offered us by an out-of-council counselor named Jen, an unusual woman whose head was never without its variety of multi-colored bandanas. She had an apple-shaped figure, exaggerated by the green Girl Scout shorts she always insisted on wearing. We only wore ours on formal flag evenings, a distinction we secretly believed made us cool, which separated us from her even more. "A shower," Jen insisted, sitting in the circle with us as we planned. "A shower is practical;

we don't have one in this unit. And it will teach you so many basic skills." I cannot remember the basis of my resistance to her idea. It was, I believe, more about my resistance to her. She just wasn't cool enough to meet my sixties standards of image and flash. But for lack of another, we adapted her idea. The Applenook shower was underway.

First we needed to cut the little maple saplings. I was very engaged and relaxed in this aspect of our project. I loved our Girl Scout hatchets. They fit so perfectly in my hand, and seemed to be of the perfect weight. I had no doubt as to my complete competency in chopping. I welcomed the little blisters that appeared behind my knuckles, at the base of my fingers, palm-side up. They affirmed my full participation in this adventure. And chop we did, chop and de-branch, and gather. I might have been an unannounced leader in this chopping process. Our pile of fallen saplings grew. Someone with a bigger-picture mind, at some point, figured out how many trees we needed—perhaps it was Jen, maybe with Gladys's help. She was more a thinker than I, my best friend Gladys, fondly called Cauliflower or Cauli, her camp name, for no particular reason. Our pile of trees completed, after a few days of strong and focused work, we moved to the lashing phase of the project.

I was never a very efficient or caring lasher. I found it dull and a bit too girly. The practical often did not hold my interest. Yet in this moment I can remember the specific smell of the lashing twine, its big, hairy ball sitting in front of me as if it were yesterday. Other people lashed, I imagine, weaving tree to tree. I was bored and anxious and probably found other things to do, or pretended to be busy. We lashed together the trees, scouts with more skill than I, getting the right tension of twine, sapling to sapling, a circle being woven of tree and twine and purposeful intent.

After all of our labor under the hot and dry sun, somehow we managed to right our little shower, getting it to its feet. Without too much forethought or planning, the structure made its way to standing with some prodding, some pushing, some intuitive Girl Scout manipulation. Someone figured out how to divert a hose from the wash stand, and threw it and secured it over the trees. There was our shower, completed, from nothing to something, from wilderness to civilization, from concept to reality, from energy to completion. It was remarkable to my fourteen-year-old heart.

Nobody ever used the shower, of course. We knew this before we began. Perhaps one would be too exposed, at the tender ages of fourteen and fifteen, too vulnerable to the public eye, to indulge in it. But Jen, our strange and visionary outsider, christened our shower. I remember being in a giggling gaggle of girls, hiding in the tent that buttressed the shower, snickering while she disrobed, climbed in, and turned on the water. Why was this funny? Why did we not take our turns, gracing our wondrous creation? I am not certain: perhaps we still needed her to be the outsider. Or perhaps we were too controlled by our teenage modesty to risk such public disrobing. Or maybe the creation of it was also the completion—to be baptized by it was just somehow counter-intuitive. Yet I remember the glory of that chopping, the coming together of those little maples, the collective lashing, and communal creation of that shower as a high point of my teenage years.

How blessed I was to know the feel of a hatchet that fit so perfectly in my hand. How graced I was to work next to others, shoulder to shoulder in creation of a shared venture. How honored I was to walk that path at night, flashlight in my pocket, heart opened to the darkened summer sky, my guide, my source, my self.

The Lord is good to me.

And so I thank the Lord.

"This was the place of my soul's purpose."
(top row, third from left)

6. Mr. Galucci and the Open Range
1956 –1965

It all started because of cowboys. Cowboys lived the life that I needed. I knew this early on. They lived on the prairie, ate beans around a campfire, drove a covered wagon, rode a pinto, and slept on the ground with a saddle as their pillow. I knew the cowboy life was a way out of the pain and constriction in *my* life—I needed the wide open spaces and somebody to save, too. I was compulsively addicted to all cowboy programs on television. But I was always monogamous with one cowboy hero at a time. There was no way I could love and merge into more than one per television season—my heart was too committed, too passionate for that. I loved Paladin for one season, in *Have Gun Will Travel*, the flashy bounty hunter from San Francisco. I loved the theme song, "Paladin, Paladin, where do you roam? Far, far from home." And the Lone Ranger, my favorite avenger riding on his beautiful white horse, stirred me when he pulled his horse up on two legs and hollered, "Hi, ho, Silver, away!" I was also committed to *Wagon Train*, Ward Bond playing the decent, dedicated wagon train boss, striving to get his travelers to safety. The themes of dedication to others, of correcting injustice, emerged early for me.

I had all the paraphernalia one could have. A series of Daisy Air Rifles passed through my hands, my favorite being a girls' model, its stock and barrel heavy, cool, and white. I had leather boots that smelled real, soft chaps, and a great broad cowboy hat. There were spurs, too, fake metal spurs that spun, but were always somewhat complicated to hook onto the boots. The holster was the best, however, a key item in the outfit. It was made of cool stiff leather, and it wrapped around my leg with a strap. I do not remember any specifics about my hand guns, but I do remember thinking exploding caps were silly and redundant. It was all about the outfit. I remember lying in the grass on our front lawn, facing down toward Roaring Brook, wearing my entire costume, Daisy Air Rifle poised—waiting, protecting, and guarding.

The best of all was my cowboy jacket. We were in New York one winter for a weekend, probably when Daddy closed the store for Christmas. In Port Authority we found a store called Teepee Town. To my child-heart's delight, it was completely dedicated to cowboy apparel. I was in heaven. Somehow I found and negotiated for the best cowboy jacket on earth. Its leather was a soft buck in color and smelled of Montana, of open skies and clear air. Its fringe was long and perfect. The pockets were deep, the buttons covered in suede. The lining was silky and slidey. I wore this jacket fiercely until it no longer fit my growing body.

But there was still something missing—a guitar. I saw my first guitar during a cowboy movie. Its image and sound spoke deeply to me. My hands needed to stroke a guitar, to strum some casual chords. My arms needed to hold a guitar, caress the origin of such perfect sounds.

My mother and father agreed: yes, music lessons would be good for me. My sister, L. took piano lessons with Mrs. Leva, the fancy teacher in the big house. L. would practice her annoyingly loud practice chords, and it got on my nerves. The piano was not right for me. I needed a guitar, a cowboy guitar. I needed to hug it, hold it, become it.

My mother, robbing time from her duties in the store, took me to Mr. Galucci's guitar store on Lackawanna Avenue, downtown across from Shookey's Delicatessen. She was busy and harried, so our silent pace was tight and quicker than I needed. I was eight years old and it was wintertime. I remember the boots I was wearing, with fuzzy tops, boots that made my feet stomp loudly in the snow. Angelo Galucci seemed old then but he was probably about forty. He was a medium-built man, with a receding hairline and broad planes of forehead and face. His movements were graceful and quiet. I remember the ring he wore on his middle finger, a distinctively red gem that stood out on his skin, a ring like nobody in my family ever wore. His complexion was sallow, his voice quiet, his manner soft.

But mostly I remember his store. It was narrow and deep, and guitars lined both walls, high and low. Such beautiful guitars! Electrical guitars of deep colors, folk guitars of all sizes, multi-colored straps, and an occasional out-of-place drum set. It was overwhelming. Over the many years that I took lessons with Mr. Galucci in a little studio behind the storefront, I always adored walking in the store, sauntering down that stunning gauntlet of guitars, a thrilling reception line for my happy heart.

I don't remember much of my first meeting with Mr. Galucci—I was painfully shy, my speech already limiting my interaction with others. But this is what I do remember: he and Mommy talked, he softly said hello to me, and they agreed we would try some lessons. To do this, we would rent a guitar, to see if I "took" to it. He turned to go get one, pivoting quietly on his soft shoes. He returned and handed me a guitar. I saw it floating through space, larger than life, making its cosmic way toward me. As it landed in my hands, I inspected my new companion. It had a dark brown shiny finish, and stenciled on it, in deep black, was a cowboy riding a bucking bronco! I was astounded that life could manifest such perfection. My mouth gasped open. My perfect guitar had been provided—the journey had begun.

Took to it? Yes, I took to it. This little guitar unleashed the next level of my fantasy world. I played and played, imagined and imagined. I was on the plains, dashing on my horse to help the settlers. The young beautiful woman needed me. I was in heaven on the open plains.

Mr. Galucci and I would sit in our weekly lessons on folding chairs in the little blocked-off studio with a window that looked out to the store. My fingers ached as the strings bit into them. The more they hurt, the more determined I became. I learned to read notes over the years, and began to stretch my little girl fingers into different chords. I do not remember Mr. Galucci's style of teaching. I do remember how he listened as I played along; I remember him not judging, and his sharkskin pant leg with its perfect crease folded over his opposite knee.

He encouraged, smiled, showed me other things. Most prominently I remember his gentle presence, his quiet ways, and the exercise books he would write in. They were blank-paged music books, soft pages with a hard cover, and each week he would write me my lesson. I cherished those books, a map of my development, and poured over them. Many years later, I left them all behind me in a quick exodus from a painful lover—the music books, not the relationship, being the catastrophic loss.

Lessons went on, Wednesday afternoon after Wednesday afternoon. I graduated from simple folk songs like *Red River Valley* to more complicated chording. At some point, the little rented guitar faded away, replaced by a stunning Gibson nylon stringer. And over the years, I learned to play melody up high on the frets, which was very cool and rock and roll-ish. Guitars stayed with me as the center of attention throughout grade school and into high school. I remember my foray into electric guitars, playing with amplified sound in my pink-and-green bedroom. Long after my cowboy obsession faded, playing music still gave me a sense of freedom, competency, and self.

Grade school with its confusion peeled away into the maze of feelings called high school. Around sophomore or junior year, I began learning to pick melodies out of chords, synching up with folk music and Mary Travers, my true love. At the end of my career, about age sixteen, I began to blissfully play some simple classical music.

There was only one downside for me and guitars, and it was the death knell to my playing. As profound as playing was, it was a wholly private experience. I could never comfortably play for anybody else, just Mr. Galucci. He was the only one, by definition of his role, who had access to that part of me. Surely I must have played for Mommy and Daddy at different times. But it was always a forced and frightening event. Any attempts to "go public," any attempts to play for friends at camp, never worked, and just created anxiety. Alone I was fluent, free flowing, little fingers leaping from note to note, from string to string. With anybody near me, the creative juices dried up, my fingers stiffened, my self-consciousness reigned.

Midway through high school, the apex of my lack of self-confidence and wild rampant shame put an end to my guitar playing. I shut the guitar case with the beautiful gold fuzzy lining once and for all on my stunning Gibson.

I am not sure why playing alone and with Mr. Galucci was not enough to sustain me forever. I don't know why the solace of the notes sliding into one another, the feel of the rhythm soaring through me, the oneness with the ringing instrument was not enough. Perhaps the pleasure was too great, the personal achievement too delicious, or the need to please others too strong. But that guitar case remained closed, as I remained closed to self-expression, to music, to the wide open spaces of my soul. Any futile attempts to renew my guitar passion in adulthood were unsuccessful. The cowboy had left town, the chuck wagon faded, the fantasies died. Now just the silence and the emptiness of the struggle echoed around me.

7. Dream, Dream, Dream
1956

The reality of my little world was all-inclusive—besides camp, Beach Haven, and an occasional trip to our Aunt Syl's fancy house in New Jersey, my world was defined, specific, and painfully narrow. Yet movies, television, and our yearly trips to New York City shook my preconceived images of life. Taking the train from our home in Scranton to New York City was joyous and exhilarating. The train station in Scranton echoed, its high, arched ceilings decorated with elaborate murals, the slippery marble-ish floor like none other in my world. Its elaborate façade was a contradiction to the town's general grey grunginess.

When daddy closed the store for a few days on and after Christmas (nobody shops then, anyway—all of the orders, the Christmas fruit baskets that mommy created with such labor and beauty, were all sold, all gone), we took the train, the Erie Lackawanna line, that linked Scranton with Hoboken, NJ. The train was called *The Phoebe Snow*. I loved that our train had a name—it delighted me. Once we were in New Jersey, we took the "tubes" over to New York. My little world was shot out of its cannon of familiarity as I burst into the new light of possibility, landing in the unpredictable and bustling world of New York City, 1956.

My excitement about the train itself was almost uncontainable. The rocking movement felt so different from anything I had experienced— exciting yet lulling, humming with difference and possibility. Crossing in-between the cars, seeing the trains hooked together, noise accelerated, shaking exaggerated, was terrifying for me. I was certain the train would de-couple, and I would land, broken, on the tracks. I had seen enough movies to know this catastrophe was possible. It took a superhuman push of adrenalin-spurred bravery for me to make the leap over. But leap I would, into the safety of the next car.

We would eat dinner in the dining car, making our way through the train, finding a table, with beyond-starched white cloth on it. The waiters were all black men, something I was not used to, and I felt shy in their presence, not wanting to do it wrong. Their white jackets were as starched as the table clothes, and accentuated the difference of their skin color. They were polite, quiet, and always seemed to look downward toward the floor. To order, we read the big heavy menu our waiter offered us, and then mommy wrote out our order on a cardboard ticket and put it in a silver container that looked like a napkin holder. This fascinated me in its difference. We ordered soup and chicken and spaghetti (for me), and waited. The silverware was heavy, the china thick and seemingly luxurious. Dinner came clanging and rolling with the motion on the train. How could the waiter carry that heavy tray with so much shuddering of the floor beneath him? Our meal was a miracle of tossing and rocking, of flavors accentuated by the hum of the engine, the lull of the unfamiliar, the whisper of things to come. Eating and jostling, sitting at a table while moving, were delicious paradoxes of delight.

Landing in Hoboken, navigating our way to the connecting train, coming over to New York, all remain a blur to me, faded out against the bright light of memory of train and City. But in New York we did end, standing on the street near Grand Central Terminal, buildings touching the sky, people in winter coats hustling by us. Christmas trees lined the streets, filling the air with the smell of pine and the hope for a post-holiday purchase. We stood, the four of us, bundled in our coats, almost circled together like a wagon train to gather our wits, daddy holding our bags. So profound was the difference in everything about this City. It was as if we were vibrating at a different frequency than the pace, the site, the life all around us. The very buzz of the City thrilled me with a shiver and a chill.

We yearly stayed in the Hotel Abby in "midtown," as my daddy said to the taxi driver who sped us there on screeching tires. I remember Daddy leaving money in the little cup in the plastic divider that separated driver from passenger. The amount of tipping was always a point of deep, quiet discussion and contention between Mommy and Daddy. I somehow knew that it remained an issue unresolved.

The hotel's modest, darkly lit lobby seemed to my child's eye to be all shiny mahogany and deep-piled rug. The handsome, dark-haired desk clerk superciliously checked us in. Our encounters here in the City proved again and again that we just didn't quite fit in, our differences written on our winter coats for all to see. I remember we shared a room, two beds: one for L. and me, one for mommy and daddy. And I remember room service—more heavily starched cloth, stiff napkins, and heavy silver on a rolling cart, like on the train. How beyond decadent was room service to me at my young age—to have food brought to your bedroom by somebody that wasn't your mommy! I loved that.

We would walk, walk, and walk through the streets. We looked at the store windows, their Christmas decorations startlingly elaborate— moving dolls, singing figures, Santa Clause alive in the Lord and Taylor's window, Macy's window shimmering with snow and elves and angels. We waited in line to see the Christmas tree in Rockefeller Center, a tree so tall that my neck could not bend sufficiently to see its tipsy top. On another trip in later years we skated there, I think, in that fancy rink with those fancy people, my coat too thick, my skates too tight, my ankles too weak to eek any fun from it. I was subtly aware that it was "expensive" to skate there, more silent tension between my mother's financial caution and my father's laxity, and it sucked pleasure from the process.

And Broadway—over the years, we saw mind-boggling plays: *Carnival*, with Anna Maria Alberghetti, whom I loved and wanted to hold close to me. I wished I could meet her at the stage door, smile broadly and fall into her waiting arms. We saw *My Fair Lady* (Mommy didn't feel good and fainted in the theater's bathroom—that man thought she was drunk, my mommy who would never do anything wrong!). We saw *The Sound of Music*, and more, so many more. Broadway was exhilarating: those moments before the curtain came up, the orchestra playing their musical introduction with such gusto, unleashed a delirious bubble of excitement in my belly. This was It: this was life, these were cool people, this was culture. This is where I knew I needed to be. This is who I wanted to be—a cool, worldly New Yorker, spending money with no thought, wearing the right clothes with no effort, going to events with no rattle of nerve or caution.

Over the years, several events were burned into my memory: eating warm chestnuts from the street vendors was one. My daddy loved the warm chestnuts that were sold on every street corner. I can smell them now, their almost-muskiness advertising a taste explosion. The man would take my father's quarter, and in exchange, wrap warm chestnuts into a cone of brown butcher paper. You had to crack the shell just right—Daddy showed me how—to fully expose their flesh. Some were better than others, those elusive chestnuts. A few would explode into a taste so specific, so chestnut-y, that my mouth waters in the memory. Others would be the bummer crop—molded, bitter in the mouth. I joined my father in his search for the perfect chestnut. I loved them alongside of him, and just the memory of them today awakens my taste buds to the glories of the past.

Another memory: New Year's Eve. We went to Times Square, with thousands of others, to watch the ball drop. I was too young to understand the concept of "ball" dropping. I kept thinking of a basketball falling from the sky, which made absolutely no sense to me at all. The crush of humanity, the push of excitement toward the New Year was so intense, that I found my little body actually being crushed by the hordes of New Yorkers. In some way I was able to communicate this to my daddy, who hefted me up and carried me on his shoulders, hero-style, all the way back to the Hotel Abby. He carried me the three long blocks back to the hotel. Every step on the shoulders of that man was a victorious lap, every step as I rode above the crowds, above the shift of year, above the torrent of humanity, was a step of bliss. I can remember the waves of people, from my vantage point, the ripple of movement in the crowd. Did Daddy have chest pain that night? Was it my fault, my fault—ever my childhood mantra—*my fault?*

And the crowning memory: later in our lives, when I was a preteen and L. a teen, we walked as a family down 42nd Street. The marquee outside the theater advertised a live rock and roll show, listing a cavalcade of stars. L. begged to go—her fifteen-year-old self aching for the community of other boppers. Again, I became hyperaware of the tension between my parents: it was a lot of money. Another mantra: *a lot of money*. My mother resisted, my father coaxed. My mother, who was the grown-up parent, held ground; my father, always the manipulative and delightful child, cajoled. I remember my father's wallet opening as he counted out the cash for the four of us. *A lot of money, a lot of money.* That worry overrode all else in the moment for me.

Into the theater we cautiously strode, four hicks from Pennsylvania—one fifteen-year-old teenage wannabe, two cautious parents, and one eleven-year-old, guitar-playing, stuttering, lesbian-to-be. We entered a theater of explosive, rocking sound. The show had already begun. Teenagers of all shapes and sizes bopped, clapped, screamed, and hollered. Policeman lined the base of the stage, to prevent the onslaught of hormone-awakened youth. How did we find seats? We did, and I sat, terrified at the noise and excitement. Somehow I was able to eventually block out the screams and hysterical gestations of the crowd and find the stage. I became fascinated, glued to the performers.

I wanted to be on stage, a boy/man, swinging my hips, shimmee-ing my shoulders, gyrating my pelvis, announcing my sexuality, my private passions, to the world. I wanted to wear tight boys' pants, with that secretive bulge, that mysterious bulge, that bulge that I so wanted for my own.

I remember Jerry Lee Lewis, wearing a gold lamé jacket with a broad black lapel, dancing, singing, and hopping at his piano, screeching out *Great Balls of Fire*. I saw Jerry Lee Lewis, with my child-eyes, my awakening child-body, and I rocked on with him. Silently, in relative stillness, I fully participated inside myself. He was a writhing, twisting, squirming barrel of rock and roll. His too-loud sounds almost annoyed me, but his movement and hysterical presentation thrilled me:

> *Goodness gracious,*
> *Great balls of fire!*

I remember Chuck Berry singing *Johnny Be Good*. Each new performer brought the pitch of excitement to a new level, and his was complete rhythm and loose-limbed movement. The lyrics amazed me with their promise:

His mother told him "Someday you will be a man,

And you will be the leader of a big old band.

Many people coming from miles around

To hear you play your music when the sun go down.

Maybe someday your name will be in lights,

Saying Johnny B. Goode tonight."

Go go

Go Johnny go

Go go go Johnny go

Go go go Johnny go

Go go go Johnny go

Johnny B. Goode tonight.

My sister swayed in her seat guardedly, sliding into the rhythm of the group experience. I glanced at my parents: my father looked tense (he later said he was ready to scoop us up and carry us out of there if a riot broke), my mother's face a blur of concerned disapproval.

But most of all, I remember the Everly Brothers, Don and Phil. Of course I had heard of them on our radio station, WAMC, the one I listened to on my little pink transistor radio at night. Their voices floated together like blue and sky, like water and ocean. Their harmonies were heart-stopping to me:

"Dream…dream, dream.
When I want you, in the night,
When I need you, to hold me tight,
Whenever I want you
All I have to do,
Is dream."

They sang my world, they expressed my heartbreak. I was stunned.

But the real epiphany was yet to come—that was about the guitars. They played together; they played the chords, like I learned with Mr. Galucci. And then their words became the melody. So many times, Mr. Galucci would play the chords, and I would stumble out the melody, without an understanding of the relationship between the two. But today, I saw, I felt, I finally got it in my body. Melody slipped inside chord, one within the other, where they flowed and moved and danced, carried by the river of harmony, the movement of sounds. I got it, deeply and wholly. My world view shifted. I understood rock and roll that day. I understood so much that day. I had hope that, even if I never could become a "real" teenager, there was solace, somewhere inside a chord. Somewhere inside a city, there was a melody that was mine.

Memory blurs again, my mind's eye dimming—back to the hotel, the vacation winding down, the train home. The reverse trip was a depressing one, a constriction, a return to what was, not what might be. All the varieties of people in New York, the compelling excitement, the stores, the opportunities, all were coming to an end. My hope, my connection—to the people, the busting, bursting life of New York—dimmed, too. I sat in the seat of *The Phoebe Snow*, the scratchy plastic irritating me, squeaking as I shifted. My heart closed down, my belly ached.

But the melody lived on inside of me:

All I have to do is dream, dream, dream—dream.

8. Leslie, Etc.
1962

Her name was Leslie Greenspan. She was in eleventh grade, and I was in ninth at Central High School. Her hair was honey brown, light tinges of soft blonde flicking through it as the sun caught it just right. She had a bouncy pageboy haircut, which seemed to have a life of its own. Her skin was golden. She was taller, more grown up than I, with a lithe figure that startled me into sensation. We were in the same study hall, an absurd proposition that gathered students of different grades and forced them into silent study. It was a large group, maybe forty-five, with a mean teacher—the old and dried up typing teacher, Miss Litterri—who became our captor every seventh period, so near but not yet the end of the long school day. Because Miss Litterri would call roll, this was a hard period for me. We sat alphabetically and would have to respond to our names with an affirmative response. I would sweat my wait, practicing generating sound in my throat, saying silently to myself, "*Here.*" *Here* was easier to say than *present*, that initial *p* sound a real obstacle for me. *Here. Here. I'm here.* (A voice inside my head screamed, "Where the hell do you think I am?")

And it would inevitably happen: "Nan Futuronsky?" she would bellow her demand.

Terror unleashed. Breath gulped, sound forced. Some guttural response would release from me. **HE**-*re. I'm here*, my heart would scream. *I'm right here in front of you!* My voice just would not obey. The teacher would look annoyed, wait a long, glaring second or two, and move along.

43

"Susan Gaines." And the roll would continue. Stress released out of my body like helium out of a balloon. I would heave and relax my guard, knowing that I was now safe in precarious anonymity.

Leslie sat at the front of the third row, where I could quietly observe her. Her outfits were Villager, the cool line of teenage clothes in 1962. She wore blue pleated skirts, high blue socks, brown Weejun loafers (no pennies in them, that was the coolest way), and a Villager round collared blouse with a circle pin holding the collar together. She was perfect to me. I wanted to hold her, to smell her and cuddle with her. And oh, how I wanted to kiss her. She attended to the schoolwork in her binder with a casual and confident air while I fumbled my way through my dreaded Spanish vocabulary, each word a menacing foe, as I kept Leslie in my side vision. She was like a goddess to me, one I wished I could hold close to my own aching heart.

I had known for a very long time now that something was very wrong with me. I wanted to kiss girls. I wanted to be the boy, so I could be on top of girls. I never liked the boys—they were silly, short, and uninteresting. My mind, my heart, my awakening body was always called to the body, the breath, the world of women, where safety, excitement, and beauty lived. This was a life-threatening secret for me to keep. I knew when I was very young that nobody could ever learn this about me. So I hid it. I hid it so well that I got lost to myself.

I loved Mary Travers, from Peter, Paul, and Mary. I always wanted to touch her hair, to wake in the morning next to her, to whisper into her ear all the smart and beautiful things I knew about the world. The way she shook her head, the intensity of her presence, stirred me in places I knew a girl should not be stirred. Not by another girl. So I hid.

Except at night. At night in bed, I wrote stories in my head while hugging my pillow, the pillow that became a beautiful woman. I imagined wonderful, sexy, hot stories of damsels in distress, of Mary singing to me, of Leslie needing me. The endings were delicious, with rubbing in just the right places, with hot kisses of release and freedom and endless gratitude, the crisis always averted by my brilliant bravery. The reward was always the body and love of the woman.

Except it wasn't really me. The hero of my stories was a boy/man, handsome and smart, who had a series of complex names and identities that shifted like the tides with the many different plots. I lived each story vicariously through the boy. I merged into him, I became him, but all in the name of writing, all in the guise of telling a story. I was only the writer, just the writer, doing nothing, nothing wrong. Kissing my pillow, nothing wrong; writing a plot, nothing wrong. Nothing. I was not even offered admittance to my own fantasies as a girl. Girls weren't the heroes. Girls didn't kiss girls.

Everything was wrong. I always knew this. My thinking inside my head did not match what was happening outside of me. When Gladys and I saw the movie *Splendor in the Grass* with Natalie Wood and Warren Beatty, I wished I could be Warren Beatty, to hold and caress Natalie's long dark hair. What did Gladys think sitting next to me in the darkened Strand movie theater, Saturday afternoon after Saturday afternoon? Did she know?

There was one time I wanted somebody to know, a few years in the future. Her name was Janice, from New Jersey. We were best friends that summer at the other camp, monogamous and inseparable best friends, that painful summer when, because I had grown too old, my own camp was closed to me. This camp was for rich girls, located in Stroudsburg, where Janice and I worked together in the kitchen. It was a summer of darkness and abandonment, but for the light of Janice. Her eyes were dark and filled with silent surprises. She spoke quietly with breathy pauses that captivated me. We walked in the woods, spent every moment together. Sal, the cook with the dirty white t-shirt and rolled-up sleeves, raised his eyebrows in mock concern when we came in together, sending shivers of the cold dread of exposure up my spine.

Camp was ending. Janice would be returning to New Jersey; I would be going back home. How would I see her again, my heart despaired? We walked in the woods that last afternoon, circling back behind the bunks, headed to our favorite spot, the pine tree grove, with its yummy smells and semblance of privacy. I desperately wanted her to know: I wanted to kiss her. I had to tell her. She would let me. We could kiss, I knew it. Blood beat in my face, heating me with hope.

"I have a secret. I want you to know." My voice and my words shocked me awake as we sat together, shoulder to shoulder under our pines. My inner voice leaked out, without my permission. I had no intention of saying those words aloud. I terrified myself to the core in the speaking.

"Oh, good, do tell," she said, eagerly turning to me, hugging her knees to her chest. Her long black hair was loose that day, circling her face in soft wisps of curls.

Time stood still. The hollow echo of my own heart clanged in my ears, with possibility, with dread, with hope. The moment was long and achy.

"Oh, nothing. Just that…" my voice floundered, seeking a way, any way, out, "just that it would be good to see each other at Christmas, at the Christmas break, maybe." My words gained speed as they lost meaning. "We could maybe meet half way, maybe in Allentown or something." I was on a roll, words tumbling me away from reality, away from my longing, away from my aching heart's desire.

I never did see Janice again. We talked once, I think, on the phone that year, months after camp. Our talk was distant and empty, a fumble for words, the magic of that summer in the woods, the potential of that moment under the pines, long faded. The healing victory of loving a real friend, not a singer, nor a popular girl in another class, eluded me then. I was shattered by the loss of Janice and even more isolated, even more disguised to myself.

But I've gotten ahead of myself in the story. In 1962, I sat in study hall and watched from afar, as Leslie, my golden Leslie, shook her hair, closed her book, and waited for the bell. I noticed the set of her shoulders, the curve of her perfect neck. I knew how my lips could fit there, could love her there. I could almost taste her, there. I closed my Spanish book and waited for the bell.

I waited and waited.

PART TWO: BECOMING

9. Levitating with Big Grey
1967

Diane took another toke of the joint as she shook her blonde, straight hair to emphasize her righteous indignation. She inhaled deeply, sternly focusing her grey-blue eyes on me and studying me carefully as she passed the joint. I anxiously grabbed it. Its warmth touched my lips and traveled toward my throat and chest. This drug, my newfound companion, served me well. I breathed in deeply, relaxing around the inhale, the smoke loosening the muscles in my face, filling me with a tingling not unlike what I imagined 7-Up in my veins might feel like.

Diane went on with her virtuous tirade:

"And then the evil of this fucking unjust war will come to an end, and the symbol of the military-industrial complex will be ground to a halt. We'll confront the war-makers. We'll encircle the Pentagon and then levitate it, LEVITATE IT, from the force of our positive energies."

Diane was my neighbor on Vine Court. We were both sophomores in a college that had dorm space only for its freshman students. Because of this we lived off campus with assigned roommates. Vine Court faced the ocean. My apartment, number 10, was three units from the beach. Hers, number 4, was adjacent to the beach. I met her outside the apartment the first week of school. When I first saw her that September day, the ocean crashing behind her, her blond stringy hair blowing in the wind, her waif-like figure clothed in her uniform of bellbottomed jeans and pea coat, my heart was taken prisoner. I wanted to know her and didn't know how. I was certain that I was not cool enough to be with her. I anxiously nodded hello, as she walked over to greet me. We talked of our schedules and carpooling, since the college was a few miles away. I was an English major, she an art major, so we shared no classes. But since I had a car, we agreed to drive in together to campus on Tuesday and Thursday mornings.

She walked away with a tilt of blasé that thrilled me. At her door, she paused and lit a cigarette with her purple plastic lighter, took a puff and, with a slight attitude of assured arrogance, walked in to her apartment. Flattered and confused by her attention, I stumbled my way into my own apartment, tripping over boxes strewn throughout the living room waiting to be unpacked, boxes that held the necessities of my life: a bulletin board, towels, sheets, a frying pan, a mysterious box labeled "MISC." in my own handwriting, dishtowels, an old teddy bear, and my favorite books.

Diane instantly fascinated me. I was too cut off from my own sensual and sexual longing to recognize my attraction to her. I just knew that I wanted to be near her. I wanted her world, whatever it was, to become my own. To me she represented cool, hippie, druggy counter-culture, not like the sorority sisters I had met the previous year when I pledged. They all looked the same, sounded the same to me, polite and right-acting. Diane was edgy, different, and I wanted that for myself.

I knew why she was interested in me. It was because of Big Grey. Big Grey was my first car that I had bought the month before from Roger, my sister's boyfriend, for $50. The car was a 1956 four-door Pontiac. Big Grey was two-tone grey, had sharply pointed fins, smiling grill-work, and just a little distinguished rust around the two back wheel wells. The inside was amazingly luxurious—the front seat was like a grey couch, spacious and deep, with lots of leg room. The gears were remarkably push-buttoned. Grey's only tragic flaw was his vulnerability to moisture. The car didn't start consistently when it was rainy or damp, and this became a problem living near the ocean. But because of Big Grey, Diane and I started driving together to campus.

She smoked Camels and always reeked of tobacco, which I found compelling. Her appeal to me was the allure of the counter-culture, the beckoning of divergence. She knew art, Dylan, cool movies, and political theory—or so I thought. She enticed me. She had a boyfriend at home in North Jersey, Ray, who came down on weekends. I loathed him from afar whenever I saw his red MG parked in front of number 4 Vine Court, like a never-changing red light. She let it be known that she was not available to me on weekends, no matter what.

We got high together most nights, usually at her apartment, often with the pot I got from a friend. I lost interest in my newly gained sorority sisters. Their teas, gatherings, and meetings seemed flighty and petty. Diane and I were having important discussions. We were dropping out, tuning out, as Dr. Leary urged. We were willing to confront the bigger issues, like the war, the unjust, illegal war that was killing young Americans, Vietnamese, and innocent civilians. Being stoned really helped me relate to her and to these issues. This bridge of marijuana created an avenue from my limited, small-town world to hers.

I was transfixed by her presence. My roommate, Antoinette, didn't like her, calling her "skanky." I felt affronted and angry by her comment, and wanted to defend Diane. But, as far as I understood the slang, this was sort of true. Diane was kind of grimy, almost slutty, but in a cool, mesmerizing, and politically correct way—challenging the traditional values of our culture was a powerful political statement, I thought. I decided not to challenge Antoinette. What did she know, anyway?

My skin came alive when I sat near Diane. Her smells lived inside my nostrils, on my flesh. Perhaps my attraction was the remains of my fixation with Mary Travers. The casual flicking of that long blond hair was such a turn-on to me, although at that point in time, I didn't realize it as such.

"So what do you think? Wanna go?" Diane's question rocked my reverie.

"Umm, go where?" I hated to admit that I had no idea what she was talking about. Not following conversations happened to me often. I wasn't plugged in, my fantasizing mind creating its own reality.

"Hello. Earth to YOU. To D.C. For the levitation of the Pentagon."

Oh, to D.C. If it meant spending time with her, if it meant sitting next to her and feeling her presence vibrate within me, if it meant no Ray, then the answer was easy.

"Sure. How will we get there?" I asked innocently.

She laughed. "We'll take Big Grey, of course," was her knowing response. She had no doubt of her capacity to manipulate our shared world.

I instantly felt my stomach sink. My agreement with my dad, upon buying Big Grey, was that the car was for local carpooling only. It wasn't a safe car, not a respectable car, not a highway car, my dad reminded me. I understood and agreed, knowing the inherent danger in highway driving, the irresponsible nature of using a substandard car on the open road. My family had instilled in me a compulsive respect for highway safety. Terror of risk-taking in general was clearly embedded in me. Life was not safe; something terrible was going to happen—those were the cornerstones of my parents' worldview. I would never drive a car like that on the highway.

Until now. In an instant, my values dissolved. Now I knew I had to drive us to D.C. in Big Grey. To confront the military industrial complex. To end the war. To confront the war-makers. And to be nearer to Diane.

We bought fluorescent paints and skinny brushes, and went to work on my proud car, transforming him into a mobile peace-nick. We painted large, demanding, not-to-be-missed neon orange peace signs on each door, and tiny florescent flowers all over his hood and trunk. If the car could have talked, I am certain he would have said, "Stop this silliness. Respect my age; I demand it." But I overrode Big Grey's response as I overrode my own internal knowing. Diane wanted to go. We were going.

It was late October, and I had spoken to very few people by that point in the semester—Diane was my monogamous focus. I told nobody I was going to D.C. Not Antoinette; not my sister who lived just a few miles away, newly married and teaching first grade; and certainly not my parents. This was a covert operation for me. And I was deeply terrified.

We left before dawn on the twenty-first of October, weather grey and damp—not Big Grey's forte. I drove us cautiously toward the New Jersey Turnpike, peace signs blinding anyone who dared to drive around us, fluorescent flowers advertising free love and peace to all who could see. Big Grey couldn't go above 45 mph, so we crept along in the right lane, the car almost inherently assuming a posture of dignified embarrassment, ignoring his own blatant advertisement to freedom. Diane sulked in the passenger's seat, smoking her Camels. My hands shook on the wheel. We were going to levitate the military industrial complex, confront the war-makers. That's all I needed to know. And Diane was next to me.

Within the first twenty miles on the highway, my eye caught something blinking on the dashboard. It was a red flashing light indicating engine trouble. My heart rate shot up. Something terrible was surely going to happen now. We cautiously inched into a gas station at the rest stop, where a young, amused attendant with bright red hair fished down deep into Big Grey's bowels, came up with his dip stick and proclaimed, "Yep, down a quart and a half of oil." We needed oil at every rest stop between our New Jersey school and Washington. Big Grey was kicking up his heels on the Turnpike and its adjacent roads, but needed his constant lubrication. So oil he got.

Diane navigated, smoked, read, and generally ignored me as I strained at the wheel, tension gripping my shoulders. We eventually limped our oil-compromised way toward D.C., joining an invisible horde of other fellow levitators. Where were we all? Diane directed us toward the Mall by the Lincoln Monument. We found our way there, somehow parked our noble chariot, and wandered coolly into the open spaces filling up with people. I said my silent goodbyes to Big Grey, hoping yet not imagining how I would find him again. We found a spot on the damp earth, put down our ripped Indian bedspread, and settled in among our peers. The speakers urged our righteous indignation and celebrated our wholehearted participation. I was tired and had to pee. But I began to relax a bit, my drug buzz from our pre-dawn joints wearing off, the stress of driving beginning to release.

Here I was, at a cool demonstration, with Diane. This was all good. We made it safely. This would be a cool and good day.

"Hi, is there room on your blanket for us?" bellowed an ominous male voice above us. I looked up to see two guys who looked like all the other guys—beards, long hair, blue jeans, down vests, denim jackets, boots. Clearly there was no fucking room on our blanket, no room in our world, for these guys. I felt affronted by their mere request—couldn't they see we were full up, had no room, were there only with each other? We had everything we needed in one another. What was the matter with them? Why would they even ask?

"Of course there's room. Sit on down." It was Diane's voice I heard in disbelief. I looked at her. I could see she was into them. Despair flooded in. The thin tall one was Lenny, his shorter friend with the greasy hair, Frank. They were "from Princeton," which increased my intimidation even more. Princeton.

I could not voice my disagreement. I was supposed to be somebody who would be open, interested, flattered that these two guys wanted to hang with us. That's who I was supposed to be. I had to swallow my reaction.

They joined us and they stayed. They stayed during the speeches. They stayed during the teach-ins. They stayed during our march to the Pentagon. They stayed during the levitating, which, as far as I could tell, was more like a big circle of screaming people. They stayed when we walked by the MP's. They stayed when we, after hours in the cold, went to a coffee shop to get warm—finally, a bathroom. They stayed when we talked over coffee.

And they needed a ride home.

"You can ride with us, can't they, Nan? It's not too far out of the way," my betrayer informed me.

I mumbled my response. *No* was not yet part of my vocabulary, certainly not with her. I was a victim, robbed of my beloved, betrayed by that very same beloved. Our special day, our special time, was stolen from me. So they joined us, these two boys/men "from Princeton," as we hunted for Big Grey, whom we found sitting humbly in his parking place, unmolested, as out of his element as I. They filled the car with their maleness, their smells, their hairy hands, their dominating conversations, their boy-laughter. We smoked pot and I drove Big Grey out of the city, weaving our way back to the highway that led us north, led us home.

I wished that I could be beamed up to my bedroom on Vine Court and find myself tucked in bed. Beamed up like on *Star Trek*, so I would not have to sit here, on Big Grey's handsome front seat, and feel the shame of my broken heart.

Lenny and Diane took up the back seat with their flirting, giggling, and innuendos. The greasy guy sat in the front passenger's seat, looking out the window as he tried to ignore me and I tried to banish him from my line of vision. Big Grey illogically seemed to have his fill of oil now, so we coasted north without stopping.

I winced, almost ducking at their kissing sounds, their little moans. I died and kept driving north, willing them out of the car, willing myself home to my apartment, willing my brave car safely ensconced by our ocean. It was a never-ending and shame-filled night. Lights from the other cars on the road pierced my burning eyes, eyes stinging from un-cried tears. Finally we found "Princeton," after driving hours out of our way. The car door slammed behind them, leaving us in empty, hollow silence. My broken heart ached, my cheeks flushed with unspoken humiliation. Diane wordlessly crawled into the front seat and settled against the door, napping. I continued driving alone now, not even my fantasies as companions. They had abandoned me hours ago.

Vine Court appeared in the ocean mist twenty-two hours after we left. I pulled up in front of number 10 shaking with exhaustion, and turned off the ignition. Big Grey coughed into silence, his noble pilgrimage complete. Diane roused herself, looked around, and grabbed her army backpack from the back. She looked at me, shrugged her shoulders, and said, "Later," as she opened the door and headed toward number 4. I sat for a moment in Big Grey's silence.

Like the colors of penny candy, the paint came off the car in messy, sloppy smears of liquid fluorescent. I sat on the curb the next day, paper towel in hand, somehow knowing that more than my car was being cleaned. Somehow my heart, too, was being scoured. As far as I could tell, the Pentagon did not budge beneath our indignation. Diane faded away, not answering my calls, and eventually dropping out second semester, so I heard, going to a school up north. I sheepishly made my way back to my sorority, where I found some easy-enough, kind-enough friendships. My classes engaged me more in the new semester. Big Grey returned to his job as a commuter vehicle, shuttling me without fanfare up and down Cedar Avenue.

And the war raged on.

"…sharply pointed fins, smiling grill-work…"
A Big Grey Look-Alike

10. Delta Phi Epsilon
1968

The music was crushing and indistinguishable as we walked into the darkened fraternity house. After a few moments, I realized it was Gracie Slick and the Jefferson Airplane, screeching out "Go Ask Alice." The garage-like room was packed with people, dancing and moving, drinking and talking, smoking and laughing, kissing and flirting. The strobe lights were disorienting and dizzying to me. In my heart of hearts, I just wanted to go home, home to our funky sorority house on Broadway Avenue, with its mismatched and comfortable furniture, home to my sisters whom I loved—especially the dark-haired Murph. I wanted to go home, to smoke pot with my friends, to laugh in the warmth of our shared and non-threatening world of women. But it was Friday night. There was no choice. I had to go to a fraternity party.

Gracie and the Airplane blared:

One pill makes you larger

And one pill makes you small

And the ones that mother gives you

Don't do anything at all.

Go ask Alice

When she's ten feet tall.

I was with two friends from Delta Phi Epsilon, my sorority—Linda, whose blond pageboy hair was sprayed perfectly in place, and Murph, the young, dark-haired new girl, a transfer from another school, the one I really liked. Smart, petite, and vivacious, her green eyes spit fire when she talked; her passion grew as she became more engaged in any discussion. I was fascinated by her level of intense energy, and the long smooth planes of the curve of her neck. We all wore the uniform—bellbottom jeans, tie-dyed tee-shirts that we had colored together last weekend, and Frye boots. Mine badly pinched the toes of my right foot, but they, too, were without choice, another inevitable response to 1968. Wear them and pretend you are cool.

And if you go chasing rabbits
And you know you're going to fall—

And you just had some kind of mushroom—
And your mind is moving slow.

Go ask Alice,
I think she'll know.

Linda skirted away to find Brad, the lug-like jock whom she was dating. He both bored and frightened me. Bored by his thickness of neck and blandness of conversation, I always wondered if he saw through me, if he could sense from his island of ultra-masculinity the perverted thoughts that I secretly held. I kept my distance from him, and felt consistently and surprisingly heartsick when Linda would morph into his girlfriend, trading her soft, kind ways to become a brasher and giddier girl.

Murph and I hunkered down for a moment in a corner. She pointed toward the beer kegs and the garbage pail of punch, pantomimed drinking, and went to get us two drinks. I tried to catch my breath, to quiet my drilling heart, as I surveyed the scene. Gracie Slick continued to sing about Alice and her descent down the rabbit hole. I wished I had a rabbit hole which offered escape from the stark confrontation this party presented.

When logic and proportion

Have fallen SLOPPY dead—

And the white knight is talking backwards

And the Red Queen's LOST her head—

Remember what the doormouse said.

Murph handed me a plastic cup with a pink beverage in it. "What it is?" I screamed in her direction.

"Hawaiian punch and grain alcohol—it's delicious and will really stone you out," she responded, her hand cupped around her mouth, funneling the words to me, eyes on the crowd, her body beginning to move in turn with Gracie and the Airplane's rhythms. She transferred the plastic cup to my hands and her fingers grazed mine. My stomach flipped its response.

The punch tasted both sweet and pungent and I gulped at it, as if straining for air in a high altitude. I needed the oxygen of bravery, the air of willingness. I drank some more, smelling Murph's presence—she smelled like lemons and Jean Nate, like cool evening air. Her short hair bobbed with the music. I stood still and drank. She said something I couldn't hear. I tried to ask her to repeat it, but she wasn't listening. She was elsewhere. Her eyes scanned the room, surveying the crowd, looking for someone to be with. I was not that person, and I knew it.

Murph danced away, heading for the dance floor. Looking behind her, as a second thought, she gestured me to come along with her. I nodded a "no" and continued standing and drinking, willing myself to invisibility. I could feel the drink beginning to loosen the tension in my forehead, my jaw releasing, a flush rising in my cheeks. The music shifted to more Airplane. I loved their promise of psychedelic release, but not here, not now. Here I could not relax. Here I was prey waiting to happen and I needed to assess the situation.

Feed your head—

Feed your head.

I learned a strategy of survival during this year of painful Friday night fraternity parties. If I could find a somewhat creepy guy—as long as he wasn't *too* creepy—a guy who was alone, and somehow attach myself to him, I would be safe. He would serve as sufficient cover to get me through the night. I craned my neck for a candidate.

"Hey, hi." The voice came from my left side. Its owner was Ralph, a thin boy/man from my U.S. History class. He wore denim overalls and a flannel shirt, with too-thick glasses and a fiery blotch of pimples on his forehead, unsuccessfully camouflaged by Clearasil. But he was alone and decent enough, and asking.

"Hi," I said, unable to hear my own voice thorough the throb of music, the jumble of the crowd, the beating of my own heart, and the rising response I was having to the punch. I realized that my lips felt numb—I bit at them, trying to will them back into full functionality.

"Wanna dance?" he asked. Could I dare to be seen with him? Was he too creepy? Or was standing there alone the real curse of death? I nodded, not knowing how to rebuke him, and needing him, too, as he undoubtedly needed me.

We made our way toward the heat of bodies moving on the dance floor. I saw a glimpse of Murph, my Murph, dancing with a blond football-player-like guy wearing a madras button-down shirt on the other side of the room. She looked happy. My heart dropped at the sight of her enjoying herself. I wanted her all for myself.

Ralph and I attempted to dance. Space did not open up for us, so we wedged ourselves in even closer to the center of activity and tried moving. My legs were rubbery, I thought in a giddy moment. I never realized that rubbery legs really felt like rubber. My cup sloshed in my hand as I pretended to dance.

Ralph went to get us a second set of drinks. We continued to attempt to dance. We didn't share the same rhythm, and although it was initially embarrassing, with the second drink it mattered less to me. By the third drink I was sweaty and without self-consciousness. It all became funny to me, Ralph and his overalls, Murph across the room with that handsome boy, my Frye boots eating at my toe. Time was warped in the gleam of alcohol. Alcohol got me through.

Somehow I found myself in a quieter and even darker room, couples strewn about in different postures and silhouettes of embrace. I came to and noticed that I was against the wall, Ralph grinding himself into me. He smelled of sour sweat, beer, and some hideously strong aftershave. His lips were pursed against my own, his hand groping for my breast. His tongue felt like a wild snake forcing its way into my mouth. In a split second I was dead-sober and pushed him away, hands on his chest, catching him off balance. He toppled to one side and fell over, onto a pile of coats. Unleashed, I made my way back to the main room.

My eyes strained to find Murph. I knew Linda was fine and ensconced with her Brad. But where was Murph, my Murph? Didn't sisterhood dictate that I find her, make sure she was safe, and take her home? I forced my eyes to readjust to the light in this room. Finally I saw her, sitting on the lap of the large blond boy. They were kissing, and there was no pushing away going on there. Heartsick and alone, shocked and yet not surprised, I turned to leave.

The night air was cool and inky black. My little blue square Rambler, named Fred because of his good citizenship-like appearance and stellar behavior, waited patiently for me. I jabbed the key into the lock and fell in to the front seat. As Fred's door closed behind me, silence and familiar smells surrounded me. I heaved a drunken sigh of relief. The party, its noise and tumult and disappointments, was behind me. I shook my head, willing sobriety to clear out the fuzziness. It was time to drive home. I could do this.

The ignition turned over with Fred's dependable and familiar consistency. Releasing the emergency brake, backing into reverse, I cautiously inched my way back and out of the parking space. The street was quiet and empty, just an occasional car swishing down its length. It was a straight route home, down Cedar Avenue, right on Broadway, and straight down to our stone house standing next to the funeral home. I could do this. I assumed a driving posture and attitude of ultra-conservative caution. I assessed and predetermined every move of my car, and handled Fred with the impeccable focus of an obsessive compulsive drunk.

Inch by inch, Fred and I moved along, all focus and caution in full alert. Turning onto Broadway, I relaxed. Ah, another red light. It was a long light, long enough to warrant a rest. I laid down on the front seat, taking up the passenger seat, the seat where Murph should have been sitting. I pretended that I could smell her and feel her presence. I rested for a few moments, waiting for the light to turn green.

"Murph, will you love only me?" I asked. I rested, savoring her imaginary response.

The light changed, and I sat up again reluctantly, drove a few more blocks, only to be stopped at the next red light. Here again I lay down and rested, and communicated some more with Murph, waiting for yet another green light to urge me forward.

"Murph, you're so beautiful. Please kiss me, kiss me forever," I pleaded, and she responded so fully, opening her mouth so completely to me that, as I dove in, as I dove deeply inside of her, I unlocked myself along the way, wet and released and all-tingling.

Up and down a few times, my little cat naps were refreshing and renewing, my conversation with Murph profoundly satisfying. I made my way back to our house, turned into the driveway and turned off the engine. I opened the door and vomited violently into the pebbles of the driveway. I watched fascinated as my vomit coated and covered the stones with unique pattern of texture and design.

Red light. Green light. Stop. Start.

Never let them know.

Never. Never.

Red light.

Stop.

11. Peace Corps Volunteer, 103 Degrees
1971

The relentless and unforgiving sun beat upon my shoulders—there was nowhere to hide from its unfair intensity. As I waited for the jeepney, one of those small, brightly painted buses, to take me into town, my teacher's uniform, green and shiny, was so tight across my back and shoulders that it seemed to harness me against my will into the moment. The uniforms were individually made, mine needing several bolts of cloth, rather than the usual one, since my American body was so much larger than my Philippine counterparts. The dressmaker, needles like spokes coming out of her mouth, laughed heartily at my size. Not a small girl at age twenty-two, the moisture I retained in the intensity of this climate filled and rounded me out even more, puffing out my cheeks and padding my hips and butt. In this culture, I was a large and giant woman. I felt even larger, swollen and constantly uncomfortable in the soupy heat. I shuffled my sandals and the dust kicked up in billows of dryness. I coughed. Waiting for the public transportation here was always an exercise in angelic patience. A few tiny kids huddled around their mother across the block, shyly hiding behind her skirt. My whiteness, my otherness frightened them. I waved at them, played a hide-and-seek game, to their shrieks of hysterical delight. The kids, adorable and eager, were worth it all, I thought

I felt neither adorable nor eager as I stood at the jeepney stand. My purse cut meanly into my shoulder. My assignment in the school outside our central barrio, now complete, had been an exercise in frustration. I was teaching English as a second language to children in elementary school and serving as a teacher trainer. However, the administrators within my school system, the Butuan Central Schools, were eager for me to be their trophy Americana. Their need was to display me, to show me off, to have me perform at teacher gatherings, wanting me to dance and sing their folk tunes. It humiliated and frightened me, and I refused, to their dismay and shame.

My need was to be useful, according to my twenty-two-year-old standards. I had yet, in my twelve months here, found a way to sink into my job and feel a helpful part of it. All I wanted to do was to serve, just like JFK said, in that first black and white Peace Corps documentary I saw during my sophomore year in high school. The New Frontier. To serve and offer yourself, to make the world better, our young and handsome president said. When I watched that thirty minute special on my parents' little television set in 1964, I knew the Peace Corps would be a way out, and a way in—to help others, to have somewhere to go. But living on this island was nothing like the documentary I had seen. With a sigh of frustration, I shifted my bag's weight.

Suddenly I felt sharp, painful sensations all over my left foot. I looked down, only to find my foot covered in a swirl of tiny red fire ants. With a rush of adrenalin, I shook it wildly, trying to get them off. Their bites were painful and deep and escalated unendingly in intensity. The more I struggled, the harder it was to get them off. The woman and children from across the way ventured closer to me now, cautiously considering my jerky movements. After a futile long minute or two, I realized that I had to use my hand to slap and swat these bugs off me. The tapping and patting was hard work that hurt my hand, along with my foot, and several more even longer minutes were needed for me to become ant-free. At the end of the siege, I was trembling from the physical assault, the exhaustion of the struggle, and the isolated fear it brought me.

Another day as a Peace Corps Volunteer, I cynically thought.

I had several other physically frightening experiences during my in-country stay that activated this particular flavor of fear. One stifling and quiet afternoon as I lay sprawled and reading on the bed under its canopy of mosquito netting, a huge spider, hairy and long-legged, sauntered out of my underwear drawer. I was not one to fear creepy, crawling things, my Girl Scout training secure. But this spider was outrageously thick and black, and so assuming of its space. A chill shot through me, leaving me shaky. I backed out of the room, book abandoned, leaving the spider to have its way with my undergarments. I tried to laugh this incident away, yet it disturbed me deeply, and somehow activated some specific worry I just couldn't put my finger on.

Another time I was driving back from Cabadbaron, Honey's little village, about sixty minutes away from our town of Butuan. Honey, my friend, Honey, my support, Honey, my love. She was driving her father's jeep, always a tad recklessly, today no differently. Her black hair was blowing in the wind, smile lighting her face as she challenged herself and the vehicle to screech around unpaved, muddy curves. Her strong, muscular arms held the wheel almost at bay, commanding it to do her bidding. I held onto my door, my absorption in her stronger than my fear. As I watched her face, forever fascinated, I saw the change before I heard it. She slammed on the brakes as we jerked to a stop. Right ahead of us, there had been a terrible accident—another jeep had gone off the embankment, missing the bridge, and was crushed below us, maybe fifteen feet. Someone was already there trying to help. The screams of the dying people haunted me, driving home to my core the distance in miles, in culture, in climate, in everything, the miles that separated me from my family, from my home. Hearing and trying to not watch death pulled from me a silent plea: *Oh, please God, do not, do not let me die here. Please do not let me die in this country.*

We were blocked in, another vehicle behind us. So we sat with death that day, never mentioning it to each other. I hardly mentioned it to myself. But in those long minutes which turned into hours, as I sat with death, I could not keep from myself the realization that I had learned to ignore in this country—that this was not and never could be my home. This could not be the place that I died. The intensity of such fear freed up the reality of this strange culture's distance from my own. I was yet again a stranger, but now race, culture, and language cemented me even further away from others.

My foot burning from the ants, finally the jeepney came carousing around the corner, laden with people and bundles and chaotic movement. It chugged to a stop, voices urging in a language I could almost grasp to hop on board. Although it seemed inconceivable that another body could fit, hop on board I did, along with the mother and her three babies. Somehow the crowd absorbed us, making way on the wooden slabs that served as benches. The boy whose job it was to collect money approached me. Webbed through his fingers were colored bills of all denominations, his portable cash register always available. I handed him some pesos and received some change, in an exchange I did not fully grasp. And on we traveled, headed back to the city, to Butuan. The air was trapped without escape inside this little bus, its temperature much higher than outside. It was a soup of hot air and I sat within its center, bubbling.

There were two seasons here, dry and muddy. Mud offered a completely new experience of mud—not Pennsylvania mud, not Girl Scout Camp mud, but mud black and monstrous and dangerously thick and sticky. Mud that had the capacity to draw you down into it and pull you in, a life force of its own, overtaking your body's will. Dry was constant, unending, up your nostrils, in between your toes, in your ears and hair. Dry was fine-particled sand that was inescapable.

That day, it was dry on our island of Mindano. We chugged over the road, jostling and slipping from side to side, clouds of dust erupting around our staggering vehicle. I noticed some pressure behind my right eye, a headache emerging, perhaps some response to the attack of crazy ants. I tried to ignore it, smile at the children, and overlook the leers of the small, greasy men staring at my breasts. They always stared at my breasts.

Over the bridge into town we went, the road sliding from dirt into pocked pavement, the noise around us increasing. Somehow I managed to crawl off the bus as gracefully as possible at the central bus stop without making much more of a scene, and attempted to keep to myself as I curved my way home. Through the open-aired market I walked, eyes down, through the remarks of the men, "Hey, Americana. You want some, babeee?" I felt their eyes on me always; even the upper class men that Dina, my Peace Corps buddy and fellow Butuan City-ite, and I had met expected us to be loose women. We were Americans—promiscuity was synonymous with white American woman. Only a few more blocks to go, my feet heavy now, my head aching in the heat and the heaviness of the moment.

Into our little complex I walked, relieved, neighborhood children bidding me hello now. Honey and I had lived here for a few months. She was back from her university in Manila on break. A provincial girl who attended the big university made her a special character; her aunt—the rigid woman who looked disapprovingly down at me when I met her in Manila, her rich aunt whose husband owned the lumber company—helped Honey pay for college and offered her a place to stay. Back in the providences, Honey was like a fish out of water, liberal and aware and bored, looking for fun. We Peace Corps interested her. Dina and I had met her through some mutual teacher friends. She and I were instantly drawn to each other.

She was small and compact, with a tidy and strong body that defied its need for cultural submissiveness. Her hair was long, free, black and alive, and I was instantly lost in it, a wanderer looking for a home. She was brown-skinned, too dark for her country's or even her family's approval, yet delicious to me—like a dark coffee, skin smooth and inviting like toffee. None of this did I know, not quite yet. For now I was simply captivated, captured by her bubbles of laughter, her world of assurance, her guidance in such a strange land. We spent all our time together, my school commitments uncharacteristically pulling to the side of my awareness.

We moved in together into this little apartment, an act that was almost scandalous to my fellow teachers. Honey didn't want to stay in her parents' village, wanting to be "in town." After my hard experience in my first host family's home—barred shut at sunset, my host mother jealous that her husband and I spoke to one another—I, too, needed new housing. In a leap out of the cultural box, we moved in together, a complete oddity in this world. Linda, one of Honey's family's helpers and poorer relatives, lived with us, sleeping on a mat in the kitchen, the kitchen where we killed a dozen huge rats before we moved in, rats as big as cats in my New Jersey world. Honey and I slept together in the one bedroom, each of us on our own little cot.

It was so strange and difficult for me to have a "helper," a servant in this tiny house. But we could not stay there without her, Honey explained when we first talked of moving in together. Having a helper made it culturally acceptable. Almost.

I trudged up the stairs of the building with leaden legs and heard Honey playing her guitar. I smiled to myself. She always played for me, amusing me and touching my heart. My guitar experience was well behind me. I never once touched her guitar, ruffled its strings, or joined my voice with hers. I just listened.

My heart lightened as I walked into the apartment and saw her sitting cross-legged on our makeshift coach, an Indian blanket covering a tattered mattress. She was wearing a red hooded sweatshirt, cold in this heat that drove my boiling heart to despair. She played guitar well and had a strong and evocative voice. She was practicing her favorite song from *Tommy*, the rock opera:

> *See me, feel me*
> *Touch me, heal me.*
> *See me, feel me*
> *Touch me, heal me.*
> *Listening to you, I get the music.*
> *Gazing at you, I get the heat.*
> *Following you, I climb the mountain.*
> *I get excitement at your feet.*

She saw me, grinned, and put the guitar down.

"Nannie," she said, her voice smiling its welcome. She often called me Nannie, her soft *a* sound warming the syllable like nobody else could. "You look wiped out. How was it?"

Somehow when she talked to me, I felt as if I was the only person on earth. All things around me melted into a soft and fuzzy invisibility. She existed as the focal point of my awareness. I relaxed.

The evening passed slowly and languidly. We ate some chicken, rice, and beans that Linda had prepared. We ate, we talked, and the night softened as the darkness settled around us. We had electricity for a few hours erratically at night, and tonight the artificial bulbs were busy offering out their light. Time softly passed.

I started feeling ill after eating. This illness slid into me quickly and with silent stealth.

I stumbled to my hot little cot and rode the waves of sensation. My headache increased, ratcheting itself up on the breath and the heartbeat. Nausea swept like torrential waves over me, bringing me to the edge of physical possibility, then releasing, and crashing me backwards again. I felt my fingers bloat and grow fat and stubby, cigar-fingers increasing as my breath intensified. How strange to have cigars as fingers, I mumbled, laughing and crying, feeling them dilate, expand, and contract again. I thought of my mother, my beautiful quiet mother, so far from here, so worried for me. I thought of my father, literally sick over my choice to leave him and his world so far behind. I cried their names and asked them for help, all the while my head crashing, my stomach churning violently, my fingers now as large as the dirigibles that would float by us at the Jersey shore on our Beach Haven summers. I cried and sweated and yearned for help. My body's shape was outlined in sweat on the little cot, sweat of disease, sweat of delirium.

Honey's presence was quiet and competent. Somehow she got water into me, hoping to encourage me to vomit. I spit it up quite violently and it only brought me more suffering, and now a wet and soggy bed. She sent Linda, quiet, almost motionless Linda for a thermometer and one appeared mysteriously in my mouth. Trying to remember not to bite it, the sweat blinding me now, I laughed and cried at this seemingly impossible dictum: don't bite the thermometer!

"One hundred and three," Honey said solemnly, her voice called to me from a distant echo chamber.

In my delirium, I thought she meant that I was a hundred and three years old. My confusion seemed hysterical to me and I roared my amusement, peed, and cried some more. I thrashed from side to side, trying to find a place that would release me from the growing intensity of my body's revolt to this food poisoning, as I would find out later.

Honey, in a seamless series of slow-motioned movements that unfolded before me, moved inch by inch on top of me, in an attempt to quiet and contain me. She laid her body full on mine, breasts to breasts, belly to belly, leg to leg, and held me fast, her wrists pinning mine down to the mattress.

Life stopped. My breath froze. I felt her in every cell of my body— her warmth, her soft brown deliciousness fed me. I sobered into the sensations of connection, illness banished. Woman to woman I was held.

"This feels great!" I gasped in silence inside myself, and shuddered. My body opened up even more, swooned into a place of untouched sensuality. I was opened and unlocked, unfolded and released, more and more, spiraling down into myself.

The moment blurred, stopped, and went silent.

I had to be this far away from home—15, 000 miles. I had to be this far away from everything I knew and loved and identified with—mom and dad, college and pot, my sorority sisters, the righteousness of the anti-war movement, my white tidy house at 207 Arthur Avenue, Madison Avenue Temple. All of that. I had to have a fever of a hundred and three degrees, wrecked out of my mind by some foreign disease, to be able to feel. To simply be able to feel: the body of another woman against my own.

It felt great.

"The jeepney came carousing around the corner, laden with people and bundles and chaotic movement."

12. The MacDougal Street Café, NYC
1974

We rode into the City on that hot Sunday afternoon, Paul puffed up at the wheel. His moustache seemed unusually burly, perhaps the humidity of the day accentuating its bulk. His thinning black hair, bald spot sweaty in the heat, was long to his collar. He wore his faux hippy outfit—polyester bellbottoms, light sea-green colored shirt unbuttoned to reveal his protuberance of black matted chest hair. His words drifted over me, unanchored in relevancy. I watched the New Jersey turnpike scenery, refinery after smoky refinery, roll by. Each breath sat heavy in my belly, leaden like the heat of this August day.

I already felt like a sore-thumb tourist, identifiable from afar. My clothes rested upon me with an uncomfortable and unfamiliar pull. I seemed to always lack the capacity to look right or to be comfortable with either myself or my clothing. My short rayon Indian skirt gathered behind my knees in little bands of sweat. My Indian gauze shirt was wrinkled and clingy. I wore Birkenstocks, my footwear of choice. A nice Jewish girl from the suburbs of New Jersey, a hippie-wannabe, I headed into the West Village to see the sights. My hair was cut in a shag, close to my head yet long in the back, generating sweat at the base of my neck. My heart was numbed, my body disconnected. I lived from my earlobes up, not landed on earth.

My husband drove and talked incessantly. He always talked incessantly. His words were of film, of theater, of people, of anything that he felt he knew—and since he knew everything, he talked of everything, always the eager-to-please expert:

"….and in that final long shot, Altman hit it just right, having Warren Beatty and Julie Christie look at each other, the way he panned back to the…"

He was talking about *McCabe and Mrs. Miller*, a wonderful movie we had seen the week before. I secretly longed for Julie Christie in that movie, as she played the madam of the whore house in the Wild West territory. I was drawn into the wide expanse of her eyes. Her determined gentleness colored the screen, and it colored my heart. I left the theater emptied and so lonely, with Paul at my side, almost heartsick with loss, deeply touched, still clinging to Julie's seductive softness.

Paul and I met in college. He, a friend of a friend, was from another college in northern New Jersey. On paper, it looked right. We were interested in the same things: film, writing, the counter-culture. We both taught English in different inner city school systems. We surely shared the same interests, interests from the earlobes upward. And Paul was not a sexual threat—he accepted my pulling away, my subtle shifts of body language, my nonchalant excuses, with a chagrined casualness.

He was not a bad man, this husband of mind. Clearly, he was caring and progressive in thought. He didn't have a mean bone in his being. But he talked and nattered and tried to prove his point, over and over again. He had gotten louder over those two-and-a-half years since we were married. He got louder, as I got quieter. He got more frenetic as my body became more immobile. He got busier as I got more depressed, looking to my high school students for connection, looking to marijuana for meaning. Together Paul and I saw many movies and much theater, listened to the Moody Blues, smoked a lot of pot— usually before, during, and after such events—and generated many wise and meaningful thoughts. We were together in these endeavors, yet so alone. Bergman's films were my favorites; the Doors and the Moody Blues my psychedelic love; Ram Das my hero. But although we shared activities, there existed no connection between Paul and me in heart, in belly, in arm, in hand, in leg. His body was a beached whale, strangely landed next to me in bed. I was occasionally puzzled about how he landed there, and often just simply numbed to his presence.

Paul navigated the red Volkswagen Beetle through the crowded streets of the West Village, maneuvering and cursing his way into a parking space hardly big enough for us. We staggered out into the afternoon heat, amidst the energy and sights of Greenwich Village, 1974.

The touch of his sweaty hand at my elbow, moving me through the crowded and colorful walkways of Washington Square Park, was not unlike his handling of the car—determined and gruff. I didn't want him to touch me, didn't want to feel his moist palm cup my elbow, his stubby fingers squeeze my arm. The awareness of this physical rejection was instantly wrung out of me—there was no available spot inside of me for such displeasure to abide. I just continued shuffling next to him, asleep to my own disconnect.

The crowd swarmed around us, rich with colors and sounds and the joys of a summer afternoon. There was a long-haired rocker, his rats' nest hair contained by an American flag headband, screeching his rebellious rhythms, his guitar case opened beside him for donations. It had been years since my guitar playing screeched into silence. Watching his passion was a painful reminder of my lacking. There was a white-faced mime, swamped by a multitude of eager tourists, escaping from that invisible room that only he could see, movements seamlessly and strangely realistic. Somehow this man's act made me uncomfortable, the gag about sightlessness not funny to me. There was a man and a blonde, happy dog playing a wild and joyous game of Frisbee, cute happy dog with smiling eyes and a goofy dog-smile flinging itself into space with such trustful abandon to catch the red rubber Frisbee. That dog was the best part of the park for me that afternoon—his eagerness, his grace, his connection with his partner-person, a connection I so lacked.

There were tables of men of all shapes, sizes, ages, and colors playing chess, eagerly and excitedly tapping the tops of their time clocks. Paul understood chess, or so he said, and hovered over one table's game. I looked around feeling so bored and disengaged that I felt I could drop to my knees and sink to the pavement in exhaustion. Nothing in this park touched me, nothing could enter my heart. I craned my neck to find the fuzzy blonde dog, the only heart that touched mine. The dog appeared to be gone now from the scrubby grass, dissolved into the filmy heat of the day. I missed him.

We walked away from the Park, following its side streets aimlessly, the noise and tumult fading a bit. Shops advertising all kinds of wares beckoned us in. We strolled by intimidating art galleries, a huge used book shop with a mustiness that wafted out into the street, a store announcing itself as *The Pink Pussycat, Sex Toys for All*—no need to go there, I thought with bitter relief—*All You Need is Love*, a vast and hip-looking used clothing store, dramatic churches, and impressive brownstones where cool people must have lived. We wandered. Externally I imagined we looked like any suburban couple in the City for a few vicarious hours. Yet internally I knew that I did not belong—not with Paul, our passionless marriage empty; not with myself; not with anybody. I was unhinged, disconnected, and utterly and despairingly alone. I was so alone that, in some real sense, I didn't know it. I was sleepwalking, going through the motions of a life that I did not really inhabit. Like a near-death experience that hovered and lingered, this lack of self-awareness seemed never-ending.

Yet there was a moment of insight. Months before, Paul off at his film course, leaving me blessedly home alone in that cute yet unsatisfying apartment with the black Parsons table and the red vinyl chairs, I found myself making the bed, our marriage bed. As I fluffed up the pillows and arranged the sheets, like a bolt of lightning, it struck me: this bed was a farce! There was no passion here, no sex here, no man and wife here. There was nothing here but the denial, the hiding, the pretending to him, to myself. My eyes found the round pink container of birth control pills that I took daily, no matter what, an essential brick in the façade of denial. In that moment of openness to truth, I saw the absurdity, the pathetic masquerade of this marriage. And then I chose to forget again. I chose to submerge myself back down into the land of sightlessness, like the mime, working to escape a room I could not even see. So sightless was I that even the room, the prison, faded from sight. I couldn't know the pain I was in. Not yet.

We entered the café that hot Sunday afternoon, its hand-painted, flowery sign an intriguing invitation: *The MacDougal Street Café*. Wood floors with sawdust on them, posters covering the walls, this cool and dark environment, a relief from the heat, was everything I wanted the legendary West Village to be—counter-cultured, hippied, ripe with the smells of incense, strong coffee, and stale beer. We sat in rickety chairs around a rounded table with a slightly stained red and white checked tablecloth on it, with a glassed candle in its center. I sank into shame, I sat into numbness. Paul talked on, as I floated away some more, nothing to hold onto, nothing real to embrace as mine.

The coffee house was quiet and sparsely inhabited. Our waiter was a thin and graceful young man. A few customers sat at the counter, mugs in hand, mouths moving silently.

My mug was filled with iced coffee. I took a tentative sip, and looked around me.

And then I saw them. It was another lightning bolt cutting through the clouds of my own unconsciousness. There were two women whom I hadn't yet noticed, sitting to my left. They were sitting at a rounded table, heads close, whispering, sharing some conspiratorial moment. I saw them and I felt them and I knew, for the first time in my life, that they were lovers. It was the tilt of their heads, the closeness of their bodies, the air around them that announced their affection. They were women, and they were lovers, and they shared this coffee house, this afternoon, with the rest of the planet. And this was possible. Women could be with women. My mouth literally dropped opened in response to this extraordinary realization. Women could love women, and go to coffee houses, and have coffee together. Somehow in my twenty-four years of life, even in my loving and holding Honey in the Philippines, somehow this realization had eluded me.

Women can be with women. Women can touch and hold each other, can laugh and cry and walk down the street. Not all streets. Only these streets. But there was somewhere, somewhere to be a woman who loved women. This moment was the harbinger of magic, as it sliced though the deadness of my life, and whispered quietly to me of possibilities to come.

Paul nattered on. My moment faded. As we drove home that drizzly evening, the New Jersey turnpike was thick with cars headed everywhere. The wheels of the VW made their haunting hum, like a plea beneath me. As I headed back to that wall-less prison of my suburban life, a tiny door had opened and then abruptly closed, deep inside my heart.

"I didn't know how I landed there."

13. I-95
1974

The drive to Florida would never end, or so it seemed. I felt doomed, prophesized, ordered, to stay captive in this Volkswagen Bug with this man, my husband, for an endless road trip. It probably wasn't a very good idea, this heading south on our Christmas break. Although Paul and I worked in different school systems, our vacations were similar enough to make a joint vacation possible. It was his idea:

"Let's drive down to Sarasota and see your Peace Corps friends, Joe and Char, over the break," he suggested with his usual air of joviality.

Certainly this was an innocuous enough invitation—some wives might have actually been interested or perhaps even excited to share a holiday voyage together with their spouse. But not me. Not this wife. This wife had been married for two and a half years, without love, without sex, without emotional connection. This wife had rebounded wildly back to Paul after a love affair with Honey in the Philippines, a love affair that was unable to cross international borders. This wife was tired and alone and so heartbroken. This wife didn't know yet that the man next to her was not the one, not the person with whom to share bed, to share bath, to share meals, to share ideas and love and touches. This wife didn't know yet that life did not have to be so painfully, violently, horrifically empty. This wife didn't know yet that she deserved more. This wife still complied, believing without thinking that existence was this hollow, that having it "look right" was the most important charge one had in life.

This wife said, as all good wives might, "Sure, good idea." She imagined thoughtlessly, this wife that I was, that the Florida trip might offer an escape, a way out of the feelings of profound and debilitating isolation.

And south we traveled, bathing suits, shorts, and sandals hastily packed. Our joints were disguised in Paul's Camels pack, a hideaway he swore was fool-proof and police-proof, a ruse that never met its test.

The charade began on the New Jersey Parkway, and the states started to boringly melt into one another. New Jersey flowed without fanfare into Delaware. I lost track after that. The bucket seat of the car held me, a comforting hand of support. Sitting in its palm, keeping awake became the greatest challenge. My eyelids were so heavy. They just wanted to close, to shut, to become sightless. My ears wanted to permanently fold over themselves, rendering me hearing-less. I wanted to sit stock-still so that I did not have to hear him, see him, feel him. Somehow being completely still would keep my charade unchallenged—husband and wife, on a trip; young married people, headed south; life partners, sharing the moment. In my stillness denial was held, cemented in place. Cracks were erupting on the surface of the façade of my denial, so I could not risk agitating reality in any way. Stillness and silence were my response, the deadening refuge that I sought, the only solace that seemed effective.

Paul appeared not to notice my silence. As he smoked a joint, he rattled on about a poem he was working on, its meter a challenge to him. His investment in our collective denial must have been a huge burden for him—it kept him talking, kept him in motion. He was a good man, just a man sitting in the wrong seat, next to the wrong woman. I attempted to respond with the least amount of effort, so I might not be rattled from my cage of unconsciousness. I settled more deeply into the cradle of my seat and watched the countryside blandly roll on.

At a rest stop in Virginia, we took off our sweaters and winter coats, reaching into the bag of foreign-feeling summer clothes. Shorts and tee-shirts, sandals and sunglasses made their way to the surface of the moment. Peeling off our winter layers, we bared our pale, northern skin to the warmer temperatures, to the heat of the truth waiting to burn off the layers of self-deception beneath which we both hid.

We stayed in a motel in Virginia Beach. The room was musty; the bed was lumpy and smelled like moth balls. We got stoned and watched the public television channel. The nature program portrayed the workings of spider ants—they built nests, created colonies. It seemed remarkable to me. How had they been able to create what I did not yet have? *To be a spider ant,* I half thought. *To have a colony, a home that fit.* The words were vague and unformed, but their ideas were whispering, blossoming, and gaining strength deep within me.

My heart was preparing itself for eruption.

Finally, after an indeterminable amount of time on the road, we pulled into Sarasota and easily found Joe and Char's place, which was alive with the fragrances of warmth, honeysuckle, and sweetness. Tucked away near the bay, the small yard tended, their picket fence whitewashed and trim, their house, small and compact, felt like them—tidy and easily available. Char came out to greet us, larger-than-life Char, earth-mother Char. Grin huge, wiping her hands on her apron, hair asunder in an auburn beehive of disheveled activity, there was Char. She always seemed older to me, ever since the first time I met her in Peace Corps training in Vermont—the wise woman, a bit more experienced, a bit more worldly, a bit more wise to the ways of the world. She was a safe place, a friend from the heart who had seen me though some strange and disconcerting Peace Corps experiences. Her support was wordless. It was the support of a smile, a hug, a touch, an encouraging nod. A delicious joint, never far from her fingertips, made her love all the more tasty. As her all-encompassing hug held me close that day, something deep inside of me shuddered.

Joe was kind and quiet, bespectacled, a bit older than we were, a quiet and good man, wearing dungaree shorts and a yellow tee shirt. His tanned bare feet seemed to keep him grounded, connected, one with the strangely sandy earth. As he smiled his love upon me, an icicle of my internal New Jersey frost began its long-awaited defrost.

We ate greens from their garden, talked of politics and life, and smoked a few more joints. Darkness fell over their knotty pine rumpus room. Their skinny calico cat, Tiny, wound her way around the labyrinth of my legs as I sat cross-legged on the floor. I never wanted to move. Frozen I sat, in the face of the warming Florida night as the light of the day slowly faded, reducing itself to a soft and sweet twilight.

"Nan, honey." Char was calling me. I looked up from my drugged stupor of disappointment and heartbreak. "Come on in the kitchen, sweetie. Come on and help me out."

Although standing on legs I did not believe I had seemed an impossibility, stand I did, for it was Char. Char was one of the few things left in my life worth standing for. On wobbly legs I followed her into her kitchen. The kitchen was soft yellow, not unlike Joe's tee-shirt. Soft flowered curtains caressed the windows, and plants sat everywhere, offering their colorful and undeniable beauty. This was a kitchen that was lived in, I thought. This was a home where love lived.

She turned to face me, looked me dead in the eyes, put her hands on my shoulders, and said, from her core to mine, "Dear, are you all right? Are you all right with him?"

Her words were breathtakingly powerful, visceral, physical, and gut-wrenching. They stung the breath out of me. I had to gasp for air, to keep my nose above the intensity of her inquiry.

Was I all right? Was I all right with him? That was the question.

In that moment, the answer, crystal-clear, emerged. The answer I had run from, denied, ignored, manipulated, feared—the answer was as simple as the next breath, the next moment, as obvious as the red geranium on Char's oak table. It was simply here, available, now fully accessible to me.

Was I all right?

No, I was not all right. Not with myself. Not with him. I was hiding, pretending to be someone and something that I was not.

It was profoundly simple, astoundingly and stunningly simple. In my dumbfounded silence, I looked at Char, who looked at me. Tiny the cat purred, rubbing against my leg. There was no going back. The truth had revealed itself, plopped itself down in the center of my heart, freed. My heart literally and instantaneously lifted. This yellow kitchen of love had given birth to my truth: I was a woman who could not live with a man. Not this man, at any rate. Perhaps I could not live with any man. But this I now knew—I needed to find out.

Paul left the next morning before dawn, after a long and sleepless night of his pleadings and my refusals, his demands and my steadfastness, his disbelief and my detached strength. My moment of truth in Char and Joe's yellow kitchen altered the air between us. I was released, able to advocate for my own needs. That simply and that quickly, after two and a half long and hideously painful years, it changed instantly.

He took the little red car and headed back up I-95 alone. I stayed with Joe and Char to continue south, to be joined by Peace Corps friends from Wisconsin, Mary and Marty. We traveled to the Everglades in Joe's pea green Volkswagen bus, and camped on the gentle earth. My friends wildly championed my new independence and restored me with love, light, laughter, and hope. We built fires and howled at the full moon. We kayaked in the ocean and napped on the sandy grass. We laughed and cried, smoked pot and drank cheap wine. We ate spaghetti and hash brownies, snickered about our past and dreamed of our future. We played wild Frisbee and sunbathed on damp, sandy towels. We were together, a family of friends, a heart of community. With heart released, I was enlivened, awakened from my deep slumber of denial. The world was bright, the light was clear, the colors were glorious, and all was possible. My tears were authentic, my laughter raucous. I was funny, sad, born again, renewed. The earth held me, the ocean warmed me, my friends believed in me, my heart freed me.

At the end of a glorious week, the chugging VW bus, its sunburned inhabitants intact, wove its way through the cement maze of the departures gate at Miami International Airport. I extricated myself from the bus and offered each one of my friends a full-bodied goodbye. After diving down into Char's arms, I righted myself and gazed at her. She took the back of her hand, brushed my cheek clear, and nodded me toward the gate. I turned away, sandaled feet heading toward airport security, a single tear in my eye.

It was the last time I would see or hear from Char. Yet, as the fluorescent lights and the hollow noises of the terminal flooded me, her touch radiated on my cheek. The sanctity of her indelible blessing moved me forward, one step at a time.

I gulped myself back to reality. Holy shit. Now what?

Chapter 14: Jumping on Suits— Angels in the Bathtub
1974

Paul looked liked he hadn't slept in a month. Slouched at our black Parsons table, he was unusually disheveled, his denim work shirt rumpled, his hair uncombed. He had a dark stubble of beard splattering his cheeks and chin. He eyed me warily through narrow eyelids. I was internally disorientated by his appearance. My separation week in the Florida Keys had been one of sun and light, healing and health. I slept and rested and played and renewed, was tanned, and felt better than I had in years. He, my dark counterpart, glared at me from across his coffee mug.

He spoke of reconciliation, of therapy, of possibilities, of hope. His hands moved jerkily as he spoke. A tiny nervous tick played with the muscles around his right eye. He kept his eyes down, facing the table, never meeting mine full on. His words faded into meaninglessness, his voice whiney and on edge.

I looked around the apartment, the red vinyl chairs, the Parsons table, the comfortable coach with the matching black and white striped chairs, remnants from his mother's house. It was a great couch for sleeping, I thought, remembering how many nights I had left my marriage bed, sleepless, companionless, heartless, to find my only solace there. It was an attractive apartment—it looked right—but it was emptied of energy, of love, of inhabitants. I knew what I had to do.

"No." My voice spoke this complete sentence quietly. This simple sentence had been absent from my vocabulary for a long, long time now. "No," I repeated, a little louder.

He looked up, startled.

"No. It's over. I need you to leave this apartment now. I need to be alone." Was that really my voice, growing in both volume and firmness? It was a voice speaking its needs, planting a flag of honesty in the earth of reality. It almost didn't sound like me, such a stranger was I to my own ears.

I didn't have a roadmap for this moment in my life or for the moments up ahead. I had absolutely no idea what would happen, where I would go, what I wanted. But I knew one single thing with profound certainty: he must leave this apartment to me tonight. I could not spend another night, another day, literally not another hour with him inhabiting the same space, sharing the same air as I.

He sputtered his disbelief, wordless, furious, face jerking around from side to side, some spittle covering his lips. The foundation of his world was shattering beneath his feet, while mine was emerging with graceful unfoldment. We were vibrating at different frequencies, Ram Das would have said, I think. Ram Das, whose book *Be Here Now* I pondered, studied, idolized, memorized, and hoped into reality.

There was no room in his reaction for my words, no space here for my perspective. No matter how formless my reality was, it was mine, and I needed to claim it. I sat without movement and practiced not listening to him, keeping myself tightly protected from his frantic response, wrapped away from his righteous intensity. This surely was not a time for logic and calm reasoning.

A deep internal switch inside me was coming to life. This switch had been unused, frozen, rusted into stillness for years. The heat of the Florida sun, the love of my friends, the week away from him, thawed and oiled it into aliveness. My mind got quiet, my thoughts hushed.

My passion took control—my anger, asleep for years, boiled into reaction. My voice was found. The switch turned on.

"No fucking way. NO FUCKING WAY. NOFUCKINGWAY. Get out of here. Get out getout GETOUT!"

Like a stranger I observed myself. I watched the fury move me; the nice girl evaporated, the good wife spontaneously combusted. I watched my eruption with a detached and somewhat amused interest. This other person was nutty, unreasonable, furious, illogical. She was passionately alive. She amazed me.

My fury continued to grow without reason. I was suddenly wholly and completely enraged. The moment was beyond thought—I was beyond thought. I was simply energies moving, change happening, woman enlivened. I rushed to the hall closet, as if to prove my point. Flinging it open—this was not a plan, I was completely spontaneous, such a new place for me—I grabbed two armfuls of his suits and tossed them on the floor between us. The gauntlet was drawn. I briefly remembered the shopping trip before we were married with his father, Joe, who bought these suits for him. I remember not liking the clothes at all, and not saying a thing—their polyester feel uncomfortable between my fingers, their cut old-mannish to me. The pile heaped between us, Paul looked dumbfounded.

I observed myself as if in slow motion, taking a leaping jump onto the pile of Paul's suits. I started jumping up and down on them, up and down, in rhythm with my beating heart, in rhythm with the flush of blood racing in my head. I jumped as if I had never jumped before. I proclaimed my personal space as it was never proclaimed. I declared my needs with a silent power that would have turned Goliath around in his tracks. Paul crumpled beneath my rage.

He left the apartment with a handful of clothing, shoulders slumped, face ashen. Trembling with the strangeness of victory, I hung his suits back up, one at a time, in utter disbelief at my own power. He came during the week when I was at school to get the rest of his stuff. Afterwards I changed the locks. I never saw him again.

I decided to abandon the marriage bedroom completely, and to live in one section of the living room. I made a little bed for myself, my bed, my self, and slept deeply held in the arms of the universe. I ate there, too, on a tiny stool, eating from a single bowl. Still on winter break for a few days, I danced around the apartment, rearranging things, moving things, taking fancy sheets and matching towel sets to Goodwill, renouncing my redundancy. During those grey winter days, I recreated my world, rearranged the physical space around me and explored the quiet space within me. This was the first time I was alone, the first time I lived alone, in my twenty-five years.

I was joyous, by myself, and freed.

One night I found myself elegantly soaking in a delicious bubble bath. I wiggled my toes, creating a playful community of bubbles. I rubbed my knees together forming tiny bubbles that sang in delight when they popped together. I enjoyed myself thoroughly. Out of my pleasure with self, my pleasure of self, a prayer emerged from deep within me. I proclaimed to myself and anyone who would listen:

"I will never again in my life do anything that I don't want to do. Never."

I laid back, resting against the porcelain tub rim, allowing my proclamation to sink in, breathing in its power and possibility.

I will never… I will never.

And then I heard them. They were the voices of women singing wordless chants, softly at first, almost a whisper, in harmony. I sat up in the tub.

Wait a second, I thought to myself. *Am I stoned? No, absolutely not. I am not making this up.*

Their voices grew in volume, in intensity. Without words, they proclaimed a song of celebration, an honoring of my newly found freedom. My rational mind was on overload—was this inside my head? No, clearly it was outside of me. My heart stilled, my breath quieted, as my serenade erupted into a toning of ancient magnificence, surrounding me, lifting me up, humbling me, healing me.

The singing of angels filled my bathroom.

My prayer had been witnessed and consecrated.

15. Leon and the Holy Grail
1975

I didn't know the way. I knew what it was, and even where it was, but I didn't know how to get there from here. I had been reading Paul's *Village Voice* newspapers regularly, packed full of heady alternative ideas, announcements, and advertisements: "Men Seeking Men," "The Hidden War of Richard Nixon." The ink of the long, thick paper blotted my hands, but I didn't mind. Somehow the ink stains emerged as a Rorschach test of alternatives and options. Read this ink blot, my palm seemed to beckon, and view your future prospects.

The classified section on the back cover was thick with opportunity, and was almost overwhelming to me. One could attend a festival of Wicca, or a greenmarket in Central Park. An open-minded citizen of the island of Manhattan could participate in the New Age Health Fair this upcoming weekend, or attend the Saint Jude festival in Bryant Park. None of this computed with my suburban New Jersey world or made much sense, but it compelled me to keep searching the ads week after week, looking for a harbor into which I might sail.

Finally, I found what I was looking for one week in early November. Halfway down the left column, it read: *Lesbian Feminist Liberation— LFL—Coming Out Sunday. Join us as we affirm our lesbian voices and claim our personal and political truth—Sunday, 11/11, @ 2:00, 751 14ᵗʰ Street at Union Square.*

Even just the reading of this titillated and thrilled me. *Lesbian Feminist Liberation.* Those words were stirring, terrifying, energizing. What did they mean? Enough denial had lifted from me, and through the lifting fog, I realized that lesbians were people in New York—and maybe other cities?—women loving women. I didn't know if that was what I was, but I knew I needed to find out. *Feminist?* The Women's Movement, I guessed, all that stuff that really didn't matter very much to me. And *Liberation?* What did that mean? Who was being liberated? I didn't know and I didn't care. My visceral response to this advertisement was all I needed to understand. I had to attend this "coming out Sunday." With Paul gone from the apartment now, I felt so released and different. It was time to move forward, and moving forward toward 14ᵗʰ Street was the only option that had materialized.

I found myself returning to the ad over and over again, rereading its invitation. Even the reading of it evoked a dangerous and shameful excitement. I kept it under some papers on my desk, even though I was alone now in the apartment. There was nobody to see it—yet I feared invisible detection.

But where was 14ᵗʰ Street at Union Square? I almost knew how to get to the Holland Tunnel from our New Jersey apartment. I had watched Paul do it over the years and had memorized the intersection of roads—the New Jersey Parkway North to the New Jersey Turnpike North to the Holland Tunnel. It still brought shivers of fear to me as I imagined both driving and navigating our red Volkswagen that far away from suburbia, through those treacherous and busy New York roads. But I was compelled. I had to.

The New Jersey Parkway North to the New Jersey Turnpike North to the Holland Tunnel. It rang like a litany, a memorized mantra of new beginnings. Could I do it? I had to try.

Inside of myself I struck up a dual bargain with life. On Sunday, 11/11, I would leave my house at noon. I would undertake this perilous trek to the Holland Tunnel. Once there, I would make my way and venture into the City, as Paul would call it, with his usual flip familiarity. If I found this "Union Square," and if there were parking spaces available, that would be a sign from life. Then I would attend this Lesbian Feminist Liberation meeting. Those two obstacles, once conquered, would be the energetic green lights in my process: to find

Union Square from the Holland Tunnel, and to be able to park at 14th Street. The Holy Grail awaited—I just lacked the map. If the obstacles were not overcome, I would return home and be assured that this *LFL*, as it was called in the ad, was not my course

Of course I could have called AAA, or figured out a more mind-centered and effective way to assure my navigational success. The more logical response to this process never occurred to me. Perhaps I was too ambivalent to take that much control of the journey. Circumstance and chance needed invoking. I was not committed enough to be sure of anything.

The day dawned grey and damp, with a light sprinkle of rain/snow smearing the horizon. I woke early, cattycornered on my long and newly liberated marriage bed (that was liberation! Maybe they meant that?). Brushing my teeth and eyeing the storm warily, old family fears of "bad weather" began churning around in my stomach. What if the roads (*The New Jersey Parkway North to the New Jersey Turnpike North to the Holland Tunnel*) were icy? My family history told me that precarious weather upped the ante to life-threatening. Icy roads, snowy roads, were one of life's sneaky ways of getting you; they were to be avoided at all costs. I shuddered in worry and knew that nevertheless, I had to go.

The weather did hold, the thin precipitation coming in light and airy waves throughout the morning, the day stabilizing itself in a grey and moist void. I wore my jeans, boots, a black pea coat that I hoped would be acceptable, a neutral sweater of maroon with a cabled neck. How to not be too obvious? How to not stand out? How to fit in enough? Even these questions were too far away from the facts of the moment—first, the dual challenges.

The red Volkswagen bug named Ruby somehow became mine in the separation. I loved this car. It felt as if it were an extension of my self, my arms and its steering wheel one, my foot and its pedal connected. It huddled around me, a red protective shield, as I backed out of the apartment complex at high noon and wove my way toward phase one: The New Jersey Parkway, North.

The thread of road to road moved me forward. There was thick Sunday traffic heading north along with me, families and singles flowing to outings and dates and family gatherings, events with much more definition than mine: a coming out Sunday at LFL. Surely I was the only person on this entire highway headed to such an event. Perhaps I was the only person on the planet, for all I could imagine. I stayed in the far right lane and kept my speed moderate, for it seemed I could careen off the road with high-speed anxiety. I progressed north. Somehow the Parkway led me directly to the Turnpike, the letters of its huge sign indisputable, its merge multi-laned and uneventful, despite my doubting and trembling nerves. A thin stream of sweat, despite the cool air, trickled down my spine.

Eventually, in what seemed like an eternity of travel, signs announcing the Holland Tunnel appeared before me. *And now the journey really begins,* I thought with irony. I managed to yield in the direction of the Tunnel, and before me it waited, its mouth cavernous and open, cars streaming in, awaiting me. The sight of it, with its neon name HOLLAND TUNNEL advertised above it, was almost too much for my jangled nerves. In a moment of near-panic, I pulled over into the bank of gas stations that lined the right of the road. I happened to land at a Texaco station, its flying horse an omen.

My trembling hands rolled down the window, as an attendant headed toward the driver's side of the car. He wore a faded Texaco jacket and grey almost-matching work pants. His name, *Leon,* was stitched in a red oblong above his heart. My awareness of him was hyper-sharp—I could see with great detail his soft brown face, the stubble of white beard, the dirt under his thick nails, his carefully trimmed wooly hair. His eyes were vague and undetermined. This messenger of my fate approached me.

"Help you, Miss?" his voice asked, with a detached neutrality.

I struggled for words. Not trusting my voice, not the form nor its content, I gulped out a question.

"Hi, how do I get to Union Square?

His eyes came into focus and met mine. I saw him, as he saw me that day, gaze to gaze, human to human. I could feel him softening in toward the window where my trembling heart sat.

"Oh, very easy, Miss, very easy. Go straight through the tunnel and bear left…" his voice had a lilt to it that whispered of a warmer, brighter place; a place of beach, I imagined, of beautiful children, of easier days. I found myself stuck on his voice, and was unfortunately unable to keep hold of its content.

"Umm," I responded, willing somehow to ask again, "I don't really get it. Can you…"

No second request was needed. Prompted by something—goodwill—a sense of karmic purpose—simple kindness, perhaps—Leon pulled a small spiral notebook out of his back pocket, its blue cover dog-eared, and, with an accompanying blue Bic pen, he began to draw a map. His map for me to get from here to there, from the Holland Tunnel to Union Square, from separation to connection, from isolation to community, from shame to the possibility of esteem. His map was clear and concise—even my confusion could not have blurred its simple effectiveness. He took time with me, surely several minutes, going over his directions several times. With a gentleness and kindness that brought the pressure of tears behind my eyes, Leon drew me a map to the Holy Grail, his eyes concerned and smiling the whole time.

I drove away, waving my awed thanks over my shoulder. The Red Sea parted, traffic opened up for me, as Leon's magic map guided me, without hesitation, without interruption, without one single red light, in a flow of ease and magic. We flowed, my car and I, effortlessly through the strangely emptied streets of lower Manhattan, headed north according to Leon's blessed directions, and with no doing, no stressing, no trying, landed on the doorstep of 751 14th Street. There was not a car parked on the block. I had my choice of a dozen parking places in which to deposit the Volkswagen.

I parked and, without thought, got out of the car in disbelief. I took a deep breath and headed toward the building, haloed by Leon's blessing, and walked forward into my new life.

16. Summer Solstice
1978

The drum was the heartbeat of the circle. Drum-Woman's only job was to keep the pulse beating, to keep the rhythm going through this, the shortest night of the year. Sixteen women were readying themselves to begin this circle, gathering around the altar, organizing on-the-floor seating and cushion arrangement, chatting with each other. They were my sisters in prayer, consciousness-building, political change, and spiritual commitment. I was Wing, thirty years old, a member of this community of radical lesbian feminist spiritualists. The core of us had been together for several years now, celebrating the four season changes, the equinoxes and solstices, sitting from sunset to sunrise in a ritual we created loosely based on Native peyote circles. The season changes were only one form in which we bonded. We shared consciousness-raising groups, political actions, and ritual circles throughout the rhythms of the month.

During the Solstice and Equinox circles, we asked the Earth Mother to guide us. The rattle would be passed from woman to woman, each one of us singing, chanting, howling, proclaiming, offering our prayers. The altar that we gathered around on this night was beautiful, staggeringly vibrant with candles, flowers, melons, feathers, fruits, and photographs, all covering the pulsating colors of the altar cloth, a Guatemalan weave. We would pray for health for our planet, peace for all people, the cleansing of the hated evils of racism, sexism, homophobia, and ageism from our earth. We would pray from sunset to sunrise with committed focus. A self-declared guideline was staying attentive throughout the night, sitting upright. The roles of the circle—Drum-Woman, Circle-Woman, and Light-Woman, whose job it was to attend to the many candles over the hours—were interchanged regularly, so that those who wanted responsibility could assume it.

Matti was Drum-Woman for this summer solstice. She was clad in a stunning chartreuse headband, feathers spiking up from it, ocean blue tank top, colorful beaded necklaces, and random sweat pants. Her face was painted with yellow and orange swirls, which seemed to deepen her attitude of concentration. As she prepared the drum for its evening mission, her face was studied and focused—none of the silly Young MattiGoat was visible now. She was prepared for this rite of passage for herself, and prepared to shepherd us through it, too.

The rest of us were dressed in a variety of bright attire, loose pants, scarves and shawls, colorful vests, mirrored blouses, and feathers adorning all. We were sitting on pillows and cushions—creating effective seating for ourselves became a perfected and woman-specific art. I sat on several soft pillows, with harder pillows behind me for support, my particular set up.

Dressing for the circle was a fascinating search for politically correct comfort. I wanted to be festive, special, colorful, yet practically comfortable. I had chosen well, I thought: my favorite brown long-underwear shirt, with a yellow magical galloping horse on it, a mirrored corduroy vest, my favorite yellow tank top underneath for layering, and my favorite yellow parachute pants. It was all good, I thought. I wore earrings of moons and stars, and beaded wrist bracelets. I was, in a lesbian feminist sense, bedecked.

Bethia, our Circle-Woman, prepared to open the circle. She was small and grayed, with angled features, an elder in our community, an intense and righteous woman. Her role tonight was to initiate the different prayers and processes to keep the circle moving and to deal with any issues that might arise. She held our full sanctioned power to respond to circumstances as she saw fit, and to make decisions for our group. She embodied our trust and held a huge space of respect in the community.

The circle was traditionally opened by invoking the four directions. Bethia's plaintive, wailing voice evocatively drew the qualities of each direction to us, drawn into our individual selves and into the collective circle.

> *To the east, renewal and beginnings,*
> *To the south, fire and passion,*
> *To the north, wisdom and knowledge,*
> *To the west, homecoming and infinity.*

At the prayer's completion, Matti and the drum began their haunting rhythm. The magic mushrooms, psilocybin mushrooms, were passed from woman to woman on a gloriously alabaster shell. Each one of us held up our portion of the mushrooms, offering the outcome to that power that was greater than ourselves.

The shell made its way to me. My hands reached out to accept this sacred offering. I held the colorless, strangely shaped dried mushrooms up to the heavens, offered my prayers of gratitude, and brought them into my mouth. They were bitter, moldy, and I struggled with every bite Hard to hold them down, my gag reflex strong, I had to work, to talk myself through, in order to finally succeed in swallowing the magic offering. I instantaneously felt warmed and dizzy.

The energy in the room was light-hearted, almost giddy. Summer solstice was a gift, the shortest and easiest night. We had been through harder, longer times together. We all knew we were able to hold this space together, to bless the earth with our consciousness, to be blessed by the consciousness of the earth. Summer was so much easier, shorter and lighter in energy than winter solstice, the longest night.

The first round of rattling began. The rattle was a foot-long pod from the Amazon, its shaking sounds hollow and reed-like. It was passed from woman to woman, each one of us singing or chanting our commentary. In conjunction with the drum, the sounds of our voices were eerily haunting and evocative. They filled Allyson's Park Slope apartment. *Good thing her neighbors are out of town*, I thought. *We can really relax.*

A growing pulsating rhythm was generating in my stomach, churning, throbbing, alive with energy. Colors in the room were beginning to shimmer, to merge with each other. Sounds intensified, the drum magically echoing in my head. I loved the out-of-control waves of sensation that drugs brought me, the gifts of the Mother.

River received the rattle first, her red, spiky hair glimmering in my eyes. She sang of gratitude for the return of the sun—it was touching, deep, and authentic. Susie was to her left, and received the rattle next. Her coquettish, pouty attitude was always a turn-off for me. She chanted about her struggles with her boss, and ranted about the abuses of the patriarchy in her life. I found myself bored and annoyed, my judgment tasting bitter in my mouth. "Get a life," my lower self hissed to her, with the bile of guilt on the next swallow. Artemis, always the poet, next in line, sang of freedom, of summer and possibility, her high-pitched voice rising above the rattle's humming. She passed the rattle to me. I felt its sleek aliveness, its presence in my hands. It seemed to rattle without my initiating it, to have a life and energy flow of its own.

My words felt like a gentle wind in my chest, rustling, blowing softly, looking for access, for exit, for listeners. The rattle opened the way for my voice to follow. My words flowed effortlessly:

"I want—to—offer—my—blessings—to my friends—my sisters—my lovers—my teachers—my mirrors. I want—to—remember—where I came from—the pain—and separation—of alienation—and isolation. I want to commit—to remember to commit to connection—to sisterhood—to oneness—no matter—what I'm feeling."

My sing-songy voice found its rhythm. I always found the rattle a profound and powerful tool, a gentle scalpel through my lingering fears of stuttering in public. Somehow the almost singing of chanting brought a rhythm that eased me. I was fully home in the circle, returned to my element, the rattle unlocking my throat's hesitation, the drug opening my heart, my friends touching me deeply. The rattle was the key that opened the door of self.

"I am blessed—to have escaped—the bondage—of my old life. I have found—a place—a community—a family—of sisters—to love me—and hold me—and cherish me—no matter what. I could have died—in isolation—in an empty marriage—but I was lead to the graces—of this community—you, my friends."

I finished with words of hopefulness—for summer, for light, for love, for us, all. I reluctantly passed the rattle on to the woman on my left, Meadow. As our eyes met, I saw the violet sparkles in her eyes, burning and flickering with life. She was wearing a billowing white cotton dress with yellow embroidered daisies on it. Her dark, long hair was tied back, creating a breathtaking contrast to the color of her dress. She was exquisite, a feast to my eyes. Her beauty stunned me.

And on the circle went, each one of us offering our thoughts, fears, hopes, and prayers to the group. As the intensity of the mushrooms peaked in me, I felt expansive and open to each woman, and to life in its fullest. After they crested, the next hours of the morning brought sleepiness to my eyes, tiredness to my shoulders, constriction to my heart, more judgment to my mind. "I wonder what time it is," I said to the emptiness inside my head, as I assessed the outdoor light peering in through the window-shades. I couldn't wait to see Janna.

Janna was my lover. She was out of town with her traveling theater company, her return scheduled for later that day. We'd had our rendezvous planned for weeks.

Light slowly seeped into the stale, tired room, crawling its way in strips across the wall and floor, finally flushing full in its softness, filling up the space. We kept the rattle going, the drum alive, in spite of our puffy eyes, our flagging energy. Finally, after what seemed to be forever, Bethia, her face drawn with exhaustion, declared the circle's end, holding the rattle skyward, uttering her final words, "The circle is open but not broken." The drum stopped, dropping us into a vibrating void of still silence, which we held for a few long, powerful moments.

Upon Bethia's cue, we yelped, hooted, hollered, and hoorayed our completion.

We stretched, drank tea, shared fruit, massaged each other's shoulders. I was ready to pull away from the group to prepare for reunion with Janna. Separation from the group after intense experiences was always a conundrum for me—never wanting to leave; wanting to dash. I quietly said my goodbyes, gathered my scattered belongings, collected myself, and headed for the front door. It opened heavily, soundlessly, exposing another reality. I walked out into the clear and crisp Park Slope morning.

The street-cleaning truck made its hissing noise down the middle of 7ᵗʰ Avenue, leaving streaks of moisture behind like a leaky snail ineffectively making tidy its world. The sight made me giggle. There were only a few people about, one busy man right ahead of me, head down, newspaper tucked protectively under his arm, coffee in his hand, headed busily toward the cross-street. I walked down the block, my step light and strangely disconnected. The air soothed me deeply as I breathed in this new, fresh day.

Janna's apartment was a just a few blocks from Allyson's, and I savored the walking. My head was surprisingly emptied of thought. I was physically tired yet emotionally awakened, enlivened to the beauty in this new morning. The sky was a pale blue, framing the brownstones with the possibility of a warm day. Effortlessly and in what seemed just a few breaths, I found myself on Janna's block. She rented a room in a beautiful old brownstone on a quiet Brooklyn side street. I found the key that I had compulsively kept track of during her two weeks away. There it was, safety pinned inside my pack, just as I had seen it yesterday, and the days before. Snickering at my own obsessive nature, I opened the pin, got the key, and fiddled with her lock. It opened with some effort and a bit of a push forward. I entered the first floor apartment from the side door, and made my way to Janna's room. Opening the door, facing her empty room, I felt her presence so powerfully.

The room looked and felt like her, with her usual blend of organization and quirkiness. Tidy, all life in its place, she was quite organized. Yet her funny little politically correct chachkas decorated the large, sunny room with such uniqueness: mallard hunting decoys hanging from the window and swaying in the breeze; Mexican prayer candles standing guard around a crowded, potent altar; red chili pepper Christmas lights decorating the other window; a Navaho spread on a mattress on the floor, a faux tiger skin rug piled in its center—oh, so Janna. And that particular smell, a scrubbed, orangey smell that seemed to float around.

I dropped my pack with a "thunk" and stripped, stepping out of my over-worn worship clothes, twelve hours ago fresh for ceremony, now droopy and done. I shook them off of me, leaving them in a pile that gathered around my ankles. I finally freed myself and wandered toward her bed. Diving under the bedspread, soft red satin sheets met my tiredness. I smiled, closed my eyes, and drifted off to a floating sleep of pastel fuzzy images, muted voices, and delicious waterfalls. I floated, I slept, I dreamed.

The door opened with a click, stirring me awake. "Who is that in my bed?" I heard her say, humor dripping out of every exaggerated syllable of her Goldie Locks imitation.

I stretched and opened my eyes. The light in the day had shifted and changed. I had no sense of the time. Mid-afternoon? I stretched some more, and turned to look at her. She was a sight for body, mind, and spirit.

She walked toward me with a typical Janna gait—determined, smooth, fluid. She had a smile building across her lips, preparing to explode into a full-fledged grin. She took off her white Mets cap, shaking loose her long, dirty-blond hair. She was a hat kind of girl. One could expect of her seasonally appropriate headgear, always her fashion statement. In winter she wore a red plaid Elmer Fudd hunting hat with ear flaps, which simply made her even more beautiful. In summer, her headgear was up for grabs: a variety of baseball caps, a straw cowboy hat, a fishing captain's white cap—one never knew what might sit atop her head.

As she walked toward me, I was warmed by her eyes, smiley blue, like robins' eggs. Her face was rounded and soft. I always saw her as the lesbian feminist's Candice Bergman, with that little pointed nose, high cheekbones. She wore overalls with a red sleeveless tank underneath, disrobing while she moved forward. She was mine, all mine.

She slid onto the bed, half jumping, half falling toward me, creating an explosion of blanket, sheet, and bedspread. She wiggled and slithered her way under the covers, finding me, winding herself into me. She was half dressed, half softly naked, kicking and fussing her remaining clothes off. Finally our legs met, intertwined, locked, and together we rolled our greeting, our longing, our delight at the presence of the other. Arms encircled, legs intertwined, bellies one, breasts coming together in a multitude of sensation, we laughed together as one. Lips finding lips, tongues merging into one, we soundlessly, wordlessly merged into the other. Our passions grew, softened, grew again and released in explosions of blessed sensation. Time floated, faded, evaporated, as we continued to touch, lick, kiss, smell, celebrate, and adore the other. Satiated finally, we released each other, and took long, thirsty looks at the face of our beloved. Without a word, Janna smiled again, cuddled up into my armpit, squirmed herself in, sighed deeply, and floated to sleep. I closed my eyes, my lips muttering a silent prayer of thanks.

Summer was here.

PART THREE: LANDING

17. Sorry We Stole It
1979

All I wanted to do was to go home and watch M.A.S.H. But they kept talking and talking, discussing it from all angles. I was stoned, that drained and past-the-peak stoned. Obviously I had to disguise my boredom, both to myself and to them, yawning into my hand as I sat on the lumpy couch in Shatzi's lavender living room. Oh, why did they keep talking? I was supposed to be interested in this.

"It is our moral responsibility. We cannot sit around on this day and enjoy ourselves. We must express our rage at the rape and pillage of this country. Does everybody agree?" Shatzi was calmly passionate—when she got excited, she got quieter and more still. Right now she was motionless and deeply calm. I knew we were treading with her through some seriously existential waters. Shatzi was round in face and body, short, soft, and close to the ground. Her hair was cut in a soft brown pageboy, like something straight out of the 1950's. At fifty-four, she was one of the elders in our community. I loved her dearly, yet her talking drove me mad. She was our voice of depressive, calm reason.

"What are our motives?" Bethia asked for the eighteenth time that night, itching for a contradictory philosophical counterpunch. Bethia, on the other hand, was intense and tightly wound, like a top ready to release and wreak havoc all around it. Her hair was short, silver-grey. She, unlike Shatzi, got twitchier and more frenetic as her excitement grew. Bethia was the voice of passionate and feverish integrity in our group.

And on and on for another forty minutes. The others would chime in—Athena, in her quiet, intense, annoyingly nasal way. She was short, tiny-boned, and very butch, with close cropped black hair. I hated her—she silently threatened my place in the group. I knew she didn't like me and it made my stomach tighten when she entered the room. There was a competition unspoken between her and me, a fight undecided, a contest unnamed. We had "energy" between us. And there was MattiGoat, young and sweet, smart and silly. Round glasses traced her pensive eyes, and she peered out at the world with slightly detached wonder.

My every contribution to our discussions had to be carefully planned. My only goal was to say something that sounded right—maybe I would take a thread from one person's speaking, then a thread from another, weave them together, and try to make it my own. I would slide into the conversation, hoping it counted for something. It was exhausting. I had no capacity to know what I thought, what I felt, or what I believed. I kept myself too busy trying to fit in to allow any real sense of myself to surface.

"So it's agreed, then?" asked Shatzi.

Yes, we all agreed. On Thanksgiving Day, next Thursday, we would dress in black, wear black veils, go to Saint Mark's Place—an incredibly busy intersection in lower Manhattan just a few blocks from my house—and wail. There on this public corner, we would have a wailing circle, to demonstrate our contempt, heartbreak, and disapproval of the thievery of the white American men who stole this country from native people.

I half ran down the winding steps of Shatzi's old walk-up tenement building. Busting outside into the New York night, I bundled my black pea coat tighter around me and released a noisy sigh of relief. It was cold and windy, with some freezing rain coming off the East River behind me. I was always relieved to get out of our meetings, I had to admit. My round "Witches Heal" button was pinned to my jacket lapel as usual, my orange badge of self-proclamation. I moved quietly through the streets where just a few people wandered—a homeless person on the other side of First Avenue rummaging in a dumpster, a quickly moving skinhead type smoking a stogie on my side of the block. I walked the six blocks home through the slushy melting city snow, though it was hardly snow at all—more like frozen rain with packed debris in it. The late November air cleared my head. Traffic seemed slower, softer, taxis lessening their fevered pace up First Avenue.

I did make the last fifteen minutes of M.A.S.H. Lighting a joint, sinking down into my bed, and pulling my blessed down comforter around me, I snickered at Radar's intuition, his ability to respond to the colonel's needs long before the colonel even knew he had them. Hawkeye got into some mischief that gave me a chuckle. I turned it off and began to float off to sleep.

Then it dawned on me, cutting into my approaching cloud of sleep: "Damn. A wailing circle. How do you wail? It sounds hard. What if I can't wail right?"

Oh, no. Something to worry about.

Somehow I did get to sleep, and, of course, as per my usual obsessive self, made it to school early the next morning. The high school where I taught was awash in excitement with the Thanksgiving holiday pending. The halls were humming between bells, the classes smaller and jangled with added excitement. My inner city high school students were not concerned with the theft of the land by white American men. My attempts to raise their awareness were for naught:

"And the white man consistently betrayed their treaties with the native people over and over again. Thanksgiving should be a time of national shame," I patiently explained to my bored seventh period sophomore class.

"You bugged," replied Tyronne Johnson, sitting in the third row picking his teeth clean with a gold toothpick. That was it: I was bugged. End of discussion.

Somehow the days clicked away—Thanksgiving was rapidly approaching. I had not been committed to my family on Thanksgiving for years. It was a day for me and my New York political sisters. Nevertheless, my mom's voice sounded slightly melancholic on the phone as she asked me, "Where *are* you spending Thanksgiving?" I didn't know how to explain to her that I would be publicly wailing to symbolically embody the rage of native peoples at the thief of their land. So I said, "At Joyce's." Not a complete lie, I thought. We would be gathering at Joyce's to write our signs and put together our outfits. Outfits? What was the politically correct word? Costumes? No, that's too derogatory. Uniforms? I really didn't know.

"At Joyce's," I told her. She seemed quietly content with my response. But you never knew with my mother. You could never tell what she was feeling or thinking. My father, on the other hand, would broadcast his every feeling with a single "hello" on the phone. They were bookends, my parents—Mr. Emotionality and Mrs. Hold-Your-Cards-Close-to-Your-Emotional-Chest. And they both were certainly alive inside me.

The Wednesday in school before the long weekend was a nightmare. Kids were crazy, running the halls, setting off fire drills. The very thought of turkey, stuffing, and cranberry sauce, with four days away from Malcolm X Shabazz High School to boot, drove these kids wild. No illusion of schoolwork could be mustered. We were in mere survival mode. We had several code red alerts, where we were locked into our rooms while security guards combed the building for the suspects of the misdemeanor of the moment. Finally it ended at 2:32 p.m., my favorite time of each weekday. I beat the crowd of kids out the door—ahh, the benefits of a first floor eighth period classroom—got in Ruby, and sprinted my way toward the Holland Tunnel, my umbilical cord home, my lifeline from Newark, New Jersey to the East Village of New York City.

When I thought about the next day, Thanksgiving Thursday, my heart sank. All I really wanted was what my high school students wanted: turkey, stuffing, cranberry sauce, some good or bad television. I quietly longed for time to savor the holiday, not to confront the military industrial complex on actions taken so long ago. I clearly did despise the actions taken by our government—the dismantling of the cultures of native peoples, its inconceivably hideous genocidal actions—I did despise all that, and felt really shitty about it, too. But I just wanted to have some turkey, watch some videos, and get stoned. That sounded like a fine response to injustice to me.

Bummer of bummers, Thanksgiving Day was cold, rainy, and bleak. I was savvy enough in the ways of political action to know that our demonstration would not be cancelled because of the weather. I moped around my apartment in the morning, bored and trying not to smoke any pot, wanting to have a fresh high for the kickoff of our action at noon. The morning was long. I spoke to my family on the phone, "Yes, yes, to Joyce's. When? Later. A later afternoon meal." As I hung up my red princess phone, I felt a little homesick. I half-wished I could be with them in Pennsylvania. I could almost smell my mom's house on Thanksgiving—her turkey and stuffing mixed together in a harmony of delight and smell. And her fabulous pumpkin pie—not too sweet and the perfect consistency, with just the right amount of nutmeg. I watched the Macy's Parade with a half heart. I just couldn't sink down into it—I couldn't relax. Wailing was on the horizon.

We met at Joyce's at 10:30. Eight of us were there. We put together our outer layers of black, to top off our black pants. I wore Matti's mother's black cape. It was heavy and smelled of mildew. Shatzi had sewn black material into veils, with small holes for eyes and mouth. I tried mine on, looked in the mirror, and snickered in embarrassed amusement. Bethia gave me a cool stare and I quieted down. *Yikes,* I thought. *This is going to be hard.*

We smoked some good hash before we left. I was relieved when Allyson took out her pipe, since I needed the support to get into the spirit. My head tingled with every inhale, resulting in escalating, incremental fuzziness. We offered a prayer over the pipe, a prayer that our actions be effective, loving, and powerful. I prayed to get through the day.

Then we made our way across 7th Street to the busy, pivotal intersection of Saint Mark's Place and Second Avenue. The New Yorkers we met on 7th Street, bundled up in their winter coats, brims of their hats pulled over their eyes, arms filled with bouquets of mums or paper bags silhouetting the shape of wine bottles, ignored the eight black-clad, veiled women traipsing down the block. They had seen stranger things in their New York days.

We waited on Second Avenue for the light to turn before we crossed, being the good citizens that we were. There was the spot we agreed upon—the northwestern corner, by the newsstand. That's where we would stand. My nerves got tighter and tighter with each passing minute. Maybe it was the hash. My small, elaborately scripted cardboard sign read, "Return the Earth to Its Rightful Owners." Shaking, I held it tentatively in front of me as we'd agreed. It felt like a protective shield, keeping my innards safe from any retaliation a representative of the military industrial complex might direct toward me.

We gathered in a circle on the sidewalk, clogging the intersection. We made eye contact with each other, as limited as it was considering the constraints of the makeshift veils, just like we had agreed to do. My veil was itchy and stiff. Moisture from my nose was condensing on the inside of my nose hole in the veil and turning cold, almost freezing. I was instantly cold and uncomfortable.

As previously decided in our interminable planning meetings, Shatzi began the wailing. Her voice went up like a shot of electricity into the cold, grey, infinite sky. It stopped the crowds of pedestrians in their tracks. The folks headed down the subway steps halted in mid-step, looked around, and noted us. Shatzi's cry was plaintive, piercing, high-pitched, and sustained. I was amazed that that sound could emerge from such a spherical body. My other sisters joined in. The pedestrians around us gawked for another moment or so, and then continued their Thanksgiving pace—off to friends, restaurants, bars, movies, all the sane places one might spend a Thanksgiving afternoon. The pace around us seemed to return to normalcy.

I opened my mouth. No sound came out. I tried again, thinking of all the horrid things this government did to native children. I conjured up murderous images and tried to wail. A little hum emerged. I tried again and again. Nobody in our group seemed to notice my lack of participation. They appeared to be fully engaged in their own private experience of mourning. The passersby just shuffled past us. No policemen confronted us. We just wailed and sobbed and cried, pleading our case to the grey November day. I finally found a bit of a wail, a wail Wing-style, I thought. It was tentative, but mine nevertheless. I did my best to own it and to appreciate it fully. I couldn't continue it for very long without having to stop, take a big breath, and reenter the collective hum. Others amongst us seemed to have the capacity for sustained wailing.

The hash wore off quickly. It was a long afternoon.

Time seemed to stand still. My feet froze and no longer existed beneath me. The cape did not protect me from the icy drizzle, which intensified both the taste and the smell of lingering mildew. Standing still was uncomfortable and hurt my lower back. Did I not wear the right shoes for wailing? Inside my gloves my fingers seemed to ice over with a layer of inexplicable moisture. Physically I was a wreck.

The mostly yuppie pedestrians walking by us during that endless afternoon gave us a first glance, and then seemed to continue along, off to take their unperturbed pleasure elsewhere, to seek shelter from the inclement weather, to receive comfort. That sounded good to me. There were no scenes around us, but for the one being staged inside my head.

It seemed the day would never end. I had nowhere to put my body, nothing to do with my hands. I was really sorry the earth was stolen. But I was just cold and wet and longing for turkey. I imagined I would die, simply drop down dead from embarrassment in front of the yuppies, from shame in front of my sisters for my insincerity and incompetence in wailing. Death seemed easier than standing there, struggling with my wail, seeing the New Yorkers' half-amused faces as they passed us, sensing my sisters' presence and judging my own shoddy participation by my projections onto them.

But it happened—finally our two-hour commitment ended. I walked home alone, tearfully grateful to be solitary again, shoes squeaking with wetness, dismantling my veil on Second Avenue. Its damp material had leaked on my hands, leaving me with pocked splotches of dye. Once inside my steaming warm apartment, I looked in my mirror. There I stood, de-uniformed and de-veiled, looking bedraggled, red-eyed, and pink-cheeked. My only thought was: *oye*.

I decided not to go back to Shatzi's for our debriefing that evening. I couldn't face my own sense of failure in the experience. Yet not going to that meeting felt like a profound betrayal of my political family unit. Prioritizing my own pleasures was outlandishly selfish, so selfish that I needed to create a tiny lie for justification purposes. I left a message on Shatzi's machine saying I had a sore throat. It was true. My throat was sore—sore from attempted wailing and aching, aching for turkey, for comfort, and for escape.

I went to the diner on the corner of First Avenue, looking up and down the avenue surreptitiously before ducking in. I didn't want anybody to see me reduced to such elementary pleasures. I got a hot open-faced turkey sandwich with all the fixings to go, went over to the Saint Mark's theater, and bought a $3.00 ticket to see *Manhattan*. It was exactly what I needed to do, I thought giddily, looking all around the lobby for a face that might witness my betrayal and superficiality.

Snuggling into the ripped movie theater seat, dry and finally warm, surrounded by the smells of marijuana and popcorn—my favorite combination of smells on the planet—holding the aluminum take-out container close to me, I grieved the rape of the earth. In my own way, I really did. *Sorry,* I thought. *Sorry we stole it. I'm so sorry we stole your land,* I ruminated, as I bit into a fake cranberry, savoring its artificial, sweet taste.

I sighed, snuggled lower in the funky seat, and prepared to share the next two hours of my privileged, shallow life with Diane Keaton and Woody Allen.

18. Push, Push, In the Bush
1980

My self-determined professional rule was clearly defined: no pot before fifth period lunch. Only special events could permeate that boundary. Those extenuating circumstances, in order of importance, were: a pep rally, extended homeroom, special testing, or a holiday. Under all other habitual circumstances, I was committed to myself to wait until lunchtime, fifth period, to drive around Weequahic Park with Annie, the gym teacher and my one cool friend at school, to get high.

My ironclad rule was profoundly pragmatic. Getting stoned at 7:30 a.m. was fabulous for the few morning hours that the buzz lived on. But the slump came early, by 10:00 a.m., with so much of the teaching day looming ahead. The headache, the listlessness, the lack of patience—all those symptoms were magnified while standing in front of thirty-two young and challenging high school students period after period. Not good. Also, trying to get high again at lunch, to recreate that morning lift-off, just hadn't been working so well for me lately. So I decided to pick and choose my morning buzzes at work. Today would be one.

It was homecoming at Malcolm X Shabazz High School. I had taught here for seven years, dancing between a love relationship with the kids (mostly—except when I didn't), and a hate relationship with the system that betrayed them (mostly always). Being part of the tyrannical system of racist and classist oppression was confusing and horrid. But it paid my way in the world and gave me an identity. I still continued to believe I could make a difference in individual kids' lives. Some days it was harder to believe than others.

115

Homecoming at Shabazz. Always a trip. *It'll be fun*, I thought.

I maneuvered Ruby through the streets of lower Manhattan, heading toward that major landmark of my work-a-day world, the Holland Tunnel. The streets of Manhattan were waking up slowly on this cool fall morning. The street cleaner truck lumbered its way down Houston Street, leaving streaks of moist schmutz behind it as it slithered its way forward, that slimy snail thing again. I loved these occasional snatches of quiet city life, betraying the frenzy of Manhattan, the waking up, the going to sleep, the up-close-and-personal neighborhood moments of New York City, my home. People, real people, lived here. I loved knowing that, feeling that, and being one of the anonymous people living in this cool, massive series of ethnic neighborhood after different ethnic neighborhood.

Ruby and I flowed easily into the Holland Tunnel. Per usual, the outgoing traffic was light. Entering the Tunnel was like descending into a familiar cave, so accustomed was I to the yellowed lights, to every dip in the road. Each bend and curve of pavement was anchored, memorized in my cellular self. Five times a week, four weeks a month, ten months a year for seven years. Fourteen hundred trips. *I am one with the Holland Tunnel*, I thought, and reached for the joint I rolled just for homecoming purposes. My rule was that all smoking of pot on workdays was begun in the Holland Tunnel. Starting here in the Tunnel, I would finish the joint and have a few minutes to integrate before arriving at school. The Tunnel was just "one joint away" from Malcolm X Shabazz High School.

I lit the joint with my funky pink plastic Bic lighter. As I drew in the familiar cloud of warm, pungent smoke, my friend and my companion, my most intimate partner, marijuana, woke up for me. It filled my chest with heat and I instantly recognized its power. This was special pot—well, let me be clear. I only smoked special pot. I was not a frivolous pothead. I would never just smoke anything off the street. I smoked mostly purple Hawaiian bud that my friend Dina sent to me in elaborately wrapped cigar boxes lined with baggies of cinnamon, forbidding detection. I marched into the central post office in midtown Manhattan regularly to pick up my Hawaiian package, not a concern in my head, so convinced was I of Dina's perfected system of shipment. We were lucky.

Another toke filled me and Ruby with reminders of Big Island, Dina's home. *This pot is good,* I snickered to myself, choking a bit. I spotted daylight ahead as we wound our way toward the Tunnel's end. Popped up into the morning light of New Jersey, I could witness the poor schmucks sitting in stilled traffic, waiting their turn to inch cautiously toward the City, as I and a handful of other opposite rush-hour commuters streamed forward effortlessly. *Poor schmucks* was my daily greeting to them, as I flawlessly and buoyantly drove up the Pulaski Skyway, an antiquated New Jersey suspension bridge. The pot was now waking me up to sensation, to the lacework beauty of the light bouncing off the bridge, to the rhythmic singsong puttering of Ruby's little, adorable motor. My hands warmed, my cheeks flushed. A deep internal knot of nerve and bone frozen somewhere in my core softened, thawed, and clicked open to the possibility of extrasensory experience, to another, different reality. I was stoned, I officially and authoritatively noted to myself. *Self to self. Make note. Stoned now.*

The fourteen-mile drive from my bed in the East Village to my desk in Room 142 in Malcolm X took approximately twenty-five minutes. I passed the ridiculous Newark Airport, a monolith of runways and terminals which always amused me for no particular reason, in the morning light. I turned onto Route 280, took it for one exit, and put on my blinker for the descent into the South Ward of Newark.

Instantly it was all different. The spaciousness of the highway and the movement of cars made way for another reality. The neighborhood settled in around me, enveloping me in its familiar, dilapidated arms. Its once noble buildings, apartment houses, and single-family homes were shabby and tired-looking. Burned-out buildings stood scarred and ripped apart right alongside functioning dwellings. Empty lots dotted the blocks, littered with mattresses, garbage, and abandoned cars. I knew these blocks well. I knew this neighborhood from inside out.

But not really, my stoned mind whispered. *You could never know, never really know.* Despite spending hour after hour, month after month, year after year with its children, I could not know the lives that were lived here. *Never know, never really know*, the wheels of Ruby hummed, as we turned right onto Johnson Avenue and pulled into the abandoned lot now functioning as a staff parking lot for Malcolm X Shabazz High School, my place of employment.

Pulling Ruby into a spot and putting on her emergency brake, I took some self-care/self-preservation actions. I brushed myself off, in case of lingering ash. I put Visine in my eyes, to dispel telltale red. I popped a Tic Tac in my mouth, to insure freshness and anti-pot breath. Like a pilot's checklist, I went down the actions, assuring myself I was able to walk in the building and do what had to be done. *Big breath in*, I coached myself. *Okay, you can do it.*

Out of the car, across the street I headed. Groups of kids stood hovering outside the low-slung brick building, which was added in the 60's onto an ancient Gothic-looking structure. Shabazz was considered modern, both in architecture and in curriculum. That was a scary thought. The kids were chatting with each other, smoking that final Newport, drinking their breakfast of diet soda. I looked at the pavement—nobody's eyes confronted mine.

Into the hollow main lobby I walked, where the head security guard, Mr. Waters, sat behind his card-table desk, reading *The Star-Ledger*. "Morning," he mumbled, not looking up, his white-shirted uniform taut around his bulging belly.

"Morning!" My response sounded light and slightly giddy to my ears. *Rope it in, babe*, I said to myself. *You can do this.*

Into the main office to sign in, fluorescent-lights-from-hell accosting me. *Oye*, I thought. *You can do this.* There on the main counter sat The Book, the sign-in system for all staff. Ellie Estevez, a nice biology teacher, was ahead of me. She was a good woman—a little too straight for me, but a nice woman. I smiled appropriately, brightly, and broadly at her back, offering her a silent good morning. My turn:

pen in hand, flipping pages to the "F's." There I was, sure-as-shooting, *Futuronsky*, the final, always the final F. Signing in with an *8:05* next to my signature was easy enough, although I did feel some giddiness bubbling in my belly. *Keep centered*, I kept reminding myself. *Keep focused.*

Over to the mailboxes I headed, where a bunch of the straighter teachers congregated, coffee cups in hands, gossiping and chatting. *Enemy territory*, I thought. I inched between them and thrust my hand into my tiny cubbyhole, pulling out a handful of useless memos. In an instant they all flew from my hand, parachuting down to the ground with surprising grace and beauty. "Excuse me, excuse me," I mumbled, slumping down to gather them up. As I bent over, a dozen or so Extra Strength Tylenol capsules leaped out of my vest pocket and tumbled between the teachers' legs. *Only Tylenol*, I repeated to myself, *nothing illegal*, as I gathered up the little renegades, my face red and my hands grabbing between Princess Towe's impressively spiked high heels—Princess Towe, senior class advisor, advanced studies English teacher, the in-crowd's in-girl. *Ugh*. Headaches came early on stoned out mornings. I needed my Tylenol to carry me though. Ellie helped me pick them up, shooting me a quizzical look which I ignored. I clutched my little pills in my hand, pulled myself together, stood up straight and tall, and happily blurted out, "Hi, everybody!" It came out with such a lilt that I frightened myself, and I slowly backed away until I could make my escape into the quieter halls.

Pretty uncool, I thought to myself. *Pull it together. This will be worth it.*

I trekked up to my homeroom, Room 482, on the fourth floor in the old building. It was a freshman homeroom, tucked away in the bowels of the building. My morning hike to an upstairs homeroom was eased by the fact that I had scored a first floor classroom for my afternoon classes. We had twelve freshman homerooms that year. By senior year there would only be enough students left in the senior class for four homerooms, so intense was the dropout rate. Opening the door with my key, I walked into the steaming room.

Heat sizzled and clanked its way through the ancient pipes, forcing air and that particular high school heat smell throughout the room. It was an amphitheater, with rows of built-in desks getting higher, echoing the days of lecture classes at what was once South Side High, quite the prominent school in the Newark of earlier and easier times. I slumped into the chair, still bravely attempting to recover from my Tylenol-Princess-Towe-high-heels fiasco. I was trembling a bit, still so very stoned.

It'll be worth it, I reminded myself. I sat at my desk, really just a table with drawers, gathering my stuff for the morning—red roll book, corners bent from wear, and my trusty Bic pen. That was all I needed. The homecoming rally would eat up the morning periods, I thought joyfully. I continued to sit and breathe, content with the silence that I knew would soon be violated. The clock ticked loudly on the wall, each second of silence precious to me.

Sure enough, the bell rang at 8:20. *So soon? Can that be right?* I wondered. Kids started dribbling in. Shahira Williams was first, as usual, busy with her plaid book bag clutched in her hand, thick glasses already sliding down her nose. Choir Girl, they called her.

"Hi, Miss Fruity," my nickname rolled off her lips with a twilled *r.*

"Hey, Shahira. How are you?"

And in they came: Nicole Williams (stunning and large and looking like a twenty year old), Jamil Jones (dapper, cool, and nonchalant in his leather pants and jacket), Malik Powers (skinny, hostile), and John Tisdale (with his endearing lisp). Characters, each and all.

We survived roll with only a few inappropriate banters back and forth between us. They, the present twenty-four students out of the thirty-five who were actually on roll, were excited and relatively cooperative because of the homecoming rally. They knew I had the power to prevent them from attending. I was happy to wield that leverage when Malik started to badger Shahira, "Hey, skinny Choir Girl. You ugly, girl. You an ugly, ugly thing." My intervention was swift, relatively unconscious, and without hesitation. It was obvious to all as to where my loyalties lay. Malik, wanting to go to the rally, stared at me with wild intensity, then rolled his eyes, sucking in his breath with a "woosh" sound and looked away from me, as if to say, "What a fucking moron stoned dyke you are." But he stopped his attack on Shahira, who sat very still during our whole interaction.

Finally the bell rang, inviting us down to the auditorium. *Finally*, I thought. *Thank you, Jesus.* The kids burst from their seats like cattle let loose from a chute—clumping down the stairs, pushing each other. My charge was to keep them together and somewhat orderly as we walked down the hall to the auditorium. In the bigger picture, it was an impossible, losing battle. In the moment, I did my best to be engaged with them, in attempted order, walking near and talking to the easier, more agreeable kids. Now in the main hallway, my homeroom students slowed down. They sauntered. They strolled. With other classes streaming in, they got cooler, wanting to appear less anxious to rush in, which was quite endearing to my heart. Finally our turn, we, like a large, unwieldy amoeba, blobbed our way into the auditorium. They were seated effectively by Mr. Cobb, one of the hugely broad-shouldered gym teachers who commanded—and received—great respect. My duties completed, I walked to the wall, leaned back into it, and breathed. I looked around.

The seats in the auditorium were filling up with kids. The very seats themselves appeared to jump into life and movement, such was the intensity of their inhabitants' energy. Movement, laughter, and shouting filled the once dignified hall. The curtain on the stage was closed—whatever was happening behind it was going to be good. I scanned the huge, neoclassical murals that lined the walls, showing Greek gods and goddesses in states of repose and study. White Greek gods and goddesses, of course. Titles like "Virtue" and "Self-Study" and "Integrity" framed them. They stood in great contrast to the slithering, writhing, constant sea of black and brown faces that now graced its seats.

I saw my friend, Annie, across the auditorium, standing by her seated homeroom. She was wearing Shabazz colors, black and gold—black sweat pants with her Lady Bulldogs state champion varsity jacket. We exchanged nods. I was sure she could take one look at me and know I was stoned. Somehow knowing that made me more paranoid. She was light-skinned, thin, and agile, both a cynic of the system and a true supporter of the kids. As the head coach of the girls' basketball team, she helped shepherd some of our more talented girls into colleges. Every lunch period we would drive to Weequahic Park to smoke a joint, get out of the crazy building, and fortify ourselves for the last hours of teaching. She was both a friend and an enigma. I trusted her fully, yet recognized that she could not really understand my world. Nor could I, hers. Subtle waves of attraction pulled at me as I saw her standing with her students. Quiet whispers of longing seeped into me, making their way sneakily toward my belly.

With a jolt and a literal drum roll, the curtain yanked open, revealing the MXS marching band, in its classy black and gold uniforms, gold plumes adorning their hats. They were performing at full tilt. Trumpets swaying in unison, legs and shoulders moving together, they high-steppingly appeared to be one squirming unit of noise and movement. Ms. Battle, young, black, and very cute, led them with great vigor. They filled the entire stage with their energy and enthusiasm.

The crowd went wild, hooting, hollering, standing, waving their fists in the air. It was a show of support, Shabazz-style.

I strained to hear. The noise of the audience almost over-shouted the band. What was the song they were playing? It was on the tip of my memory, right around the corner of conscious thought. What the heck was it? YES, that was it. It was the new ultra-disco song the kids loved, by Musique, "In the Bush":

"Get your woman on the floor,
Gotta get up to get down.
Push, push, in the bush,
You know you've got to get down.
Some of the time beats all of the time

> *And part of the time beats none of the time.*
> *You know you got to get down."*

Recognizing it, I spun out, head swimming, leaning back into the wall for support. Through dizzying memories, head light and floating, I remembered homecoming at Central High School, my school, two thousand light years ago, in Scranton, Pennyslvania. I remembered sitting in the seats of a homecoming pep rally, listening to a song devoid of lascivious content, reflecting the 60's:

> *"They always called him Mr. Touchdown...*
> *They always called him Mr. T.*
> *He can run*
> *And he can throw,*
> *He's our hero,*
> *Wherever he goes...."*

Ohmygod, I thought. *I must be ancient. From the innocence of the 60's, to this, to here, to now.* I felt slightly nauseous, time-traveled, dazzled by reality in all its many manifestations.

The band finished off-key with a flourish, to the crowd's hysterical, frenzied delight.

The rest of the program unfolded—the introductions of the football team, each cheerleader giving a player a black and gold carnation, the football players in turn kissing their cheerleader with mimicked passionate lust, while the student body counted in unison, "ONE, TWO, THREE...". The principal, Gordon Mayes, giving his speech of encouragement to catcalls and woops as he menacingly and angrily scanned the crowd for misbehaving culprits.

Encouragement and disapproval.

Innocence and lust.

Possibility and dead end.

Connection and alienation.

Just another day at Shabazz, I thought.

I felt so very close, close to them, close to their world. These kids really did live in my heart.

Yet so far away was I.

And so, so different from them.

Alien. I was an alien. I could never understand.

Clearly I was in alien land. No matter how long I was there, nor how well-intended I took on my role, the differences in culture seemed to grab at my heart, squeeze it in an iron fist, and return it back to me, emptied out, a little achy.

The band ended the assembly with an even more impossibly rousing version of "In the Bush."

Only ninety-five more minutes before Annie and I could leave for our noon pot break. *Weequahic Park, here I come.*

"It was an amphitheater, with rows of built-in desks getting higher."
(front of class)

"Ruby and I flowed easily…"

19. Some Happy Squirrels in Seneca County—
Stop Those Cruise Missiles
1983

There were five of them, local guys, with a crowd of their townie friends hooting behind them. They were husky, their hairy arms folded across their chests, threatening scowls on their faces, standing around their badly written cardboard sign that read:

Pinko Dykes Should Camp with Their Comrades in Moscow

We women activists stood before the main gate of the Seneca Army Depot staging a sit-in. We were boxed in with the locals behind us and the army depot in front of us. The barbed wire fence was lined with faceless MP's dressed in full riot gear, helmets, sunglasses, protective vests, and boots. They were holding their clubs menacingly at crotch level, like a baton of self-preservation to ward off our invisible powers of emasculation. We were a contingent of thirty women from the much larger Women's Encampment for a Future of Peace and Justice, camped next door to this huge army base in a legal summer peace camp gathering. We were protesting the shipment of cruise missiles to Western Europe. Tensions were high as we sang our chant of power:

> *The earth is our mother,*
> *We will take care of her.*
> *The earth is our mother.*
> *We will take care of her.*

Some of the townies were furious at our summer invasion—we threatened their right livelihood and the peace and status quo of their rural communities. The soldiers were hyper-cautious, on full alert, expecting the worst from this crowd of feminist activists dressed in tie-dyed shirts, headbands, sandals, and cut-off shorts, with peace signs adorning all.

I was stoned out of my mind most of the time. Drugs helped my commitment to the cause. I was elated, dedicated, excited, turned on by the adrenalin of non-violent protest, completely uninvolved in the politics of the peace camp, sleeping with Becky—a cute, young, working-class woman from Greenham Common, the long standing British peace camp—living in a cool bender in the woods, uninterested in any of the philosophy or theory upon which the camp was based, and having the time of my life. I had been there for a few weeks and was committed to spending the summer in order to keep Western Europe safe from cruise missiles.

Our chant intensified, ending in a crescendo of empowered hollering, whistling, stomping, and wild drumming from the women with the hand drums. Complete with this political action of the late afternoon, we broke up and faded away in smaller groups. The MP's seemed to collectively breathe a sigh of relief, as did I. The town folks taunted us, following us to our cars. Ruby, my red VW bug, was waiting to chauffeur several of us down the two-mile strip to camp.

Back at the camp, walking down the politically correct ramp that women constructed for disabled participants to have full access to the campgrounds, I felt the pot wearing off. It took a lot out of me. The following day was the fifteen-mile protest march, and some of my friends from my NYC political group had come up for it. I should get some sleep, I thought. Becky and I had dinner with our other friends, sitting around one of the campfires, bundled up in our variety of mismatched, tattered, and functional outer layers. I put on my red and black plaid wool jacket, my favorite. We ate beans, rice, and tofu, and went to Becky's bender to smoke another joint. After a long day of civil disobedience, I said goodnight, heading home by the light of my flashlight, knowing the next day would be a big one.

I was living in a bender, which Becky helped me construct. It was the housing of choice at Greenham Common, she told me, which secretly titillated me. We found an area in the woods where small saplings were growing close together. We bent the half-willing little trees toward each other, lashing them together, and covered the entire thing with heavy see-through plastic. It was so much better than a tent—round and high and see-through. The stars touched me, the sunrise warmed me, the trees were one with me. I loved my bender. To me it felt like housing of status, a cut above my mildewy forest green L.L. Bean tent now packed in my car. I felt some politically incorrect housing hubris, which I kept to myself.

The morning dawned with pink sky and early steamy heat. About sixty of us gathered by the main gate for our long and righteous hike to Seneca Falls, the birthplace of Harriet Tubman, carrying signs made of sheets on poles and proclaiming our cause. "Give Earth A Chance" was the lead banner. I was wearing comfortable khaki shorts, old Adidas sneakers, and my favorite sleeveless lesbian tee-shirt that my friend RunningBear had painted for me. It had on it a huge colorful women's sign, interlocked with a shimmering peace sign. I was ready.

The day got hotter, brighter, and steamier as we marched. We had permits for each part of the march and believed our journey to be legally sanctioned. I had enough sense to leave my stash of drugs back at the camp, in Ruby's trunk, disguised beneath the tools in her spare tire. I carried a plastic water bottle and got really hot and tired quickly. This was not much fun yet. People passing us in cars and pickup trucks seemed minimally annoyed at the inconvenience we caused them but were generally uninterested. This all changed when we got to the small town of Waterloo, a few miles from the peace camp.

The crowd of locals thickened, tightening in around us as we attempted to move through the streets of this small town. The bridge leading us out of town and to safety was barricaded by what seemed to be several hundred people, waving American flags, screaming taunts, and telling us to "Love America or leave it." One furious man with a stubble of beard spat at us, "Cock-sucking lesbians." Becky, with her perfect British accent replied, "Not exactly," for some instant comic relief. Our laughter dissolved quickly as the crowd around us grew in spiraling intensity.

I felt myself tightening up into a ball of rubber-banded tension. The verbal and visual impact of so much hatred directed at us was beyond terrifying. I found myself fading away, not even noticing the sweat streaming down my face and burning my eyes or the spastic quivering in my knees. I tried ineffectively to block out the curses of the righteous citizens surrounding us. Someone in our group shouted for us to sit down in circles to be safe. I plopped myself down next to Bethia and Allyson, my New York sisters, trembling in the heat of this terrifying confrontation, unconsciously leaning into them for safety. Somewhere above the din of noise I heard a bullhorn announce, "All marchers are subject to arrest for disorderly conduct." The locals seemed to pull back in the face of the police presence. We continued sitting, demanding our right to move through and out of the town, to continue our legal march. Someone in our group was negotiating with the police. I was numbed and brain-fogged with fear.

In what seemed to be a flash of a moment, police in riot helmets came closer to our circle, with one final warning. I continued sitting only because the women around me continued to sit. I was beyond making any sane or insane decision. Out of nowhere I felt large sweaty hands grab me under my arm pits from behind and begin to drag me. I struggled crazily, haphazardly thrashing about in futile movements. Another faceless policeman manifested out of nowhere, grabbed my legs, and swung me in loping movements with his partner down the block away from the sitting women. I was wildly stunned, tussling about in the air, kicking at no one. *What is civil disobedience?* I thought in panic. *What am I supposed to do? I don't think I went to that teach-in. Wasn't that the day that Becky and I found that beautiful waterfall and skinny-dipped all afternoon? Was I supposed to go limp? That was it! Go limp.* I collapsed into the air, wrenched my back in the releasing. It seemed easier to struggle than to let go.

In another moment, I was flung like a chicken into a police wagon (*a paddy wagon*, I could hear my father's voice say). I righted myself on the bench next to a few other women I did not recognize. The door was closed behind me. I sat, airless, breathless, sightless, senseless, and thoughtless. The truck began to move, carrying us away. We sat in stunned silence.

After what seemed like an eternity of bumpy, weaving travel, the vehicle came to an abrupt stop. Its doors swung open, daylight again streaming over us. Blinded in the glare, I held my hand and arm up defensively protecting my eyes. More faceless policemen pulled us out. My right foot was asleep, my legs exhausted and still trembling. I limped forward, a policewoman escorting us through the cement gates of a compound. We were in the Waterloo County jail, one of the officers told us.

There were peace camp women already milling in the outdoor courtyard, with more regularly streaming in the doors. The officers gave us lukewarm water in waxy paper cups and told us we would eventually be processed. I leaned against the three-quarter concrete wall, no roof overheard, pulling my body into the tiny sliver of shade. Packed earth was beneath me. I was hotter than hot. I saw Bethia and my other friends wander in. I collapsed down, hugging my knees into myself. Relief and confusion swirled, competing for attention in me. Meetings were held—I sat on the outskirts of one, trying to listen. Consensus was reached; we would all claim to be Jane Doe. I felt bewildered.

Eventually I had to pee so badly that walking became painful. I limped over to the long line that had formed to the one bathroom. I waited in the sun interminably for my chance at relief. Finally it was my turn. I closed the door behind me, sat on the slimy seat. I could not pee. This was my tragic flaw—I could not pee upon command in a queue. This weakness wrecked great havoc in my life. Music festivals, camping, highway rest stops, all kinds of events and venues caused me distress. Because of this, I used the great outdoors whenever possible. Here I sat and sat. Nothing. Sighing with frustration and abject acceptance, I stood, buttoned up my shorts, and walked away from the possibility of comfort and release. Back out in the sun.

Some more hours passed. We were served baloney sandwiches on white bread with stale potato chips on paper plates, with more lukewarm water. It all tasted like cardboard, had no distinctive flavor, and gummed up the roof of my mouth mercilessly. I spit it out onto my plate and stood up. I walked to the large trash can, threw my garbage into it, and wandered around the large open-aired complex, now filled with lounging women.

The sun had slanted away from us, basking us with relieving shade. I had to pee so badly that a deep ache filled me. I wandered around some more, looking for a spot in which to sit. I saw a large wooden door running from the ground to the top of the wall, and went over to this quiet corner to examine it. The doorknob was a shiny black metal. I looked around me, tried the knob. To my astonishment, it opened. I pushed the door forward, and found myself standing outside. The door swung closed behind me. I was free! *Hey, everybody,* I wanted to yell, *Come on, we can get outta here!* I tried the door. It was locked. I had locked myself out of the coolest demonstration in the women's movement. It dawned on me what I had just done. I tried knocking, then banging on the door. Nobody heard me. *Let me in.* No response.

I had successfully escaped. Then I realized, *Oh, shit, what have I done?*

I had escaped. Escape is not a tactic of civil disobedience. I had violated some unwritten code of non-violent political action.

Now I was alone, doubled over with the need to urinate, without a cent, and wandering about in enemy territory, behind enemy lines. Thankfully my survival instincts clicked in. I successfully made my way to a pay phone down a few blocks, called the peace camp collect, and somebody came to get me, sympathizing with me all the way home.

Once back at camp, after a "debriefing" with the upper echelon of camp women, I dejectedly wandered back to my bender, without my closest friends to commiserate with me. They were effectively and smartly locked up. All I wanted to do, now that I had peed and eaten, was return to jail. To no avail.

Back in my bender, fragile with disappointment and exhaustion, I started to have paranoid thoughts about the drugs that were hidden in Ruby's spare tire. My run-in with the law had opened the doors of paranoid obsession for me. I had two ounces of purple Hawaiian bud marijuana and an ounce of magic mushrooms. Scary thoughts started taking over my mind, like a tiny piece of lint, building, winding, weaving itself into a quilt of obsession: *I shouldn't drive with that stuff.*

I could get stopped. Should I keep it in the bender? That's not fair to the camp. What if we are searched? Oh, no, what should I do? I slept restlessly, uncomfortably, with paranoid dreams. In the middle of the night I awoke to the perfect solution: I'd find a safe place in the woods, plant the entire stash, note where it was, make a map, and simply return there when I needed more stuff. In this way, I would only have enough drugs with me for daily use. Satisfied, with a smile, I went back to my prison-free sleep.

In the morning the camp was awash with news of the Jane Doe Fifty-four, the women in the Seneca county jail. News media was alerted: the women were standing fast to their anonymity. Bella Abzug issued a press release of support, and Governor Cuomo was alerted of the situation. Protests were being held outside the prison, starting at 10:00 a.m. That gave me time to do my drug digging.

I made my way to Ruby, safe in the parking lot, popped open her trunk, and surreptitiously removed the drugs, putting them into my fanny pack. I had all the elements of a successful dig: a shovel in my car and a cigar box with stationery and stamps. I emptied out the box, grabbed the shovel, and headed to the woods. I walked and scrutinized the landscape, looking for the perfect spot. After about thirty minutes of searching, I found it. It was between my bender and the little stream that ran behind the tents. There was a long rotten log on the ground, a group of little spruce trees in a distinctive circle—it was all very identifiable and specific to itself. I dug a hole under the log, whistling and happy with myself. Now I could be freed up to be a more responsible citizen of the peace camp. Now I could have my drugs and be safe, too. Now I could protest in support of the other Jane Does—shit, I was Jane Doe Fifty-five, unprocessed, I thought with irony—and be responsible. I felt satisfied with the depth of the hole I had dug. I kissed each plastic bag of pot and mushrooms as I put them into the cigar box. Goodbye, see you soon, adios. I had kept out a few joints for the day in my fanny pack. Wedging the cigar box under the log, I filled the hole in, trampled it down with my foot, and stood back to survey my work. Successful, I thought. One would never know. I memorized the spot, made a map of it on an index card

I had inside my pack, waved goodbye to all, and turned my back. Off to support the Fifty-four.

After a day of ego-deflating and nerve-jangling protesting at the jail, with the real action going on inside, I ran out of pot. As was my plan, I would return to the stash to get another day's worth, and keep the rest safely in the earth. So the next morning I retraced my way to the enchanted hiding spot. There stood my circle of little spruce trees and my own rotten log. Good job, easily found, I thought. I looked and poked under the log. Nothing. There was nothing there. I shook my head in disbelief, looking all around. Surely this was the place. I spent a few minutes frantically digging under the log—still no cigar box in sight. I backtracked to my bender, walked the perceived path again, found another spot that looked similar, rotten log, spruce trees. Nothing. I spent the morning looking. My magic cigar box was nowhere to be found.

The next day and the next I searched. I was devastated, had no drugs, and had lost a lot of money. It made no sense. Ten Jane Does accepted the $50 bail offered them and were released. The other forty-four waited for a hearing. Days passed before the hearing was convened. Once it had begun, it went on endlessly, I was told, until eventually the judge "dismissed the case in the interest of justice." The women returned to the peace camp bedraggled, exhausted, and heroic. I had to borrow pot from RunningBear to get me by, and make a trip into the City to buy some inferior pot. The summer continued. We protested. The cruise missiles were deployed to Western Europe regardless of our passionate intervention. Becky went back to England, too.

The mystery of my missing stash of drugs was never solved. I drove away from the peace camp on the day before Labor Day to get ready to go back to work, still baffled by it. As Ruby and I pulled out of that familiar gravel driveway, tires clicking over it for the final time, we watched the little farmhouse get smaller and smaller in our rear view mirror. I could only imagine some happy squirrels dancing and celebrating, munching on prime Hawaiian pot and delicious psilocybin mushrooms, my contribution to the earth and to the critters of Seneca County.

"The earth is our mother."
(center, with headband)

"I continued sitting only because the women around me continued to sit."
(front row, fifth from right)

20. Chuck & Loretta
1984

He was older than the others, a purple-grey stubble of a beard appearing on his moon-rounded, mocha cheeks. He was chunky and squat, yet obviously muscular beneath his tight-fitting leather jacket, sharkskin pants, and pointed leather low boots. He kept to himself, didn't interact with the other seniors in my English 4 class. Since it was eighth period, the last of the day, the students were looser and a bit more interactive than the regular senior classes. The seniors that were still in school were not the problem kids—the problem kids had long since exited the rolls of Shabazz to enter life on the streets, or wherever their lives took them. The seniors that were still in school weren't necessarily the smarter kids, either. They were simply the more tenacious, perhaps the ones with more support from home, the ones most able to withstand the pressures from the street, the call to life's other, non-academic pursuits. As a result of all of these factors, the seniors tended to be withdrawn and non-interactive, unlike the younger kids, who were generally boisterous and uncontained. Many of our seniors seemed to me as if they were wrapped closely in on themselves.

To teach seniors was a gift of seniority. I had earned the right through my long tenure to have a calmer environment for my last period in this long, monotonous day of high school teaching.

In my earlier life, I had wanted to be a writer. I majored in English in college and was sure that, in writing, I would find, if not fame or fortune, certainly my own voice, my own experience—something I longed for so fully, something that life seemed to deny me. Then my dad sat me down in the living room at the end of my freshman year and patiently explained the ways of the world to me, saying, "Nan, you need a career that will pay you a living. What if your husband gets sick and can't work? What will you do? You need to teach." Hence both my sister and I found ourselves on the track of training to become teachers. What if our husbands did get ill? All assumption pointed in the direction, at that moment in time, of my having an alleged husband who might, in fact, fall ill.

So I shifted my major to English Secondary Education. I made fun of the education teachers in my college, finding them the least skillful and engaging of all my professors. But I student-taught my first semester of my senior year of college in a large, progressive high school in the New Jersey shore area. I loved the kids, the possibilities, the feeling of spacious control when the door closed, holding the full responsibility to create an environment of learning. That excited me. I played Beatles songs for motivation. We examined the lyrics of Simon and Garfunkle songs during our unit on poetry. My supervising teacher applauded my capacity to bring relevancy to the classroom.

If I had to teach, then I wanted to teach creative writing. Shakespeare, metaphor, and simile—all of the fabulous and fascinating things from my school background that spoke to my heart, that mattered to me. I wanted to make a difference in the lives of others. This surely was the way to a meaningful life—I always believed that.

Yet life led me to the inner city of Newark, to its South Ward, where our high school kids read at an average of a sixth grade level; where basic punctuation and sentence formation were the curriculum of senior high schools—not Macbeth, not Emily Dickinson. There was no Emily Dickinson in my future at MX Shabazz.

So I tried to know how best to teach them, how to best prepare them for their lives. I taught basic skills as best I could, attempting to communicate with my colleagues and with my department heads, to learn from them, to grow in my functioning in that specific educational environment. And I came up short.

And there sat Chuck, living evidence of my shortcomings, bent over his test, holding his stubble of a pencil in his large, fleshy hand. I could almost smell the intensity of his focus, his full-purposed intention. He was nineteen, held back from graduation once. He was slow moving, thick both in speech and body. This was the final exam, the one he needed to pass, English 4, this second time, and to graduate in two weeks, to stand up on the stage wearing his powder blue cap and gown and beam down at his family, his girlfriend, his three-year-old son, and his one-year-old daughter. This was the test that determined his future.

If I could have willed the correct answers into his head and through his fingers, made manifest onto his paper, I would have done so. I knew that Chuck couldn't read very well.

The other students scratched away at their papers, the ticking of the clock like a metronome marking their progress. The air was hushed. This, for most, was their final final, the last test of their high school career. Three of these twenty were going on to advanced education. The others, hoping for the best. For many, graduating from high school would make them unique in their families, the first graduate ever.

I didn't know how to help Chuck that year. I realized early on in the fall that he couldn't read. I tried to help teach him, but felt impotently unable. My mantra became, "I don't know how to do it. I can't."

Chuck's mantra became, "I will hang in there. I can."

So he kept showing up, and I kept trying. But I tried like a person not fully awakened. I tried like a person still wounded and limited by her own history. I tried with half-hearted efforts. It never dawned on me to take a course in remedial reading. It never occurred to me to advance myself so I could advance them. I just tried to love them, support them, and meet them where they were.

And so here we sat, clock ticking, pens and pencils scratching, Chuck's sweat dripping onto his test. The May heat and humidity gathered under my collar. It was warm, the day was long, and the results of these tests would be, I was certain, pretty discouraging.

"Ten more minutes," I announced. They were being tested in writing, reading comprehension, and vocabulary. I would be up late that night reading their essays, heart-breaking attempts at communication from people who lived full, complete lives, but simply lacked the structures in which to effectively communicate those life experiences in a traditional, accepted-by-society manner.

Chuck sat in the seat of my focused awareness. I could not get the image of him out of my mind, no matter where in the class I stood or where I looked.

Our relationship had been cordial. He was easy to get along with, an agreeable, passive guy, trying so hard to come to class regularly, despite the demands of the job he held to pay for his girlfriend and babies' needs. He got an A+ for trying, while I got an A+ for intention. But our efforts did not merge into learning and change for him. And that was my failure.

I knew I would pass Chuck, no matter the quality of his exam. I knew I would not stand between him and a diploma, for whatever that was worth. I would not stand between him and that Kodak snapshot of himself, in his cap and gown, face glowing with pride, family elated at his "success."

I had faced this dilemma before in my teaching career, and chose to pass rather than hold back several senior students who were academically lacking, where there appeared no other solution or response. My friend, Tom, a black man, told me I was "limping for the cripples." But that evening, sitting at my kitchen table reading Chuck's essay, I saw his failure as my own. Perhaps it was my liberal guilt that moved my hand toward the roll book, to write a "C" after his name as a final grade. It certainly was my failure and the failure of the system that was supposed to be committed to his education. It was not Chuck's fault.

My failures and successes were blurred here. Sometimes it was difficult to distinguish the two. Earlier in the school year I found myself headed toward the library to check out reference books for my seniors' research papers. A young girl I did not know approached me in the busy, cinderblock hallway. She was young, tall, and broad, long-armed and long-legged, very black-skinned. Not cool, not fancy-dressed—a quieter, church-going kid, I assumed. She stood in front of me shyly, anxiously.

She asked, "Miss Fruity, can I tell ya' somethin'?"

I answered, "Sure, anything. What's your name?"

She responded, "Loretta. Loretta Mack. I dreamed 'bout you last night."

That was interesting to me. I wondered what this might be about.

"Tell me about it," I encouraged her further.

"Can't tell ya' now," she said, turning and walking away.

"Come and talk to me anytime," I shouted after her, as she disappeared into the crowd of moving, flowing students.

A few weeks passed. I half forgot about Loretta and her dream. One morning in my mailbox there was an elaborately wrapped series of papers, folded and taped into themselves. My name, "Miss Fruity," was on the front in a young, cursive scrawl. Inside were four blank sheets acting as protectors for the one page on which something was written. I had no idea whom this might be from. I dropped it into my pocket and headed off to homeroom. After organizing myself for the day, I opened the note with some struggle. It was from Loretta, Loretta Mack. It read:

"Miss Fruity, what would you do if you was middle aged teenaged girl who step mother boy friend came into your room at night an all the time did what ever he want to you?"

I was stunned, my breath releasing on a sigh. Oh, poor Loretta. A middle-aged teenager. I knew I was in way over my head, but was amazed that she trusted me with such a deep and painful truth.

I sought Loretta out, finding her during her sixth period study hall. We stood in the quiet hall, talking. She could not meet my eyes, averting them, looking to the side with the beginnings of tears welling up in her eyes. She was so painfully shy and obviously overwhelmed that I now knew her gravest secret. I told her not to worry, I would figure something out. I would find some help for her, I said. She still could not look at me, and wrapped her floral jumper closer around her legs. My words seemed to make her even more uncomfortable. I told her I would have Catherine Murray help us. Catherine was a black woman, a vice principal, one of the few competent, caring administrators.

Loretta's eyes got even bigger at the mention of Mrs. Murray's name. Her mouth seemed to form itself into a little *o*, but no sound came out. I did my best to assure her it would be okay, that Mrs. Murray was to be trusted, that we would make it better for her. She would not look at me still. I asked if she had anything to say. She shook her head violently, wildly indicating "no." She escaped back into her study hall. I stood in the hall, now speechless, too.

I questioned my need to bring Mrs. Murray into this. Yet I knew I could not manage this one alone. I knew that class and race would make me even more ineffective than I really was.

I spoke with Catherine Murray that afternoon, who, with a businesslike clarity, sitting behind her large, organized desk, thanked me for my time and involvement in the process. She would take it from here, she told me, with a dismissive propriety. As far as I could tell, she worked with Family Services, and helped, over time, to remove Loretta from that abusive house. By the end of the school year, Loretta looked brighter, less inward—though I saw her only in passing in the hall.

Loretta never talked to me again. I guess I was simply a window for her to walk through to get help. For that I am grateful. Catherine Murray never enrolled me in the process in any further way. My usefulness was spent.

Chuck. Loretta. *All the kids' lives that have washed over my heart in these years*, I thought, as I drove Ruby away from the ghetto, toward the Tunnel that would return me to my world of quiet privilege.

I'm tired. So very tired, I thought, as Ruby took us into the Tunnel and home once more.

"Failure and success were blurred here."

21. The Matriarchy and Other Hopes for the Planet
1985

"It makes complete sense. A world without men. Men are the problem, the fuck ups, the power-hungry, the privileged. Women hold the secrets of life, the powers of birth and intuition. We are the earth, the earth-mothers. Men are the other. Period. End of discussion." Carol took a breath and looked around, smirking, proud of herself. Her frizzy halo of dirty-blond hair seemed to shimmer with life, excitement, and energy.

I passed the joint on to Matti. She daintily inhaled and guffawed, spitting smoke and a little tiny bit of saliva out onto the corner of her mouth. I snickered, which made her laugh even more. Trying to be cool and un-silly, we hid our laughter behind our open hands, disguised in a cough. We were discussing whether or not our political group, Radical Jewish Lesbians Rising, should break off from the main contingent of the upcoming Gay Pride Roundup and create a women-only assembly. This was not a funny discussion. Conversations like this bored me to tears, but I tried to keep focused. I knew that I needed to listen, to be a person who wanted to listen, a person who could listen.

The discussion went on and on, each one of us giving an opinion, then a counter-opinion, and then another, it seemed. I thought of Cindy. She was somebody I was dating—tall, long, blue eyes, big dimples, from the Midwest. An artist. She was cute, different, not from my circle of political friends. That seemed good. She was not of my group. I loved these women and couldn't imagine my life without them—they defined me, they were me, they taught me who I really was. But it felt good and exciting to be with somebody from elsewhere.

Serial monogamy was the lesbian joke—committing to somebody, being in that relationship until it ended, and then doing it again. It defined me and my relationships as well. I didn't know what dating really meant. Dating? Another lesbian joke asks: "What do lesbians bring to their second date?" Answer: "The moving van." I just wanted to find somebody to be with, to move in with, to get married to, so that all this craziness could end, I thought, with another toke. *To take away the pain. Somebody to take away the pain. So I don't have to deal.*

My thoughts were all over the place these days. My headaches were worse and worse—migraines weekly now, sometimes twice a week. The coffee enemas I learned to give myself did reduce the pain, as the holistic nurse suggested. But the enemas were also life's greatest rush, such a wonderful high. Cooking coffee, filtering it, holding the enema in, lying on my left side—I loved the ritual of preparing it, the challenge of holding it, the miracle of releasing it. Oh, such a rush. I was doing them regularly now, not waiting for a headache to come, but doing them preventatively. *Preventatively*, I thought. *Like, maybe I'll do one later tonight. To prevent something.* I giggled to myself.

I couldn't really concentrate on our discussion. School had gotten harder, too, recently—a new kind of violence was emerging at the high school where I taught. That frightened me. I'd been pushed by a student in the hall last month. Granted, I was wearing a ghost costume and was unrecognizable as a teacher—it was Halloween. But it freaked me out and my neck still hurt from the wrenching. And this thing with Cindy—I didn't know how to reach her, or something.

"Yes," I said out of nowhere, breaking atypically into the discussion. "Yes, no men in the roundup. Let's consolidate our power." This interjection seemed bland enough to be accepted by all, which was always my concern, to hedge my bets, to say the right thing. I was proud that there had been no men in my apartment for all the years I lived there—only that telephone repair man, once. Sure, no men at the roundup. Much time would have to pass before I discovered the friendship, the beauty, and the depth of gay men, and even longer before I could sit and listen to a heterosexual man talk.

And women, too. Women were so fucked up, I thought. It was painful to see heterosexual women as such pawns in the hands of the establishment. They broke my heart. I felt angry when I thought about how straight women played into men's hands, and how they were so used by the system. Couldn't they see it? Also, unconscious, apolitical lesbian women were horrifying, another part of the problem. It was exhausting to think about. It was all so fucked up.

As a radical Jewish anti-Zionist lesbian spiritualist, I believed that breaking away from the established system was the only freedom that life offered us. I believed that the patriarchy was a disastrous creation motivated by greed, power, and lust. I was furious at the state of Israel for its racist actions against Palestinian peoples—or so I thought. The truth was, I wasn't really thinking very well. I wasn't feeling very well, either. Getting high wasn't working so easily. I needed more drugs, more alcohol, more pills to get through the day.

The meeting ended, with the decision to not make a decision. *Damn*, I thought to myself, heading across 8th Street going home, *if that isn't just like us? A decision to not have a decision. A meeting to talk about the agenda of the next and upcoming meeting.* I shook my head. It made me tired to think about it.

I was cold and lonely. That was all and that was true. I was seeing Cindy later. Maybe I'd do a coffee enema to get ready for our date.

The early December day was crisp and pretty. The light was bouncing off the newly fallen snow and it pierced annoyingly at my eyes. When I shut my eyes at the red light on 6th Street, pulsations of light and color and sensation danced behind my forehead. *Oh no*, I thought, *shit. I really don't feel good. I hope this isn't a migraine.*

By the time I got to the corner of my block, East 5th Street, I felt really shaky. I was nauseous and dizzy. I sluggishly made my way toward my building, opened its prehistoric heavy door, and began the trek up the four flights of steps, clomping my feet heavily on every step. I tried climbing the steps without breathing too deeply, in order to prevent further activation of the headache. At my door, I fiddled with my many keys for the different locks. Methodically I let myself in to my spacious, sunny kitchen. Oh, too much light! I went down the narrow hall, dropping my coat and scarf and gloves and keys behind me on the floor. I tossed myself onto my bed, closed my eyes, and fell into a mindless, dreamless sleep, the ultimate gift to migraine sufferers.

I woke three hours later, rubbing my sore eyes. *Wow, that was weird,* I thought. *Head not too bad. Not enough time for a coffee enema.* I inched up from the bed, and reached for my migraine medicine. *Just in case,* I thought, and swallowed three pills. If instructions on medication said "take one," to me that meant two would be more efficient, and three would be appropriate. Instructions on medicine were for other people.

I got up, tidied the place, showered, and felt a little better. *I think I'll smoke a tiny joint before Cindy comes over,* I thought, *just a little.* Rolling just a tiny one, I noticed the evening coming in over lower Manhattan, the setting sun casting slanted, fading light on the apartments around my building. I could see the tips of the World Trade Towers downtown. The light reflected off them was shimmering and beautiful, and seemed to flicker and dance in the early New York dusk.

"Hell-ooo," Cindy's voice bellowed out from the street below. My building didn't have a buzz-in system. I opened the window, waved down at her, and tossed my key inside a sock toward her head, my perfected method of letting guests in. She ducked out of the way of its fall, picked it up, and made her way inside.

She knocked at the door in a few minutes. Approaching the door, I felt frightened and small, but I didn't know why. Just frightened and small. I opened the door and there stood Cindy, tall, smiling, dimpled. I urged her in, gesturing with my hand for her entry. She put her coat on a kitchen chair and stood before me. She was wearing a red cardigan sweater, grey corduroy pants and cool, ankle-high leather boots. Her hair was mid-length and dirty-blond. She was clearly cute, scrubbed looking, fresh and clean.

We sat on the kitchen floor. I had no idea how we ended up there. She was talking about her work, a newly completed installation of watercolors depicting animals interacting with people. She spoke quietly and deeply, and I had to strain to hear her. My scalp was itchy and my eyes were watering. I didn't know why.

"Are you okay?" she asked with gentle concern.

"Sure, why, fine. Fine, yes, I'm fine," I sputtered with some tingling of paranoia. Why was she asking me? It wasn't her business.

"You seem jumpy. What's going on with you?" Her voice was gentle, even quieter than before.

I reached for a joint, lit one, and offered it to her. She shook her head with a frown.

"What's up with you? You seem really uncomfortable."

Fuck you, I thought. I reached over to kiss her. She shrugged me away, replying, "I'm asking you an important question. You seem really— strange. Are you okay? And no, I don't want to smoke any of your damn pot. Why do you smoke all the time?"

Why did I smoke all the time? *Great question*, I thought, *a great, moronic question.* It made me furious to hear her ask it. I could feel heat rising to my scalp at the mere sound of her words. *Isn't it obvious to everyone with any political consciousness? I smoke to create an alternative reality, to sharpen my extrasensory insight, to see God, and most fucking importantly, to violate the abusive, fucked up system we lived in. Isn't it obvious?* I didn't have the energy and couldn't be bothered to say it aloud.

I reached for her again.

"Quit it," she said, with more energy. "You know, I've been praying for you, Wing. I think you really have a problem and I've been sending you my prayers."

That completely pissed me off. I didn't want her damn gentile, establishment prayers, her stupid Midwestern prayers. Who the fuck did she think she was to pray for me? *Fuck you,* I thought, and reached over to massage her knee.

"That's it. I'm outta here. You're very dear, Wing, but I think you need some help." She grabbed her pack, her coat, and glided out of my kitchen, out of my apartment, and out of my life.

Fuck. Who did she think she was, to pray for me? I didn't need her prayers, or anybody's. *Good, good she's gone,* I thought. *She's not one of us. It would never work. Now I can celebrate something. I know there is something to celebrate.*

The rest of the night was a blur. I remember going out finding Ruby parked on 4th Street, and driving somewhere. I don't really know what happened next. The first thing I remembered was waking up, coming to, and finding myself driving in Ruby, alone.

I had no idea where I was or where I'd been. It was pitch black, the middle of the night, and profound silence surrounded me. I had no idea what neighborhood I was in. That was the scariest thing of all. Nothing looked familiar. I could have been on the black moon for all I knew. I had a terrifying few moments, without any memory of where I had spent—how long? It was 2:10 a.m. now, my watch told me—about four hours of my life. Those four hours had gone missing. *Whoa, that's really scary,* I thought again. I felt cold and clammy and alone. Ruby's heater wasn't working, so I bundled my scarf more closely around my neck. I continued along the street and found a street sign, telling me I was on the Upper West Side. What the fuck? I didn't know anybody up there. I cautiously held onto the wheel, slowed down a bit, and traced my way downtown, down toward my apartment, trying to talk myself down, to calm myself. Once back in my neighborhood, I entered the good-luck-finding-a parking-spot-from-hell experience, something I was oh-so-familiar with. Pain in the ass. After some block circling, I finally found a space on 7th Street that was legal until Monday morning. What a score—at least something went right.

I got out of Ruby, locked her up, and tried to find my land legs. I felt shaky from the inside out. The air was cold and bit hungrily at my nose. I thrust my hands into my pea coat pocket and walked the two blocks home, shaking my head in wonder. Where had I been? Fuck Cindy anyway. *Pray for me. Fuck you. I'm Jewish. I don't need prayers.*

The nausea grew, building with every step. By the time I reached my block and my building, the bile was rising in my throat. Oh, shit. I held onto the cement wall of the Chinese laundry next to my building for balance, and found myself vomiting in slow-motion. Like on those nature shows on public television, everything was slow and long and time-warped. It began as small upchucks, then morphed into larger, more fluid, flowing streams. My vomit projected itself in graceful arcs onto a pile of fresh snow against my building. It was a remarkable thing to see—the snow absorbing the vomit, melting together into one, the vomit becoming the snow. I was fascinated. *Look,* I thought, *I am the earth. The earth is me.* I felt a tad better, and collected myself for the hike up the four flights of stairs from hell.

I made it upstairs, managed the door locks, and found my bed. I didn't bother to take off my clothes—too hard. My bed felt damp but good, oh, so good. The room spun around me. I smelled something bad—was that my hair? My hands?

Dizzy, swirling, sweating, help, let me sleep.

Fuck Cindy. I don't need her. Or her prayers.

I'm fine. All is well.

I am the earth.

The earth is me.

Forever live the matriarchy.

22. Disappearing Sands Beach
July, 1986

She was a shit and I hated her. I hated her and I loved her. If only she would have done it my way, everything would have been all right. I knew this. She knew it too, damn it. Damn her. She knew she wanted only me. Athena had to go. There we were on that beautiful island, with everything wonderful and lovely around us. What did we do? We got ourselves crazier.

The Big Island of Hawaii. The Kona Coast. Before Kona we visited Dina, my dear Peace Corps friend, in her little village of Volcano, up by the National Park. It was painful and weird. She didn't get along very well with Dina, mild and gentle Dina. She could have eaten Dina up. I could tell that Dina looked concerned. I understood that. Dina probably noticed how opinionated and judgmental she was. Dina probably thought we were crazy together, that she wasn't good for me. I knew how protective Dina was toward me. Dina was right: we were nuts together. But we were together, and that would not change. After a few strange days with Dina, we came down to Kona and found a place to stay for a while. The ocean was right outside our patio. The sound of it drove me crazier; it reminded me of something. I wasn't sure what it reminded me of. I forgot what.

The crashing of the waves all the time—it made me a little nervous. The restaurant downstairs served great Mai Tai's. The evening started out there. I had one, then another one quickly. They were coco-nutty, milky, like a milkshake with a built-in buzz. The first drink instantly went to my head. I could feel the restaurant swim around me, just like the crazy crashing waves. The second took my head off like a rocket ship. I had to pull it together. I had another one, just for the road, thinking that would help. This one tasted different. I tasted nothing, actually. My taste buds seemed gone. But I had it and it helped. It settled me. Whenever I felt dizzy I just held on to the chair and clenched my jaw tightly. That worked fine for me. She had a few drinks, too, I think.

We went upstairs to the condo, smoked some more of the fabulous Hawaiian bud we had. Then we started up the same old fight about Athena. She wanted both of us, the shit. I wanted Athena gone, just me, only me, love only me. I wanted her only to myself, and I deserved that. Our voices grew. She was furious at me, black eyes snapping her crazy rage. She turned me on when she was like that. I grabbed her, held her wrists. She squirmed, leaned into me, bit me on the lip. That pissed me off. I lit another joint. *Fuck you*, I thought to myself. *What?* She screamed. *What did you say to me?*

I reached over, pushed her down on the bed and climbed on top of her. I breathed in her delicious smells. She kicked and thrashed beneath me. I knew it would change—it always did. After a few moments of struggle she sank into the bed, moaned, pulled me with her, toward her, into her. We rolled, lunged, grabbed at each other. I was wasted, dizzy. She hurt me. I bit her neck, tasted blood. She laughed, then got mad. She kicked me hard in the stomach. I started retching.

Fuck you, I thought for the eighteenth time. *Fuck you. Fuck this.* I coughed blood into my hands. *Fuck you, you hurt me.* This time I said it aloud. I stood up, shaky, unsure. I couldn't go on. I grabbed my silver cigarette case with my joints in it, my lighter, and my keys, and staggered toward the door. *Fuck you.*

Get out of here, you baby, she cursed after me, throwing her shoe at the door. It missed me. I closed the door behind me with a passive-aggressive thud.

The Hawaiian night was deeply silent and still. There was a full moon, and the midnight black of the night was cut with slivers of silver from this pregnant, rounded moon hovering above me. This moon offered

153

me no escape from its watchful eye. I was sobbing, my breath heaving. *Fuck her. Fuck her.* I couldn't breathe. My heart throbbed violently in my throat. My head seemed to vibrate with pain—especially my eyes. The deep quietness of the night, interrupted by the rhythmic rocking, crashing waves, was all-encompassing. It surrounding me—this night ate me into it. I staggered down the steps, coughing up mucus. *Fuck you*, I thought again. A moan escaped my lips.

I walked away from the condo, the restaurant, and the lights, my steps unsteady, my gait erratic and uneven, into the spreading darkness. The pavement tripped me up and I stumbled forward. *Ouch. Fuck it*, I said to myself again. *Fuck this, what the fuck ever.* I walked away from the parking lot.

On the far side of the parking lot stood a small wooden sign announcing something. I wandered, staggered over in that direction.

> *Disappearing Sands Beach*
> *Kona, Hawaii*
> *Thank you for reading and respecting our rules.*

Fuck you and fuck your rules, I said to the sign. To the sign's left stood a little beach, vastly visible tonight in the light of the monster full moon. I wandered over toward it, and my foot sank down into the sand. I started to walk, trudging toward the shore.

The beach was white-sanded and narrow. The ocean, pitch black, was illuminated with moon shadows tracing the tops of the waves, scrolling them with silver-white moon glow. Moon, ocean, waves, sand. That was all. And me, traipsing unsteadily along, mumbling to myself.

Disappearing Sands, stupid fucking name for a beach. Loser beach. Small tiny fucking beach. Fuck it.

And then it happened. The waves of pain crashed inside of me and broke—I could not keep them away any more. The waves inside of me, perhaps encouraged by the waves outside of me, pushed away the surface of my anger, opening me up to the depth of suffering that lived in me. The pain was me—it was all that I was. It crashed me down to my knees. It took away my breath. It devastated me, laid to waste on my knees, on this empty, tiny beach of sand, disappearing sand. This ocean was relentless; it would not stop crashing. This moon, this haunting moon would not leave me alone. Pain crashed and built again, like the waves, crashed and built again inside of me. I howled, rolled on my side, pulled my knees into my chest, trying to make myself tiny, to limit, to contain the anguish. It didn't work. I sobbed into the sand. I was beaten, heaving, sobbing, wailing on this beach of disappearing sand. I was disappearing, too. I was being erased, whited out, wiped out by the pain.

No. It's too hard. No. I can't fucking do this. No. Help me, help. Please fucking help me.

I screamed into the emptiness of this beach, the vastness of this ocean. I had never said those words before. *Help me, help.* Snot clotted on my face, spit and bile covered my t-shirt. I couldn't stop heaving, almost puking, into the sand. I tried to light a joint, my lighter flickering in the wind, thinking that would calm me. I toked wildly, sucking the paper wet. I couldn't get enough of it, yet it didn't help. It didn't help. Nothing helped anymore. Nothing. I was disappearing, just like the sands.

And then it happened. A voice coming from somewhere, coming from nowhere, coming from outside of me, called to me, spoke to me:

It's going to be okay.

It was so other-worldly, so freaky, that it sobered me up and stopped my heaving, instantly taking me up to my feet. I was positive I heard it. I saw nobody around. There was nobody around. The voice was loud, clear, distinct, definitely from outside of me. It was—vast, bigger than everything else.

Hello? Who are you? I asked, voice quivering, body shaking. This was really weird.

It's already okay. It spoke again to me. *Everything is okay exactly as it is now.*

It completely freaked me out. I looked around again—nobody and nothing. The beach was stark empty. I backed away, keeping my eyes scanning forward, then pivoted on my heels and walked-ran back to the parking lot. I stumbled my way back to the condo, where I had sworn I would never go. I went back to her, she whom I swore I would never return to. As I crawled into bed next to her taut, hot body, she opened up to me, cuddling up to me, writhing into me. We made up for the eighth time that day. *Sorry, sorry. Love you, sorry, so sorry*, our ancient, exhausted mantra.

I tried to forget about the voice. *I was stoned, I made some shit up*, I reasoned. But there was no denying it: something spoke to me, something assured me, reassured me. Something contacted me. Something offered itself to me. Something was now available to me.

It would be a few weeks before I could walk in the direction of that voice. And it would be a very, very long time before I could walk away from that woman in the bed upstairs, the woman I thought I loved, the woman who was my lover. There was more pain left for me, the pain of trying to change somebody. The pain of denying myself and my needs. The pain of wanting life to be different. The pain of the illusion of control. The pain of self-imposed oblivion.

It would be a few more weeks before I could walk in the direction of that voice, my new and forever partner. But for now, more struggle. For now, more pain.

For now, another joint, as we curled up together in bed, surf pounding outside our window, moon shadows playing on our walls.

23. August 27th—Part A
1986

As I smacked my head from side to side on the ground, I became mesmerized by the unevenness of the floor. I had known for years that the north side of my apartment was higher than the south. But I had never experienced it viscerally or felt its irregular angles quite like this. Rolling first to my left, head banging, then right, head banging again, I spent a few long moments contemplating the floor, the higher north, the lower south. I continued to roll and bang my head, fuzzy, confused by the circumstances that had brought me to this moment of awareness. Time halted, my alertness magnified. As the rolling continued, unabated, I was aware of several things: the humid, scorching heat holding my body in place, the raging headache beating behind my eyes, and the dry gulch of my mouth, horrid and decimated. It seemed the rolling would never stop, that I was separate from it, that it had a life of its own. I was unable to make it stop, this relentless banging. And then the thought that changed it all entered me:

"How long have I been banging my head on the floor?"

I didn't know the answer. Was it a moment or two? An hour? Was it a day, an evening? Or was it every moment of these thirty-eight years of my life, where challenge after challenge, disappointment after disappointment, feeling after feeling, overwhelmed me, terrified me? Perhaps banging my head on the floor was really my only coping mechanism.

I didn't know. I didn't know how long I had been rolling from side to side in my skinny, funny room.

Not knowing the answer woke me up into sanity. I instantly stopped rolling, sat up on my knees, and tried to right myself. I touched my head—no blood, good. Sore and tender—bad. I staggered onto my wobbly legs. I surveyed my apartment, this long, narrow tenement space, great for a swimmer's lane, I always imagined. Things were beyond their usual state of disheveled. I didn't have real furniture—egg crates served as tables, my mom's old wrought iron porch table and chairs as my living room furniture, purple material as makeshift curtains on my long, wonderful, streaked windows. It was downwardly mobile funk. It was so cool and radical, I thought, to not buy into the system, to not have normal things like furniture. Yet perhaps the real reason for my apartment's sparse uniqueness was lack of money—much of mine went toward drugs, alcohol, and eating out. What else did New Yorkers do? Or perhaps I just didn't know how. How to what? Perhaps I didn't know how to have a home. Tears pushed behind my eyes, demanding escape.

Didn't know how to have a home.

Didn't deserve to have a home.

That last thought sobered me even more. Leaning against the wall, I stood to my full height. My body ached. What had I been doing? Where had I been the night before, or even today? Again, I didn't know. A moan escaped my lips, a tiny sound that bore no resemblance to my voice at all. It surprised me, that moan. Like a tiny, trapped animal, it eked out again, this time louder. I was frightening myself now, stomach churning, bile burning in the back of my throat.

Standing up made me dizzy. I crouched down again, using the wall for support as my head swam. It seemed easy to imagine myself dropping to my knees and recreating my rolling and banging. I felt the weight of my body pulled down by the gravity of that possibility. *No*, I thought. *No more.* "Please, no more," I said to nobody.

I staggered up again, trembling now, heading toward the telephone without a thought. It was red, had an abnormally long cord for bathtub talking, and sat on a milk crate next to my platform bed.

Sitting into the bed with a groan, I grabbed the telephone in trembling hands. Who was I calling? I had no answer to that question either, no cognitive response. I found myself dialing information. The voice of the recording asked me without inflection, "What number do you request?"

I heard myself respond, "Alcoholics Anonymous."

Shocked again by my own voice and its free-standing request separate from me, I wondered where that idea had come from. It was clearly not mine. I remembered now that my friend, Jan, had talked about Alcoholics Anonymous a few weeks ago, kindly implying it might help me. I snickered at her intrusive assumption and forgot about it, or so I thought. Until this moment.

"Connecting," the automated operator said nasally as its voice repeated the number.

Phone ringing, hands shaking, stomach gurgling, eyes watering, heart pounding, sweat dripping, I waited. I waited for an eternity.

"Alcoholics Anonymous. Hello. How can we help you?" The male voice was neutral, undisclosed.

"Is there a meeting?" Strangely, that seemed to be my voice inquiring.

"Where are you now?" his response softening.

"East Fifth Street." I somehow knew that.

"Ah, yes, the *I Don't Have A Clue* group meets tonight at 5:30, at the Church of Our Lady of Perpetual Mercy on East Fourth, between First and A." That was a block and a half away from where I stood that very moment.

"What time is it now?" I wondered, having no clue. I snickered to myself. I didn't have a clue, just like he said.

"5:20. You can make it," he urged.

The phone left my hand, spilling down aimlessly toward the receiver. Without a thought pro or con, without conscious intervention on any level, I simply headed toward the kitchen, found my battered Birkenstocks abandoned there, my keys tossed on the table along with old mail, empty wheat grass containers, and used matches. Shoes on feet, keys in hand, I mindlessly wrestled with the security bar lock on my door, sliding it to its neutral position, unlocking the bolt lock, the chain, and the second bolt lock. The smell of my hallway flooded me. Cat urine, my neighbor Mabel's stale garbage, trapped hot air, and my upstairs neighbor's Polish cooking all combusted together to form a most specific and unique smell. I gulped at it, and weaved my way down the dizzying steps, four flights down. The street door was green and heavy, the door knob greasy. I lunged it opened and felt assaulted by East Fifth Street.

It was hot and humid as only New York City can be. It was so hot that the air seemed to clutch at me and, once successful, to lie upon my skin relentlessly. The humidity slid into me, intensifying my already baffled body functions. My sweat flowed openly down my arms in sticky rivulets, and crept behind my ears and down my spine. I could have easily fallen forward and been held up by the density of the day. Sounds were screeching, buses flying up First Avenue, kids shouting and playing ball down the street toward the police station. It was overwhelming. I was not sure I could take a step.

Then I remembered his voice: "The *I Don't Have A Clue Group*," he had casually said. And I remembered how I didn't have a clue about the time. There was no decision to be made. I simply moved thoughtlessly toward the intersection, looked hesitantly at First Avenue's treachery, and threw myself into it. Instinctively I dodged cars, buses, and a nasty bike rider, and wove my way across the street, to the other side of the Avenue. I walked the short block south, the block filled with identical brick senior housing units, the black, waist-high fences corralling in patches of dry grass. East Fourth Street, a few seconds' walk away, manifested before me. I turned left, walking the side of the housing units cautiously.

Without appearing obvious, I began to scan the other side of the street, where the alleged church had to be. What did he say? The Church of Our Lady of Perpetual Mercy. What was that stupid name? I had absolutely no idea.

Sure enough, mid-block stood an aged, grey church, with a stepped entry way and a railing. All around the steps, leaning into the railing, stood people. People. I didn't realize people would be there. Like, real people. I took one glace at them, again taking great care to not appear interested at all, and knew surely: there was no way, no FUCKING way, I would walk into that ridiculous old church with those ridiculous people. They looked, what? Regular. And different, too. One woman wore leather, LEATHER, on the hottest day in America's history. There were some butchy biker men. Yuck. Completely un-political, hetero people. Breeders. NO FUCKING WAY. I wondered if I was talking aloud or to myself. I wasn't sure.

I continued walking to the end of the block, my stride lengthening with my indignation at the mere assumption that I might go where these people went before me. I felt huffy, righteous in my rejection of this possibility. At the corner of Avenue A, I crossed over to the southern side of the block, and walked back on Fourth. NO FUCKING WAY. I knew so much about the establishment, the patriarchy. I knew how I needed to continue raising my consciousness with lesbians, really with radical Jewish Lesbians. Really with Anti-Zionist radical Jewish Lesbians. They were my people. These people, these freaky church people, had nothing, absolutely nothing to offer me. They had all gone inside by now, the losers, wearing leather and laughing on such a hot horrid night. *Assholes,* I thought.

I came to the steps of the church now, my righteous indignation at a peak. Without any sensible thought, I found myself turning left, walking up those three little cement stairs, and making my way toward the voices, toward the people, and toward salvation.

24. August 27th—Part B
1986

The picture of Jesus on the wall was the largest I had ever seen in my entire Jewish life. Jesus was looking tall and benevolent, wearing a robe and slippers, and holding a lamb. It took up most of the wall, appearing practically larger-than-life-sized. Or perhaps it was me. Maybe my perception was off—I wasn't feeling very well. We were facing each other, Jesus and I, assessing each other, sizing each other up. I wasn't sure of him at all.

We were sitting on horribly uncomfortable metal folding chairs. Mine was rickety, and when I moved, which seemed to be often, the chair responded with a squeak. My already out-of-the-box self-consciousness was magnified by this damn chair that had to call attention to my every nervous readjustment. There were about twenty people sitting in a makeshift circle. I could hardly bear to look at anyone but Jesus.

We were in what seemed to be a tan rec room with faded paint, an old ping pong table off to the side, and a few battered floral couches that had seen better days. There was a coffee percolator on a rickety-looking card table with Styrofoam cups, napkins stained with coffee, Oreo cookies in their box, and a plastic bowl of hard candies. I shuddered at the obvious lack of nutritional sophistication of these people. I would never eat any of that. My commitment to my raw foods diet was impeccable.

People were talking. It seemed impossible to focus my hearing in a way that the words were individuated and made sense. They all seemed to assault me at once, these words, and pour senselessly over me. I couldn't seem to slow them down, to divide them out. What the hell was happening to me? That thought terrified me anew, and I took a deep breath, which seemed to slow everything down a little.

"And I realized that I wasn't the only person who felt like that," said a voice.

I searched around the circle to find the owner of the voice and couldn't believe my eyes. It was the leather woman. She was dressed in a black leather vest, despite the intolerable heat. She had on skin-tight jeans, knee-length laced boots with spiked heels, and a biker's cap on her dyed inky black hair. But I was mesmerized by her piercings—this was well before piercing was in vogue. She had a dozen tiny metal balls streaming down the length of each ear, piercings in each of her nostrils, and something odd and metal adorning her right eyebrow. Although I had lived in the middle of the East Village for years and had been accustomed to everybody, every shape, race, color, size, and gender blend of personal expression, this was over the top for me. I was fascinated and repulsed by the elaborate display. Surely this woman and I existed on opposite sides of the universe. I was the anti-Zionist radical Jewish lesbian. I was Nachama, the name of my grandmother's mother. She was—Pierced Lady. I believed in and lived for a matriarchy, freed from the symbols of male power and oppression. I saw her as a walking embodiment of male power and oppression.

What the fuck was I doing here with these people? The intensity of my discomfort continued to increase. I felt downright squirmy but stayed seated. I had no real alternative but to sit, to allow this strange meeting with its own particular cast of characters to play out.

Jesus met my eye again, offering me a touchstone of presence. I squirmed beneath his gaze.

I tried to take a breath, attempting to discern the words floating around me.

Pierced Lady continued, "I get really scared when I don't know how to do something."

I heard that. Those words caught me, shook me a bit more awake. *Me, too,* I thought. *I got terrified at work when I had to teach that new class in phonics last month—it completely freaked me out.* I sat up a little.

Pierced Lady went on, "I want people to like me. I want everybody to think I'm good and kind and do things right. I just don't know how to be myself, to have my feelings, to be in relationship, to show up. When I get scared, all I want to do is to drink or drug so it will go away. When I do that, I think I can show up. I try to, and everything gets really messy. Everything gets worse when I drink or drug. The problems get bigger, and I feel like shit about it all. I feel like shit about me."

I was stunned, at the edge of my chair. She, this Pierced Lady from the galaxy of biker-land, was speaking the words of my inner, most secret life. She was saying things about me that I hadn't quite said about myself, but that I knew, deeply inside, were true. They were words that I tried to forever push away. In her speaking them aloud, something inside of me shifted and settled.

She went on, describing her attempts to stay sober and clean, about how her life was improving slowly, one day at a time. I had never had the experience of being so impacted by somebody's words. It was almost as if they missed my brain and entered directly into my body, into my heart. My head calmed. I sat alert, in awe.

"Just don't use. Just don't pick up. You can outlive those feelings. Keep coming back here. Just keep coming. Thank you," Pierced Lady ended, to a round of applause.

I sat dumbfounded. She understood me, this be-leathered and odd being. Despite the differences in our costumes, despite our obvious contrary political perspectives, she spoke my world into being. She put words to my reality. Everything seemed very still in the room.

The leader, a lanky jock-looking guy in cut-offs and dirty white high-top sneakers, thanked her and said, "Let's continue the discussion with Jason," and looked to a young pimply kid on his left. Jason opened his mouth and started talking.

It happened again. And it happened again and again as the discussion passed organically around the circle. These people, these men, these strange women, each spoke something that touched me, something that held a mirror up to my own self. I had never in my thirty-eight years felt so joined by other people, people I had never seen before.

Somehow the discussion floated around the circle. Somehow the words spoken were my words, wanting to be said, wanting to be released. Somehow, when the circle's attention focused on me, without thought, with chattering teeth, I was able to say, "My name is Nachama. I'm an alcoholic and drug addict." Without thought, without planning, my wounded self was disclosed, my gravest secret bathed in the light of acceptance.

I had landed.

PART FOUR:
OPENING

25. Men and Other Such Foreign Beings
1986 – 1989

Recovering from Lesbian Separatism was a rocky, awkward process. I did it so imperfectly. Sober life was requesting that I come into relationship with at least 50 percent more of the population on the planet than I had been acknowledging for the past fifteen years. My healing and change in this arena were slow. Like a little tortoise peeking my head out of a protective shell, I inched my way forward toward the heterosexual universe, cautious, suspicious, paranoid, and yet available to the slow, gradual miracle of change.

Separatism made complete sense to me for a long, long time. Why not protect myself from the oppressors, from those who wreaked injustice and tyranny on the planet? Why not surround myself only by women, delicious, round, soft, glorious women? I celebrated having no man in my apartment for fifteen years, but for that one damn telephone repair man. I loved having no male influences beside my dad. He was more female than male, I rationalized. I adored women-only concerts, camp outs, dances, events. Walking into an event without men polluting the vibration of the matriarchy was the safest, most delicious feeling.

I recognized that, at times, our lesbian feminist culture took this philosophy a tad too far. My friend, Shelly, had an eight-year-old boy named Alex. He had orange-red hair and freckles fighting for space on his chubby, round face. He always tagged along with his mom to the Fire House on Thursday nights, when our women's group met for a consciousness-raising session. Since Shelly didn't have consistent child care support, Alex made his own way around the events, puttering here, coloring in his thick paper coloring book on the floor over there.

He was a gentle, quiet kid who obviously had learned how to tiptoe around life and to not make noise when he walked.

One Thursday night, I was coming out of the bathroom when I heard a bloodcurdling scream from the kitchen. The hair on the back of my neck came alive in terror. I thought only the worst—some awful, power-abusive crime was taking place over the simmering of our chamomile tea. In a moment of uncharacteristic bravery, I dashed toward the kitchen.

There stood Belinda, stocky, cantankerous Belinda, decked out as usual in her layers of flimsy Indian silk, hands on the sides of her head, screaming. The object of her hysteria, backed into a corner and petrified into stillness, was Alex. "There is," she screeched hysterically, "there is a PENIS in this room." She elongated the pronunciation of the word with heavy emphasis on the second syllable, pe—nis. I looked at Alex. His eyes were so rounded with awe that they took up much of his face, minimizing the width of his forehead. He was blotchy pink with defended terror. I doubted he understood that that evening, he was a potential oppressor; that his penis gave him power, status, and dominance over us women. He simply looked completely freaked out, as only a powerless eight-year-old kid might. I helped with the calming down process, with included an abundance of chamomile tea, conscious dialoguing, and banishment of Alex. Going home that night on the rocky subway, I remembered the look on his face. That terrified face put a little chink in the armor of my separatism.

For those early years of my lesbian-hood, separatism worked for me. As time passed, I hid a bit behind the very ideology that defined me. But life had a plan for me. It was called sobriety. It had my number. It knew what I needed to grow.

During my first few months of sobriety, I went to AA meetings at the Lesbian and Gay Center on the West Side. There I encountered other lesbian women who were not of my political persuasion. Some wore makeup, to my dismay. Makeup! A tool of the oppressor. Some had boyfriends, defining themselves as inhabitants of that confusing netherworld called bisexual. I found that appalling yet compelling.

Like a train wreck, I couldn't take my eyes off of them when they shared. They slept with whom? Men? I wanted to flee, but I did what my sponsor, Molly, suggested. I just sat still and listened. And yes, I did identify with their feelings. They talked about being afraid, of perfectionism, of wanting something to fill the emptiness inside. All of those issues grabbed at my heart.

If the non-political gay women were from another country, the gay men were of another galaxy. In general, they were a tidy, articulate, and friendly bunch. They terrified me. Again, I practiced saying hello and listened to their stories. They spoke of their fear of being different, of wanting stability and love in their lives. I walked away from the meetings touched, but still unable to really talk to people afterwards. I was a bolter—nanoseconds after the ending Serenity Prayer, I sprinted to and through the open door. Oh, well. I was practicing being present. Molly said I didn't have to get it right. "Just don't pick up," she said. "That's the only thing you need to do right today." I did that, one day at a time.

One day after a meeting, a cute, quiet man approached me tentatively. He stood next to my chair—I was still sitting—and coughed. "Hi," he said.

"Hi," I mustered back, clueless as to the next word.

"I related to what you said," he told me.

What the heck had I said that a man could relate to? How interesting.

"The part about being scared to go home, to see your family. Me, too. I'm going to Philadelphia this weekend to see them, and I feel so strange about it," he confided.

I looked at him more closely. He was very tidy in his neat chino pants and his nicely laundered polo shirt with a little emblem on it. He wore interesting, casual and worn, yet expensive looking sneakers. His light brown hair was neatly trimmed; his eyes were hazel, direct, clear. I liked his eyes.

"My name is Eric. Can I call you some time?"

Call me some time? Me? Why me? Well, why not? He was brave to talk to me, and something about his manner felt so profoundly familiar. He felt comfortable, like someone or something I knew well. We talked for a few minutes and exchanged phone numbers.

Eric became my friend. It was amazing—our evening check-in phone calls were rich and honest. His family dynamic, his role in the family, was almost parallel to mine, being youngest in a Jewish family, with an older, dominating sister. He was a brilliant photographer who questioned his talent. He wanted a boyfriend and yearned for a life of meaning and grace. I really liked him. He reminded me of—of what? He was becoming the kind of person I wanted to be myself.

Life had given me a best friend. And he was of the male persuasion. His were the first eyes of a man that I really looked into. And, surprise of surprises: I saw myself looking back.

I started going to my non-gay meetings, the non-"special interest groups" as the AA literature described gay and lesbian meetings. They were closer to my apartment, easier to get to, and strangely, they were more gripping. Here I encountered two other rare, unusual species in my narrow, closed world. First, the heterosexual woman.

Sitting in the Saint Mark's AA meeting one night, I half-listened to the discussion about the 11th Step. "Sought through prayer and meditation to improve our conscious contact with God as we understand Him, praying only for the knowledge of God's will for us and the power to carry that out." I was tired. The school day had been long and crazy, filled with unending fire drills and a boring, meaningless faculty meeting. The room was full and hot. I was there because I told Molly I would go. I wanted to watch television and not deal with other people. But I was struggling with this thing about God's will for me. I didn't really understand what God wanted for me. I was trying really hard to get God's will right. It was pretty exhausting.

Her voice was clear and woke me from my stupor. "The important word in this step is 'improve,'" she said. "It's not about getting it right. It's about improving."

It was Tina talking. She came to these Saint Mark's meetings a lot. She had been sober for two years, an incredible, inconceivable accomplishment in my eyes. She had mousey brown hair that was slightly teased and bouffant-y. She was small and thin. She was obviously straight and hung out with some of the really butch biker guys. She had soft blue eyes that I could see from across the room. I had listened to her share over the past few months and had attended her second-year anniversary meeting. I had grown to listen carefully when she shared.

She continued, "When I try to out-think God and make my will happen, I'm in pain. When I accept God's will, I am comfortable and free."

Hum. I really didn't understand her words, but I did feel and understand the way she said it. Her quiet, calm voice rang with some obvious truth. Hum. *Maybe I should talk to her,* I impossibly thought. Me, Queen of Bolters, had a thought of connecting with another human being. A straight woman, of all people. Hum.

The meeting ended quickly, with the scraping of chairs and the fumbles of hand-grabbing to form a circle for the Serenity Prayer. After the prayer, without thinking about it, I mustered my courage, took a gulp, and walked up to her where she stood talking.

"Tina?" my voice sounded young and tinny. "Hi."

She looked my way. I found myself bathed in the blueness of her eyes.

"Can I ask you something?"

"Sure," she said. "Of course." She offered me her full focus, turning to face me full-on.

"How do you know what God's will for you is?" I felt embarrassed at the rinky-dink nature of my question. Surely everybody knew this but me.

She smiled and softened, "God's will for you is what's happening."

God's will for me is what's happening, I repeated over and over again walking down Second Avenue. A new mantra. I didn't really understand what she meant, but I knew it was profound and important, and I could hang on to it. I understood something anew, delivered to me via a very heterosexual woman. I never would forget her words, the look in her blue eyes. Her response opened up my world. Some of my struggle softened that night.

The final category of folks into which I was immersed was the world of the heterosexual male. They sat at meetings, eating cookies, drinking coffee, sharing, and listening. They were—normal. There was no violence, except when one of the homeless guys from the Bowery who came to the meetings for the cookies fell off his chair. He hurt his head and laid on the floor in a clump, crying. Several of the guys helped him up with great kind tenderness. I felt tears sting my eyes, watching them right him up, wiping him off, ignoring the filth of his caked, ripped long and old wool coat. *Wow,* I thought, *I don't think I'd touch that guy. These very straight men truly helped this poor, helpless guy.*

One Saturday morning I sat at the Saint Mark's meeting, which had become my "home group," the meeting I committed to. A man named Greg was sharing. I had listened to him over the weeks. He was earnest, intense, yet quiet. He was a small guy with close-cropped dark hair. He had shared in the past about being diagnosed as HIV+. I was awed by his ability to talk about it. Tonight his voice rang through the room with a clarity and a grace that unlocked my heart:

"I am learning what the word humble means," Greg said. "I cannot control this disease, just like I can't control the disease of addiction. It is not up to me. All I can do is my best to live well and with balance. Something, somebody does the rest. My only job is to be in relationship with that power greater than myself."

I felt goose-bumps twitching up and down my arms. He spoke his truth and, in the speaking of it, I understood my own.

Those whom I held away from me for so very long had so much to show me.

My world was opening up.

26. So Now What?
Watch What You Ask For
January, 1989

"I just think I need a teacher, someone like a spiritual guide, to get through this 'conscious contact spiritual' thing," I said. My voice sounded a little whiney and nasal to me. Funny—I didn't feel like I was complaining. "It's so hard to know what the Big Book of AA means sometimes. Connection to a Higher Power and all that—it's a little woo-woo for me."

My therapist nodded her head with feigned interest. Our session was ending and I had pulled my typical move: attempting to deepen the conversation by introducing a new topic in the last few moments. Nancy assessed my comment and its motives, always so thoughtfully organized, just as she was always so neatly put together with her tidy, color-coordinated outfits. Then she appropriately responded, "Well, let's talk about this next time."

Very slowly getting up, in my attempt to subtly prolong the session, I continued my train of thought, "But a teacher. Really. I've always wanted a spiritual teacher."

Somehow Nancy helped me to gather myself up, both literally and figuratively, and closed the session. But my energetic request for a teacher was out there, echoing in the cosmos.

Weeks and weeks later, my request for a spiritual guide completely forgotten by me, a friend from my 12 Step program mentioned a yoga retreat center she had visited for a weekend program. "You'd love it,"

Jan said enthusiastically. "The site is stunning, the people are great, and the food is delicious and healthy. It's only a few hours' drive upstate. Oh, and there are great recovery meetings you can go to in town."

I was attempting to create my first sober, solo vacation. I had traveled much in my active addiction. Having the summers off with a paycheck rolling in from teaching got me out of the City and exploring other places and countries—Hawaii, Spain, Morocco, San Francisco, the Seneca Peace Camp. But I was never sober. Drugs and alcohol were my full-time, 24-7 traveling companions. Now, during this, my second sober year of being drug and alcohol free, I was ready to venture out on my own in a new kind of exploration. Jan's description of this retreat center seemed to meet my criteria.

It was autumn. Fall in the City was beautiful, cooler nights and still-warm afternoons, the air a little crisp and clearer. Life was so much better now that I wasn't using drugs and alcohol, but I still struggled with loneliness, with feeling that something, someone was missing. Life in the City was intense—I knew I wasn't a forever New Yorker. I just didn't know what was next for me. Work, too, was exhausting and wearing thin. I knew something else lay up ahead.

The foundation of my days were AA meetings. After figuring out my meeting for the day, I would then schedule friends and activities around that core commitment.

On the long, four-day weekend coming up, I decided to make the trip north and west to Lenox, Massachusetts, to explore this yoga center that Jan had raved about. I was going to take a program called "Retreat and Renewal." There were a lot of classes being offered, but that one sounded fluid and flexible. I was excited, bordering on fearful. It seemed a big trip, to leave my home 12 Step group, to take to the road by myself. My AA sponsor encouraged me in going, telling me I was ready for a sober adventure. Sober adventure? It sounded like a contradiction in terms to me. Using drugs and alcohol was how I both manifested and managed adventures. I made my reservation on the phone with the retreat center and was committed to go.

I left early on a Thursday morning. The City was quiet, my neighborhood waking up slowly in the unfolding, early morning light. I had neatly packed, unpacked, and repacked again, not being really sure what to take to a yoga center. I read their clothing list. It reminded me of my Girl Scout camp summer check list—bring a poncho, a mess kit, a collapsible cup, the scouts told me. You never knew when you might need a collapsible cup. The yoga people simply said, "comfortable clothes, walking shoes, raingear, a journal." *Wow,* I thought, *I'm going to be walking in the rain, wearing comfortable clothes and appropriate shoes, and writing in a journal, all at the same time.* I knew my silly thought was a response to my nervousness. Why did this feel so big? I took a breath as Heart-Throb, Ruby the Volkswagen's daughter, a red bug with a rebuilt engine, pulled away from 5th Street and headed upstate toward Albany and the Berkshire Hills. What was I getting myself into?

I had a lot of anxiety about getting lost on the road. This ancient fear seemed to rear its ugly head now that I was sober. When using drugs, if fear crept in, I guess I just lit another joint, in order to not have to deal. Now I had to both feel my feelings and strategize around them. I had printed out directions from the yoga center's website in really large font, and carefully underlined the key junctures with pink highlighter. I'd gone over them several obsessive and compulsive times in great detail. I'm not sure why being lost while driving was so threatening to me.

But once on the road, I seemed to manage, one highway at a time. I fiddled with the radio and found a golden oldies station. That helped my nerves. I danced up the New Jersey Parkway with the Supremes, was led to the New York Thruway by Jay and the Americans, and the Beatles serenaded me on the Mass Pike. The stations petered out a few hours north and I was left to my own devices. Once I got off the obviously larger highways, the smaller roads were reasonable. One ran easily into the next. Finally I found Lenox, MA, right on the border of New York State. *Good job,* I thought, my nerves a bit rattled.

There, on the top of a gorgeous hill, stood one of the ugliest buildings in America. Could this be it? Or was it a penitentiary? A mental hospital? It was brick, massive, and awkward, without any architectural sense at all, with a funny steeple on the top—all very strange. Sure enough, the sign announced it to be true: *Kripalu Center for Yoga and Health.* The grounds were beautiful, just like Jan said. Driving up the hill, Heart-Throb needed a bit of encouragement. So did I. I could feel my anxiety growing.

Finding a place to park, I pulled into the spot. A moment of indecision emerged—I could have so easily driven away. Somehow this felt just a little too risky, too scary. What would be expected of me? How should I act? So many unanswered questions plagued me. But something propelled me forward, something without thought or concept. It was just a feeling, an internal, energetic green light. I turned off the key, grabbed my pack, and walked toward the entrance. As I walked inside, another chapter of my life prepared to reveal itself to me.

The registration desk was mobbed with guests. I hovered to the side, holding my bag, feeling uncomfortable and shy. This didn't feel right. How did one check into a yoga center? Did I smile? Look serious? Look yogic? Project profoundly spiritual vibes? I felt fat and self-conscious, and downright spiritually flawed.

Finally, one of the registrars waved me over to the counter. Her nametag said "Hi, I'm Shanti." *Ugh*, I thought. *Shanti.* It reminded me of a character in a bad movie I'd seen about the 60's. Without much fanfare, Shanti very efficiently checked me in, giving me my bill and my dorm room number. To my horror, there were no keys to the rooms. What were they thinking? What about healthy boundaries? No keys! That freaked me out, but I was able to calm myself down. Shanti handed me a schedule of the Retreat and Renewal workshops and activities, which I promptly crumpled up in my pocket. I did not see myself as the workshop type. I began to walk away, wondering what the heck I had gotten myself into.

Then I remembered meetings. I had promised myself and my sponsor I would attend at least one. How did I find AA meetings around here? I looked back at the desk. Shanti was engaged with the next guest. Out of the six staff people, there was only one who seemed available. Her back was toward the counter. I walked over toward her, cleared my throat, and asked, tentatively, "Excuse me?" She turned to face me. She had dark skin, dark eyes, and the kindest smiley eyes I had ever seen. "Hi," she said, voice warming. Her nametag said, "Hi, I'm Kundan." I asked about 12 Step meetings in town. She smiled even more deeply, and said, "I'm going to an AA meeting tonight. If you want to join me, I'll meet you here at 7:00." It was perfect and I knew it, through and through. Somehow I was led to the right person.

The rest of the weekend unfolded with an equal ease and grace to which I was unaccustomed. I did not attend any workshops. That felt too threatening, too confrontational. I did run down the huge hill on Saturday morning, laughing and laughing until I fell onto the soft earth, doubled over with laughter. There was no mental joke to which I was responding. The laughter just seemed to explode out of me. I did eat the delicious, simple food that satisfied me so fully. I wasn't hungry between meals and had no need to snack—quite the victory. During breakfast they had something called silent dining, eating without talking. I liked the quiet—I didn't have to attempt to socialize, which horrified me. I did walk in the grass with my shoes off. I sat in the sun. I bobbed up and down in the whirlpool, dunked breathlessly in the bitter cold dip. I slept so, so well. I met Kundan for the AA meeting two nights in a row. Her kindness was uncomplicated, gracious, and genuine. She instantly put me at ease. The meetings were familiar, helpful, and connecting. I was having a good time. In some strange way, this was a great place to practice being alone with other people around, something very new to me.

I walked by the Main Chapel on Saturday night. There was some strange man up on the stage, playing an unusual instrument. It sounded like an accordion, but it was flat on the ground and keyed. He had long hair and wore a robe. I stopped for a moment, listening. He seemed to be singing or chanting. It was compelling, but a little bizarre to me. I found myself touched and interested, almost pulled inside. But my supreme caution won out. I moved along down the hall, forgetting all about him, and amused myself in the interesting, eclectic gift shop.

The rest of the weekend passed in ease. I talked to Molly, my sponsor, on the phone several times, and her consistent support was calming and comforting. Finally Sunday came, and time for check-out arrived.

Driving away from this strange building, my heart felt tugged backward. *That was good,* I thought to myself. *That was really, really good.* I was relaxed, rested, and deeply touched somewhere inside of me. I couldn't say it was "spiritual," but I felt quiet and easy with myself. Maybe I didn't know what "spiritual" really meant? My trip home was easy and uneventful, much less stressful since I now knew the route.

I resumed my regular schedule, back to work on Monday. School was emotionally demanding, but I was grateful to be able to get through the days there sober and not drugged. Showing up sober seemed like some feeble way of making amends for my past behaviors. Annie had been cordial when I told her I would no longer be joining her on our usual lunch period drug sessions. I saw very little of her these days, which was a painful loss. I struggled to reach my students. I knew that more meaningful work was calling me. I just couldn't put my finger on it. What was next for me? I had no idea. I continued to feel the same about New York City. As much as I had once loved it, somehow I knew that a move was needed. Change was in the air. I just didn't know what the next chapter looked like.

I did go back to the yoga center one more time that winter. I took a yoga program and actually committed to a weekend of classes. To my surprise, I found that whenever I began to do the postures on the mat, my eyes would fill with tears. I spoke to the instructor, I sweet man named Rube (what was with these names, I wondered?). He compassionately listened, and told me to stay with it, that it wasn't unusual for yoga to detoxify the body of held feelings. Held feelings? What the heck? It was a harder weekend than my first visit, but I got a good deal from it. I found Kundan again, my 12 Step connection, and attended a few more meetings with her. She was her usual easy and loving self, like a calm, loving balm for my soul.

Back home, I felt more and more restless, knowing that City life was winding down for me, knowing for sure that it was time to make a move, both professionally and personally. I was anxious and antsy, and had no clue where to go. My AA sponsor and my therapist both suggested the same technique: slow down, do the next best thing. More would be revealed to me when it was time. I felt my time would never come.

During my last visit to Kripalu, Kundan had told me about their volunteer program. One could volunteer—something called seva, or selfless service—to work in one of their departments and receive classes in spiritual living and yoga. Their entire staff was all volunteers, something I had not realized. It was an ashram, she told me, a learning center for disciples with a living teacher. Their teacher was Gurudev or Yogi Amrit Desai, the man I had watched in the Main Hall that night from afar.

I became more and more interested in the summer volunteer program. Spending my summer months in the Berkshires sounded great. I still had my paychecks coming in, so money would not be a problem. My apartment on 5th Street would be fine, with a little looking after from some of my City friends. But I had doubts. Could I really leave the City, all my program friends, the life that I knew, for that long? This felt like a huge, complicated decision.

I filled out the long, intricate application for volunteering anyway, following Molly's advice: just do the next best thing. The questions asked all about me, my background, and why I was interested in their Spiritual Lifestyle Training program. I still could not commit to it. I decided to go up for a weekend program in April called the "Inner Quest Intensive," a self-discovery program. That sounded good to me. I would use that weekend to decide about my summer plans. If it felt right, if there were signs, I would submit my application for the SLT training. If not, I would return home and forge a sober NYC summer for myself.

Application on the dashboard, Heart-Throb and I headed north and west again. Some driving anxiety lingered, but it didn't plague me now. I wove my way back, feeling more and more excited as I approached Lenox. Something always opened up inside of me when I drove toward Kripalu. It reminded me of the feeling I would get as a child, driving down the dirt road to Camp Archbald—freedom unfolding, something unknown, something wonderful awaiting. I checked in without incident and with much less self-consciousness, settled in, had some dinner, and eventually made my way toward my program's opening session.

The instructor was a thin, intense woman named Daya. We were a large group, taking up a good chunk of that main hall, maybe fifty or sixty people. We sat on the floor on these strangely comfortable things called backjacks, or little folding seats. I was suddenly swept with waves of strong and dark fear. I thought of my SLT summer application sitting on Heart-Throb's dashboard and wanted to rush outside and tear it to shreds. I wished I were in the car, driving away from here, returning to some familiarity, some known comfort. In that moment, it all felt too hard. I could feel myself trembling. *It's just too hard*, I thought to myself.

Daya welcomed us, had us look around at each other—that was very difficult for me—and then directed us to close our eyes, take a deep breath, and look inside. I did that.

Her voice was both soft and strong, calming and energizing. She said:

"Breathe, relax, and notice. Congratulations. You got yourself here. Now it's time to relax."

Okay, I thought, *yes, I did that. I got here.*

And then her words landed deep inside the core of my heart, unlocking it.

"Now it is time to enter the embrace of your own love."

And I knew exactly what she meant. I got the chills from the intensity of knowing. Now *was* the time—to enter the embrace of my own love—to learn how to be with myself, to learn how to love myself, to learn who I really was.

Now was the time.

My question about the summer SLT program was answered.

The next puzzle piece emerged.

27. Happy Birthday to Me
1989 – Summer

I really loved yoga. But I never wanted to actually *do* it. The classes were so confrontational. I couldn't sit on my yoga mat and not feel. Feel what? Feel everything. I would cry. I would laugh. I would have to pee. I would resent the hell out of the stupid person next to me doing the posture so right, that damn goodie-goodie. I would think the teacher was either God sent to bless me or a complete asshole. Either or, with nothing in between. I would berate myself for my lack of flexibility, lack of strength, for my general, despicable disregard for and separation from my body. Yoga just kicked my butt. But I loved the concept of it. It was the practice of it that was so challenging.

I had been here volunteering for six weeks, with two more left before my return to the City. Our Spiritual Lifestyle Program yoga classes were a huge part of the experience for me. There were two daily classes, from 6:00-7:15 a.m., during which I usually cried. A lot. Our second daily class ran from 4:00-5:15 p.m., during which I typically: got resentful (at the teacher), got angry (about the process), and then got disappointed (in myself and my foibles.) That was my general relationship with yoga.

But I loved it. I loved the process in the morning, waking up, foggy and fuzzy, hardly changing from my sleepwear, staggering twenty feet down the hall and landing inside a chapel. A chapel. A chapel of practice, a chapel of like-minded and like-hearted companions on the path. A chapel of meditation in motion. A chapel of commitment. A chapel of prayer. I lived next to a chapel. I found that fact in itself breathtakingly awesome. And to watch night become day, to observe the darkness soften into morning light, filtering through the huge open space, landing lovingly on the walls—oh, it was wondrous.

The chapel was silent, stunningly beautiful in the morning's deep, soft darkness. We would each and all find our usual places in the dark. I had a favorite spot, for no particular reason—on the right side, facing the altar, by the wall. I would place down my blanket, smooth it out carefully and hopefully, settle myself into a seated position for our opening meditation, and remind myself to breathe as I readied myself with building expectation. I would look around in the now half-darkness and almost feel where everybody was. Like reliable constellations, we filled up that galaxy of space: Richard from Vermont, to my left, tall, older, white-haired, funnier-than-life-itself Richard, a therapist taking the summer to cut vegetables and remember what was important in his life. Sue to his left—Sue from Michigan, on break from her university studies, Sue searching, seeking, ever-looking, Sue. Behind me was Mark, gay and young and ill, hoping to foster if not redemption, certainly some sense of healing for himself. To his left, Marge, round and bossy and older and such an annoying button-pusher for me. We were all there, in our spots, preparing ourselves to face what was given to us on the yoga mat for that morning practice. The mirror of the yoga mat. I was beginning to see how yoga did reflect to me exactly what I needed to see about myself to grow. This was a strange and interesting concept.

The teacher, a senior ashram resident, opened the class with a meditation. Today it was Suvitra:

"Settle in to your breath. Settle in to your belly. Feel yourself sitting right here. Right now. Just sit. There is nothing to do. There is nowhere to go. Whatever is happening right now is perfect. Breathe and relax."

Nothing to do? It seemed like there was everything to do—learn yoga and be done with it by figuring out the damn, endless postures, then do my seva with impeccable commitment to God, make fabulous and lasting spiritual friendships—that sounded like a lot to do. Nothing to do! Who were these people? What were they talking about?

"Create an intention for yourself for this practice. Let your prayer bubble up and place it upon the altar of your own heart," she invited.

I prayed to be present. I prayed to do my best. I prayed to begin to believe that my best was enough. And tears from the centuries of my perfectionism, centuries of my self-rejection, washed through me and filled my eyes. And I cried.

Soft music held us as Suvitra guided us through a series of postures, ancient movements that consciously generated tension in our bodies. Then we practiced the release of that tension. My mind was a little calmer today, as I focused more intently on my breath. "The breath," Suvitra said, "can integrate all. Just breathe and relax." My self-critical voice was a little quieter on this soft morning.

Suvitra led us through these series of movements, scientifically created 6,000 years ago to open the energy blocks in the body up to energy, to healing, to awareness. I enjoyed the warm-ups, noticing anew that my energy did, in fact, wake up. That was a huge revelation for me. The standing postures today were not too hard. However, the balancing one, the Tree, standing on one leg, frustrated me. For the life of me, I just simply fell. I was a fallen tree. The teachers kept saying things like, "Allow the falling, and allow the shaking. Let it be. Befriend it. Bring it into the light of awareness." I didn't really want to allow it. I wanted to learn it and get it right and get it done. It embarrassed me that I couldn't do it. I struggled today a bit with that frustration. My friend Arpana said I needed to embrace the process, not be so attached to the results. Hum.

The sitting postures were more manageable. We did hip openers (ouch), the Frog, the Boat (which didn't happen in my body—my body did not "Boat"), and the Bridge (I had a fighting chance with this one). Our session ended as usual with yogic breath called pranayama, which I didn't like very much. It made me feel like I was drowning. As Suvitra led us, I found myself gasping, gulping the air, probably not the yogic sages' intent for it. Whatever. But I tried. Then we meditated, focusing on the breath. I was certain I meditated wrong. All that happened during my meditation was my noticing my crazy, busy, speedy mind, worrying about everything. And then always, always I had to cough and cough, my inevitable physiological response to the phenomena of meditation. It was embarrassing to cause a disturbance for others in the middle of a spiritual process.

And then, my favorite part of the practice: the deep yogic relaxation. Suvitra led us thought the tensing up of our muscles, and then the releasing, guided by her wonderful voice: "Release your feet...ankles... shins...calves...." I found myself floating away, landing in a place richer than sleep, more relaxing, more valuable, more delicious. It was shockingly wonderful, better than drugs and so much easier on the body—deep, floating, profoundly beyond relaxation. Better than drugs, did I really think that?

Her voice stirred me again after a few minutes (hours? days? it was impossible to tell). "Gently wiggle your feet. Stretch yourself awake." It had ended. Time to sit back on my cushion. What a journey to get upright, and to chant together the sound of *om*, the sound of unity and peace.

I gathered my blanket, my socks, my sweater, my tissues (used and unused), my water bottle, my journal, my favorite pen, my quartz crystal that guaranteed heart opening, my skull cap (my head got cold sometimes), my Ayurvedic nose drops to help with the pranayama, all my spiritually correct paraphernalia and, dazzled, wandered back to my bunk in the big sisters' dorm. And it was only 7:15 in the morning! So much had happened already.

I saw my belief in my self. I saw it growing. I saw my judgment and my self-hatred.

I did my best. I tried.

I relaxed. I rested. I showed up.

I saw some growth and improvement in the postures.

I saw some firmly held old beliefs.

I did my best.

And it was only 7:15.

Breakfast now, silent, Kripalu-style. The delicious, simple veggie soup and brown rice, my favorite. And silence. Three hundred people eating, focused not on small talk, not on socializing, not on rushing to work, but on the taste of the food, the sensations of the chewing, and the choice of swallowing with conscious awareness. It was wonderful. Although my mind was even wilder during the silent meals, which was probably all wrong, I still loved it. It made me feel safe and freed from having to talk. I found that I ate less during the silent meals. I thought of my sad kitchen in New York, empty and roach-filled, sunny but without energy. Without others. Without purpose.

Off to seva, our work, by 8:00 a.m., a great commute down the hallway. I worked in the household department. It was my job, with a team of other "sisters," to keep the first and second floors clean. This included vacuuming, bathroom cleaning, and tending the guest rooms on change-over day.

We began our time together as a full team of twelve. Yannish, our supervisor, a senior resident of the community, led us in meditation and a "check in." Everyone had a minute or two to say what they were feeling. Marge said she "was determined and ready." I found that aggravating and untruthful, but I guess it wasn't my business. In Kripalu-speak, she was "my mirror, showing me my issues." Young Sue was wholly excited about the day. Linda, an eager twenty-year-old with stringy hair, talked about her spiritual connection to the work. I got anxious as it approached my turn. When it came to me, I said, "Gee. I'm not sure what I feel right now." There was silence. Yannish urged, "What is your body telling you?" My body? Telling me? I really had not the foggiest clue. That I was hungry? I was often hungry. That I wanted to lie down and not face this? That seemed appropriate for the moment. I could feel my face flushing with heat. It felt like I didn't know the right answer.

"There is no right thing to say now," she eerily said. Could they hear thoughts? I stammered my way through, feeling embarrassed and shy.

Yannish reminded me, "You did speak your truth today. You told us you didn't know what you were feeling. That's a victory, right?"

She was right. That was a strange, convoluted victory.

Somehow the "sharing" ended and we were off to work—I mean, selfless service.

The difference was, work was focused on the results, while seva was about the process. The process was as important as the destination, Yannish taught us. It was confusing, since certainly they wanted their rugs vacuumed. Yes, they said, the results were important, but each moment was the place to be.

So I practiced that. I vacuumed more in my first half-day that summer than I had in my entire thirty-nine-year-old life. My biggest struggle was with the vacuum cord. It was a long, extended sucker. On certain days, that vacuum cord was beyond cooperative as it lovingly looped itself around my wrist, just as they trained me. It was a submissive, obedient, ideal, ready-to-serve vacuum cord. But other days, like today, the damn vacuum cord had a life of its own, an agenda separate from my own. It tangled around my feet; it snagged me at every turn. It bunched, it gathered, it got in the way. I vacuumed over it a few times, several of them purposeful, vengeful and intentional, resentment in action. "Take that, you goddamn vacuum cord. Let me hurt you." That didn't help.

Yannish told me the "vacuum cord was my teacher." Well, it sounded absurd, but the more I practiced not getting upset and the more I relaxed, the more cooperative that damn cord was. If I chilled out, I was able to manage our relationship, cord and woman, with more "equanimity." Today we made peace, my vacuum-cord-teacher and I. We were getting along. Together we swept down the long, lengthy hallway, journeying over and over the tan rug, not a speck of dirt on it, the vacuum leaving little treads along the way. I was ever so slowly falling in love with physical movement, with the repetitious walking, with cleaning. I was falling in love with vacuuming! This was frightening. The first weeks it drove me nutty, bored, and made me time-obsessed, every few minutes an endless block of suffering. But now, something was shifting.

Oh, and the people. The Kripalu people. The residents who lived here, the more senior disciples—they were clearly remarkable and special people. Such a cast of characters. I really hadn't been exposed to so many different kinds of people until recovery. But these folks were above and beyond, so different and yet so very much the same. They were: young, old, wise, silly, serious, mischievous, vastly competent, wildly bumbling. No matter how different they were, however, all in all they were just the same in their own way: they were all fascinating, kind, open, and loving.

Kundan and I went to 12 Step meetings regularly. We were the Recovery Underground. The Kripalu guidelines for volunteers allowed only two 12 step meetings per week. Along with a few other sneaky 12 step folk, Kundan and I would go to as many meetings as we felt we needed. The Kripalu people believed you "could do it all on the yoga mat," and 12 step meetings were extraneous. I was sober enough to know that, left to my own devices on the yoga mat for fifteen minutes without AA, I would find myself simultaneously shooting drugs, drinking alcohol, smelling glue, eating ungodly amounts of organic hot fudge, and acting out in unimaginable and deadly ways. I knew this to be my truth. And because I randomly or not-so-randomly met Kundan when I was considering volunteering, she told me not to worry about the guidelines; that residents in recovery went to meetings, period. Without meeting her, I never would have known that. And I never would have come here for the summer. I never would have come to a place that would limit the amount of meetings I was able to attend. I was sober enough to know that. So, it was a miracle that I met Kundan. My recovery continued. The 12 Step principles fit into the yogic paradigm well and created a powerful unit of understanding for me. And, I must admit, I did enjoy sneaking around just a little bit to go to meetings, doing it my way. Still, perhaps always, the rebel in me pushed against the existing system. But with no wailing.

The days were rolling by. It was mid-August now. The nights were colder, the days felt muggier, heavier. The fields around Kripalu were covered with purple loosestrife flowers growing in huge quantities, colorfully standing next to hoards of so very yellow golden rod. The purple and yellow signaled the end of summer and triggered my nasal congestion. Feeling congested and sad one day at the end of morning yoga, I came outside to the front patio of Kripalu.

Sitting there on the step in the bottomless silence of that August morning, the sun rising to my left, the sky a soft powder blue, the glasslike water in the Stockbridge Bowl reflecting the beginnings of this early morning, the stillness outside of me and the stillness inside of me seemed to merge into one. I felt deeply at peace.

And from that stillness inside, I heard myself saying aloud to nobody in particular, "For my 40th birthday present this winter, I want to give myself the gift of living here for one year." As soon as I said it, I knew it was true. And as soon as I said it, I tried to will the words, the sentiment, the affirmation, back into silence. No, only kidding, just kidding, I thought. I so wanted to stay here, to never leave this place of glory, and yet, I just wanted to run like hell away from this hilltop. I wanted the ease, the predictability, the illusion of control my City life offered me. But I knew that was all over—Shabazz, 5th Street, the New York craziness and the New York healing. Something was happening here. Some work of the soul. Some work of healing the soul. Some work of finding myself, my voice, my needs, my ideas, my passion. I didn't have the words to speak any of this. I had just the deep, mysterious longing. It was stronger than any doubt, than any fear.

And as soon as it was said aloud, this intention seemed to echo and vibrate over the Berkshire Hills and all over the universe. Sitting in the whirlpool the next morning, I sublet my 5th Street apartment to a guest who needed a place in lower Manhattan for the next ten months.

That was easy.

I talked to the volunteer department about extending my stay for the year. There was dorm space for me and availability in my seva team beginning in November. I signed up.

That was easy.

I told my parents about my plan to stay. My dad's voice got tight and controlled as he asked, "But what about your teachers' pension in Newark?" Good question, I told him. I had no answer. He was silent for a moment, so unusual for him. And then for the first time in the thirty-nine and three quarter years that I had known him, he hung up on me. It would be the first and the last time he did that in our lives together. Such was the depth of his worry for me. Such was the depth of his concern about my affiliation with this cult in the mountains that would bring financial and professional ruin to his dear daughter.

That was hard.

I talked to my doctor in New York about helping me get a leave of absence at work. With a leave, I would not have to resign, something I was not ready to do. She had been worried about my stress level and my migraines for years. She happily agreed to write me a letter recommending a leave of absence, suitable for the Board of Education.

That was easy.

It was done. Well, not done. But the wheels of movement were taking me forward. It was happening.

It was and wasn't easy.

I was: ecstatic, terrified, delighted, appalled, wanting to sprint away from this place, never wanting to leave it, in love with the lifestyle, unfathomably suspicious of it, terrified, emptied of fear, full of faith, scared shitless.

And so on.

Sitting on the steps facing the lake after yoga on the morning of Labor Day, the sun was climbing with a different pace and a softer intensity, like an early autumn drawl into the morning sky. I realized this was the first September in fifteen years that I would not be going back to Newark to teach. I smiled and put my face up to the warming morning sun.

This September would find me vacuuming.

"Happy birthday to me," I said aloud.

28. By Any Other Name
1989 – Late Fall

It was a no-brainer. If I was going to be at Kripalu, and if I was going to do this ashram thing, then I was going to do it completely. I knew I had a tendency to dive deeply, to jump in quickly and fully—sometimes to my detriment—so I kept assessing my motives. But it felt right. Whenever I paused and checked in with myself, it made complete emotional, intellectual, and energetic sense. I would get initiated and become an "official" disciple on the Kripalu path.

As I understood the process, intuition was a way to deepen my commitment to my spiritual practices, to the external guru, and to the internal guru, that place of all-knowing and intuition that lives inside. It was the next best thing for me to do. The timing was perfect, too, it seemed. Initiation was being offered this fall, right as I prepared to enter the Kripalu volunteer community for a year's commitment.

After spending the summer at Kripalu, taking the Spiritual Lifestyle Program, doing yoga, working in the household department, having my study group classes with my peers, and participating in the workings of the bigger community, I made the decision to return to New York for the month of September. It would allow me to manage my transition with more space, time, and foresight. It was a decision my New York AA sponsor, Molly, helped me forge. It made sense. Rather than bolting away from my life in the City—again my more habitual tendency—I would benefit from a more conscious transition, a more mindful tying together of the knots of my New York life. I would spend the month of September in New York, return as a Kripalu guest for the October initiation program that lasted a week, volunteer for three weeks, and then November first, begin my official one-year commitment. It made timely sense.

And it didn't make sense. I was leaving a job that paid my way in the world, which offered me benefits such as vacation time, sick days, summers off, health insurance, life insurance, and a pension. I was leaving to work as a volunteer with a $60 per month stipend. I would be part of a crew doing household cleaning. Yes, it was true, all of my needs would be met by the ashram—their health coverage, use of their fleet of cars, food and boarding. Yet the element of the unknown terrified me. That's why I decided to hold on to my job by taking the leave and not quitting, which would allow me to return the fall of the next year if I so chose. And I could return to my apartment in the summer when my tenant completed her stay, rather than giving up my lease. These two uncharacteristic decisions helped assuage the anxiety of the unknown.

The month of September in New York was uncomfortable for me, living inside a life I had already renounced. The weather was humid and hot, those early autumn dog-days activating my allergies. The weather made me feel sluggish and reminded me of those horrible days when I had hit rock bottom a few years ago before, the days that ushered my way into AA. Autumn was a physically hard time for my body, I was beginning to identify. Hay-fever encouraged headaches, low energy, and resulting depression. Seeing the cycles of my energy and health was a new experience for me.

Standing in the middle of my long, narrow apartment one muggy day, I began pulling garbage bags out of my one narrow, spare closet. I had to brainstorm, organize, and move things from my apartment into storage, since there was no extra storage space in this strangely shaped apartment, in order to make way for Lilly, my sublettor. I plopped down in the middle of the floor, not so far from the spot where several years ago my bottom occurred. I sat surrounded by boxes, stuffed garbage bags, and files. I looked around.

"Help," I bemoaned.

Boxes, files, storage—ugh. Everybody's favorite afternoon event.

I reached down into a box of clothes I didn't wear much and pulled out a pair of jeans. "Whose are these?" I wondered aloud, their size harkening back to thinner, pre-recovery days where losing weight was as simple as taking a handful of pills. I tossed them aside. Grab-bagging into the box, I found another pair of jeans that looked double the size of the first. My clothes depressingly seemed to mirror not only my up-and-downs with weight over the years, but also my inability to throw things away, to stay current in the moment. I tossed the big-girl pair to the other side of me. How to deal?

Seeking escape, I turned to another box, and found myself facing old accordion files with hand-written alphabetized categories carefully printed on their individual sections: A: *appliances, air purifier, alarm clock (warranty)...* B: *birth certificate, bike helmet (extra pads)...* Help. An alphabetized magical mystery tour through my life demanded my attention, my decision-making, my reorganization.

I didn't want to face this stuff, the jetsam and flotsam of my life. Couldn't I just stuff it into a closet and let Lilly deal? Well, there was no closet in which to stuff. Life was giving me a chance to look, to lighten up, to let go. The Kripalu people, I suspected, would encourage my doing it "without judgment." How to not judge tiny-skinny-pant girl and big-fat-leg-pant girl? How not to like one more than the other? I snickered to myself. Oh, good. More opportunities to grow.

I looked at a little cut-out picture of the view from Kripalu, looking down toward the fabulous lake, which I had scotch-taped up on my wall. I took a breath and tried to remember how it felt to be there.

"Help me, please." My voice echoed in my strange, long apartment, a space that I was fond of, that held years of memories, both good and bad. A space, an apartment, a home, a time of my life that was ending.

In a very real way, this process of elimination and organization was the external manifestation of the internal process I was in—letting go of what was, in order to make space for what might be. Another damn metaphor.

So I took another breath and promised myself that I would do my best, just like on the yoga mat before practice. I reached in, pulled out musty old clothes, and began. With one box designated and labeled "GOODWILL," one for "TOSS," one for "MY NEW MA. LIFE," and one for "I DON'T KNOW HOW TO DEAL WITH YOU YET," I began. "You, to Goodwill," I said to an old soft blue flannel shirt that I lived in for several winters and hadn't touched in a decade. "Good will. I send you, this shirt, off with good will. Thank you and goodbye, shirt. Good will. Good bye." And so my mantra continued. And so my process unfolded.

I worked for an hour, then took a break, wandering to my front room that looked out over First Avenue. I would leave my mother's porch furniture, such as it was. Lilly could deal, I imagined. I sat on the shaky chair, remnants from my childhood front porch on Arthur Avenue. *Oh, the times they are a changin'*, I yodeled, trying to imitate Dylan's twang.

Looking around the front room, my eyes met a box of record albums. *Oye.* I walked over and started flipping through the records: The Jefferson Airplane, Donovan, Joan Baez, Cat Stevens, Joni Mitchell. Another retrospective of my life, this one audio-based. Obviously these records would have no function in my new world. They had been sitting here unattended for years. I decided to sell the albums in the used record store on Second Avenue, next to "Love Can Save the Day." *Later,* I thought, *I'll tend to you later.* I imagined all the songs played, all the times I listened to them, all the joints smoked while listening— years worth of listening, an audio journey through my addiction. *This is pretty damn confrontational,* I thought.

And so it went. My commitment was such—one hour focused attention, a fifteen-minute break to my own liking. Throughout the afternoon, and the next, I plugged away.

And I did it. Record by record, box by box, discarded and disregarded shirt by disheveled shirt—I decided, I tossed, I packed for Lenox, I offered to Goodwill and the universe at large.

In the meanwhile, recovery friends offered love, dinners "on them," hugs, and well wishes. The remainders of my lesbian feminist friends, on the other hand, were profoundly suspicious of my desertion over to the hetero side, my hero-and-guru-worshipping of a man idol figure.

"No, it's not like that at all," I attempted to explain to Matti. "He's a good guy. Really. It's not about him. It's about the internal guru, the sadh-guru, the deep knowing inside. Really."

She eyed me mistrustfully over her sushi roll, shook her head, and chopsticked another roll into her mouth. "I fon'tfnow," she mumbled through a mouthful of California roll.

"What?" I asked.

"I fon'ffnow," she repeated and swallowed. "I just DON'T KNOW WHAT YOU ARE DOING, NACHAMA," she hollered, glaring at me like a stranger.

I didn't either, really. There was no adequate explaining to others, to my family—oh, my poor devastated father—or to myself, really. I just did the next best thing.

And so I got through the month, one day at a time, one box at a time, one meeting at a time, one memory at a time. September unraveled, the days got shorter, the light in the sky shifted. The season was changing, and so was my life.

Molly my sponsor helped. AA meetings helped. Everything helped. And my anxiety and terror ebbed and intensified, softened and built. And so the month went.

And finally, I woke unto the morning of my leaving. My car, Heart-Throb, who had seen better days, was packed and in a garage—a grown-up and non-habitual thing to do. I was sober enough and old enough to not risk leaving my new New England wardrobe—new down coat, gloves and the like—in the car on the street overnight, to the whimsy of street violence. I woke, looked around. The last time I would be waking here for a while, if ever. So very much had happened in and around this space; good things and bad, illness and recovery, hurt and love, disappointment and hope.

"Chapter closing," I announced to my funky purple made-by-me really bad fake curtains.

"Story ending," I hollered down the hallway to my childhood porch furniture.

"Adios," I offered to the bookshelf I found on First Avenue one drunk night and had schlepped back here, up these damn steps, inch by inch, and woke up on the floor of my kitchen next to. Like a stranger-one-night-stand-lover, this stranger-one-night-stand-piece-of-furniture lay next to me unmoving in a puddle of morning light. I was horridly embarrassed at our intimacy and had to look away.

"Coming soon," I said to the blank spot on the wall where the picture of Kripalu used to be. I had already taped it to Heart-Throb's dashboard.

I dressed, tidied, and looked around one final time.

"Thanks," I said, and for the last time, managed the floor lock, then the double bolt locks, to unlock these fifteen years of my life. I closed the door behind me. How funny, that I'd be living in a place where there were no locks at all. Passing Mabel's door and smelling her many cats for one last time, I started crying. I cried all the way to the garage, up the FDR Drive, to the New York Thruway. I essentially cried the entire four hours of the trip, sometimes in little sniffles, sometimes in huge, gulping, sobbing racks of tears. Sometimes in whispers. I cried with gratitude. I cried in terror of the unknown. I cried with hope for what might be. I cried because I didn't want to go. I just cried. I arrived at Kripalu that afternoon, dehydrated, red-nosed, swollen-eyed, and exhausted. Nobody seemed to care. I was simply offered positive regard as I checked in.

I settled in. I rested.

The program I took at Kripalu my first week was preparation for the initiation process. Called "Commitment to the Path," it was made up of dedicated Kripalu guests, along with some pre-volunteer staff like myself, preparing for the ritual of initiation. It was led by two senior residents, Yogadon and Premdaya. We sat quietly on opening night as they outlined the week's preparation.

"We request that you spend the week in social silence, speaking only when needed. This will help increase your awareness of the witness consciousness, the ability inside of you to observe. We also ask that you refrain from eating sugar or meat, and lighten your diet. We'll be practicing yoga and meditation together this week, and teaching you some of the other practices, to prepare you for Friday's ceremony," Yogadon said. He was not of the Kripalu warm-and-fuzzy mold. Serious, without a crack of smile, he sat ramrod straight in his backjack, his impeccable white clothing ironed and starched to perfection. He did not inspire confidence or connection in my doubting heart.

I felt my misgivings creep into me.

Premdaya was softer in her words. "We want you to use this week as a silent retreat, to really be present with yourself. You are leaving behind a way of being, and opening up to a new level of energetic and spiritual pursuit. We are here to walk that path with you."

No kidding. I'm leaving behind Puerto Rican Discovery Day, Rosh Hashanah, and Presidents' Day as paid holidays, I cynically thought.

She continued, "And on Friday, during the rite of initiation, Gurudev will give you each a Sanskrit name. He will meditate upon your essence and generate a name that energetically fits you. It is not necessary to look up the literal translation of your new name. Sanskrit focuses on vibration of sounds rather than on literal meaning."

I knew I would be getting another name as part of the initiation process. I was excited about it—what a great way to belong, the child inside of me screamed. But I was also embarrassed. *How many names in one lifetime, God?* I inquired silently. The people in my life were getting a little tired of this name change thing, I imagined. So was I. Who was I? Out of nowhere, the line from Romeo and Juliet came to me:

"What's in a name?
That which we call a rose
By any other name
would smell as sweet."

Well, I thought, hopefully I'll smell as sweet as...as whom? As Nan? As Wing? As Nachama? *It's exhausting,* I thought, *all this growth.*

The week was deep, quiet, uncomfortable, and insightful. I felt shakier and more tentative as Friday approached, rather than more certain as I would have hoped and expected. We had practiced yoga and meditation, guru mantra which I loved. During mantra, one repeats the phrase which means, *I surrender to reality as it is*:

Om Namo
Bhagavate
Vasudevaya.

Mala beads or prayer beads mark the phrase. *Oye, my Jewish grandmother would fall off her sofa if she saw me using a rosary-like system of prayer,* I thought. But it felt good. I bought a set of mala beads from the gift shop. They were cats' eye amber and felt cool, solid, real in my hands. They fit perfectly, as if they were made for me. *Mala beads for the Jewish Lesbian-once-Separatist!*, I could hear a little mala bead-maker somewhere in Delhi holler. There were one hundred eight beads on a necklace. I would practice before bed. I found it a great way to deal with insomnia. It put me out—was that wrong?

I tried to eat lighter food, and kept away from the fabulous Kripalu bread and bakery goods. It was hard but do-able. Living in social silence was uncomfortable, but I was just a little more okay with being uncomfortable. I felt squirmy in Yogadon's company. He was too perfect for my comfort. Maybe I was jealous. Premdaya was kind enough, a little strange. Well, wasn't I? Weren't we all?

Kundan and I did get to our AA meetings and that was comforting, normalizing, helpful. I was beginning to recognize some recovery people from Berkshire County. It was a strange and long week. I half-missed my apartment, with its echo and eerie sense of empty freedom. I did not miss Shabazz High School at all, but did already miss the paycheck that would not be coming this Thursday.

I felt nowhere, neither here, not fully present, and certainly not there, in the old life.

The day of initiation dawned. I woke early and anxious. There was a bustle in the dorm around me, with hushed, whispered preparation for the ceremony. One of the disciples lent me a sari and, in the darkness, helped me wrap myself. What a strange experience. I found the sari both constricting as hell and uncomfortably revealing, with my back and much of my belly unclothed. Walking was odd. Looking at myself in the mirror, I felt like I was wearing a costume that didn't fit. When was the last time I even wore a dress, let alone constricting Indian garb? It was all too strange. My nerves were taut. How could something so unfathomable to my mind be so right for my heart?

We did not have breakfast. We entered the Main Chapel at 6:00 a.m. Sitting in alphabetical, assigned seats, I was surrounded by the N people. The Chapel was dark and cool. I felt cold and exposed, and I shivered with anxiety. A renunciate led chanting as we waited for the arrival of the guru. I couldn't find my voice and kept flubbing the words.

As the guru arrived in the Chapel, another renunciate offered out the prayer that welcomed him. He came and sat in his chair, looked around, and shut his eyes. So did I, in half-confused bewilderment and a sliver of awe.

And so the ceremony that would launch my spiritual path as a disciple began. The guru sat up on his chair in half lotus position, serious and looking around, rubbing his bare feet. He talked for a bit. As usual I had trouble understanding him, and strained through his thick Indian accent. It was not his words that touched or interested me. Sitting in my little backjack with my disciple-mates around me, I shuddered again in the cold. This was not fun yet.

He stood and began his walking through our rows. He was splashing us with water and repeating some Sanskrit words. They told us this would happen, but it was still surprising and unsettling, and somewhat exciting. I sat still and waited, trying to will the concept of baptism out of my Jewish brain cells. When he walked by me, I felt a flood of warmth, a rush of energy. The water was cold—it dribbled on my head and right shoulder. It quieted my mind, and my attention dove inside.

We repeated mantra with him for a while. That was soothing as always. Surrendering to reality—that was a good prayer for me.

And then the name-giving began, the part everybody was so excited about. I kept hearing a Juliet-like voice say in my head, *"A rose by any other name…"*

One by one, alphabetically, we were called by a renunciate to stand. As that person stood, Gurudev, in his charming/annoying accent, told them their new name.

"Alan, your new name is Atmadev."

"Amy, your new name is Malvika."

There were flurries of response in between, rufflings of saris and dohti pants material as we rose.

It took a long time to get to our row. I think it took centuries.

Finally it was my turn. Standing in a sari was not an easy proposal. I had worried about it for days, and actually practiced it with the disciples on staff for the retreat. It took focused will. I struggled with the material, and willed myself to standing. Miracle of miracles, on shaking legs, I was upright.

"Nan." (He pronounced it like Naaaan.) "Nan, your new name is:"

I held my breath. I was thoughtless, my feet shaking beneath me.

"Your new name is….Aruni."

I took a breath. *Is that it? What did he say? What?* Somehow I collapsed/sat.

And on to the next person.

*Did he say **Varuni**? **Baruni**? **Daruni**? Oh, no, what did he say? Was it Aruni? I don't think so. There was a **runi** in there somehow. That sounds silly, clown-like. Runi, Runi the clown.* My mind was like a squirrel running around, looking for a nut. Somehow I managed to stay put for the rest of the name-giving.

I looked around. Now I was the officially dubbed Somebody-Runi. The Chapel was filling with morning light now, stunningly awakened in the new day, as we were. I didn't feel stunningly awakened yet. I felt more relieved than anything.

The ceremony ended with a continuous *om*, a chant that went on and on and on. Released from our seats, we all milled around comparing notes. A senior resident handed each of us a card with our official names. Mine said in elaborate script:

Nan Futuronsky—Aruni

Aruni.

I couldn't remember it. I had to keep the paper in my pants pocket and take it out to remember, in order to respond to all the inquiries from others.

Aruni. It did not land at all in my world. I had no frame of reference for this strange combination of sounds.

Although we were told not to, a gaggle of us from the initiation program scurried to the library after the ceremony, scrambling for the Sanskrit-English dictionary, to see the definition of our names.

I waited my turn impatiently, my body wanting out of the damn sari. My turn finally, I found the definition of Aruni: *harbinger of the dawn.*

Hum. I thought. I did like the dawn—it was a strong and connected time for me. Maybe there was something to this.

Hum.

I walked slowly toward my dorm to de-sari myself.

Nan.

Wing.

Nachama.

Aruni.

What a lifetime.

I wondered what Juliet would say about all of this.

29. A Natural
1989 – 1995

In the beginning of my sober journey, it was different. As Nachama, I sat in the rooms of AA in New York and shivered with anxiety. When you had less than 90 days sober, they asked you to announce yourself. "Anybody counting days?" the meeting chairperson would ask, sitting at the card table in the front of the drafty room, looking around. Hands shot up. My hand was more tentative, not because I lacked sober pride, but because it meant I had to say the words. Holding my pseudo-raised hand at shoulder-height, sweat gathered on the back of my neck. *Find the rhythm,* I thought. *Find the fucking rhythm.*

"Yes?" the chairperson pointed to my quadrant of the room. He was a hip white guy wearing a leather vest with a blinding diamond-like stud in his ear larger than California. *Whatever,* I thought, trying not to distract myself by its glimmer. *Find the rhythm.* The twinkling-eared-dude nodded toward me.

Here goes, I thought.

"My name's *Na*"—tiny stutter—"*ch*"—another catch of breath and sound—"*ma. Igot39dayssobertoday,*" I exploded in one breath. Anxiety flooded through me, face shamed in red, ears hot. Fuck. A splattering of applause met my static-like introduction. I couldn't look around, just kept looking straight ahead, blinders on, didn't see them. The meeting plodded on.

I hated this. Sometimes I thought that being sober made my speech worse. It was a long time since I had to say certain things. For years I had manipulated my reality so that I was in charge. I taught, I had the roll book, I picked the words. I dated women. I was in control. I had the script. I was the master of synonym-izing. But here in sobriety, there were certain words, other people's words, that needed saying. There was really nowhere to hide.

Nevertheless, I kept going to the meetings. I kept sweating through it, literally and figuratively. The alternative did not exist—I knew I could not go back to what was, so dreadful was that pain. Back in New York, I would leave Malcolm X at 2:32—thank God for that first floor classroom—and, squeezing ahead of the kids, tear out the door. I would zoom home, park like a maniac on my block. Thank God also for the cop-block I lived on—parking turned legal at 3:00, perfect—and I would sprint down to Saint Mark's Place for the 3:00 meeting. Huffing and out of breath, I sat there, heart pounding, waiting my turn to sputter and stutter and spit out my name, then the days I have lived without a drink or a drug. It seemed harsh punishment.

And then the damn book. They passed it around. You had to read the steps or the traditions, or on certain days that were step meetings, actually read paragraphs from the book. The passing of the book haunted me, its random flow through the room so fucking reminiscent of grade school, of the horrors of Spanish class in high school, or even college, where I would slide into the back seats of classes, dropping down into the realm of the anonymous. Here, in an anonymous fellowship, there was a call to presence. It never occurred to me to pass the book, not to read. Somehow the trauma seemed like penitence for this Jewish girl, emotional bounty for all the shit I had spewed out onto myself and the planet. I sat stock still during the sharing. I would never, never raise my hand. Why? Why risk it?

Then it started to change. I started raising my hand. At first, one of my friends dared me, told me I would never do it. I did it to prove her wrong. It meant having to push through the terrifying introduction, "*Hi,*" (pause and big breath in, then explosion of breath and jumbled sound): "*mynamesnachamaimanalcoholicandaddict,*" in one rush of breath. But then I was free. Free to synonym around the sounds I couldn't say, free to weave the tale within the boundaries of safe sounds.

That wasn't hard. I grew to like talking about my experience, about sobriety as it was unfolding around me. It was satisfying to share what I was feeling. Nobody answered me. They just listened, or didn't. Then the next person went on. That was freeing, effortless, like dropping my individual life into the reservoir, the ocean of many lives, my little drop floating along on the waves of others' experiences.

And time passed, days without drinking and drugging passed, meetings passed. Fall became winter, which blossomed into the most beautiful spring I had ever seen, a spring of startling greens, explosions of beauty within flower boxes that dotted City windows. The beauty of spring made me happy. Once after sharing about how the season helped me to feel at a Saint Mark's meeting, a young woman sitting next to me turned and said, "I like hearing you. Thanks for sharing. I always get a lot from what you say."

Holy shit. That was heady. That was good. It felt good inside and out to hear her words, to be validated. I smiled a shy and young "thanks" back at her.

It kept changing. It surely wasn't linear, but it kept changing.

Walking down Saint Mark's Place that springtime, after the past twenty springtimes of drugging and drinking, I couldn't believe the beautiful cherry blossom trees that so majestically lined the block. They were pink and white, folding into themselves, beautifully soft. I stopped, amazed and awed, to touch the inside of a blossom. I couldn't believe someone had just planted these trees here. They were stunning.

Jose, a guy from my meeting, walked by. I liked him. He was cute and sparkly and had a flash about him that was both funny and bubbly at the same time. When he shared, I found myself smiling.

"Hey, hi, Jose," I called.

"Hey, Knock," he said, smiling his nickname for me.

"Hey, when did they move these tress here? Aren't they really cool?" I asked.

His face changed, dropped, softened, opened. "Knock," he said, more quietly, "these trees they been here for hundreds of years. Where you been, girl?" he asked with a macho Puerto Rican tenderness that twisted and ached my heart open.

Those trees had always been there. Only I had never seen them. For the twelve springs that I had lived two blocks away, for the twelve springs that I had walked down this block to the subway hundreds and hundreds of times, I had not seen them. I had been busy, busy arranging my reality, busy organizing my thoughts, busy lining up the words I could say, busy trying to get it right, busy trying to control the people and the things around me. I started to cry a little bit, and then got embarrassed, wanting to be cool for Jose. I sucked it in, nodded, and walked away.

And I kept going to meetings. And it kept changing. Over the seasons, the book stopped freaking me out quite as much. I learned to tap my foot quietly to myself, to get my words flowing. I also learned to take liberties. If a stinker-word, one that would nab me, was in my paragraph to read, I saw it coming and synonym-ized myself another word. I just simply replaced it. Most people didn't have books. It didn't even matter.

It kept changing.

I got a bit of a reputation for being a "good sharer." Of course, it went to my head. My sponsor, Molly, took me to Flushing, Queens to speak at a meeting. It was a huge speaker meeting. Standing up on the little stage, my white-knuckled hands gripping the podium for dear life, my insides froze. But I opened up my mouth and each word flowed into the next, each thought informed the next thought, each idea opened up others. "You're a natural," said Molly, sitting next to me on the subway home.

A natural. I'm a natural sharer. It was a ridiculous, ironic truth. After all the trauma and pain I lived through on account of my speech impediment, I was becoming a *natural* sharer in AA.

I was recovering my capacity to speak. I might not have been able to say this at that point in time, or recognize or realize it. But very gradually, I was recovering a part of me that never really developed. I was recovering and reinventing a profound capacity in me that the stuttering guarded, like a scab, tentatively protecting its gaping wound.

I had something to say.

Moving to Kripalu and joining the ashram accelerated the detoxing of my speech trauma to another level of both terror and freedom. Sitting in study groups with the disciples that were "my home room," students at my same level of time there, I had to confront this issue more deeply. Now I was moved into the zone of: what did I think, in relationship to others? What else did I have to say to add to the discussion? I was with people I really liked, people whom I really wanted to like me. Somehow the stakes seemed higher. I found myself shivering again inside, that trembling inner feeling so ancient, so primeval in my being.

Today we, the Interim Group, sat with Jaishakti, our teacher for our weekly study group. She was wonderfully alive and sparkly as usual, and our group was engaging. Sitting in a circle of backjacks on the floor, we were discussing bramacharyia, the yogic principle of moderation. Because it was the core philosophy behind our vow of celibacy, it was a juicy topic, with much heated discussion and "energy." I felt more and more cut off from the group, knowing I would have to contribute. *I could,* I thought bitterly, *just sit here and be a silent moron*—but I couldn't do that anymore. Damn. Somehow I knew that that silent moron gig was over; coming into relationship with speech was the healing of this moment.

"Aruni?" Jaishakti asked. I was Aruni now, Nan and Wing and Nachama had been peeled away, revealing this new naming of my self. "What do you think about what Premal just said?"

Oye. I would rather have died than attempt to put words to the moment. Pounding heart, sweaty palms, all the familiar physical symptoms of speech trauma screamed for my attention. But I noticed that my foot was quietly tapping, my old AA tool for rhythmically beginning to talk. I took a breath, followed the tapping, and launched:

"To feel attraction and to not act on it, that's powerful," I tentatively began. I paused, but didn't fall captive to the silence around me. I kept going. "To have the feelings move through me, to notice them, to not give them value, to not make them mean anything, that's pretty darn non-habitual. That's a new way of being for me." Jaishakti nodded, and I continued along, feeling the ice thawing, the glaciers of layers of silence and shame melting. The discussion moved forward, my contribution to it a link in the chain of meaning, a link in the chain of community, a link in the chain of learning, a link in the chain of my healing.

They taught me in the ashram that if you could feel it, you could heal it. They taught me that unresolved trauma and non-integrated feelings live in the body. Revisiting those feelings could literally detoxify them and free our bodies of the trauma. It sounded kooky. It sounded woo-woo. Yet it was happening. It was working in my life, both in AA and in the ashram.

I came into a relationship with that dear, terrified, stuttering little girl by feeling her feelings. I held her close. I did my best when I could, as I could, to stay with her, to not make her wrong. I told her that I loved her and that I was sorry it was hard. *Of course you are scared, dear little girl.* I held her closely and deeply in my heart. And I released her and let her go ever so slowly, without even knowing of our healing.

It kept changing.

I had been given a voice.

30. A Happy Ending—But…
1992

The sari was wrapped so tightly around me that I had trouble walking. Its tightness hugged my legs and my hips so snugly that I was able to take only tiny steps forward. *Not a bad thing*, I realized, *not really a problem*. In reality, I didn't have all that far to walk. I didn't wear saris very often, but tonight's celebration seemed to deem special dress. Arpana, my dear friend, helped dress/wrap me beforehand with her usual loving, one-focused attentiveness. She got a little carried away with her task, and tightly trussed me up.

I was standing on the rise in the Main Chapel, swaying with the music, limited in my range of motion but swaying nevertheless. The harmonium and three drummers were playing an energetic chant, a call and response, singing the Guru-Mantra, our Sanskrit prayer of surrender:

> *Om namo*
>
> *Bhagavate*
>
> *Vas-su-de-vaya.*

The translation was profound for me—*I surrender to what is*—*I honor reality*—*What is, is holy*. Repeating it over and over again was strangely and surprisingly comforting.

It was Guru Purnima, an important Hindu celebration of honoring the guru. All of the disciples in our ashram, all three hundred fifty of us, were here to honor our teacher, Gurudev, and to celebrate our commitment to the ashram. He was offering vandana tonight, too, which was a special rite only offered a few times each year. During vandana, we came up to him as he was sitting on his big, comfortable, upholstered chair. In twos, we would bow down at his feet and receive his energetic blessing. Sometimes, if one was lucky, this might include a good thump on the back, a smile, or an individualized word or two. Receiving vandana was a significant event in our community, something that I had been looking forward to for many weeks.

I looked around the Main Chapel, the celebration in full swing. The Chapel's beauty never failed to stun me. Whether it was silent and emptied of people, or packed with participants during a celebration as it was tonight, it always echoed of prayerful presence. It resonated with a sense of continuous spiritual practice. It was a room of prayer. A former Jesuit monastery, this main room was deep, long, and spacious, and had a hugely high ceiling. It had a comfortable light brown carpet on its floor, and high airy widows. A huge picture of Bapuji, Gurudev's guru, graced the center of the stage area. He looked round, kind, and strangely soft in his orange robe. His half-smile seemed to hint at some inner, amusing private joke he was savoring. Gurudev sat below the picture, in front of the white marble-like altar that was bedecked with small, simple, and lovely statues of Hindu deities. Bouquets of flower decorations spaciously spotted the front of the chapel and splashed the altar with color and splendor.

At Gurudev's feet sat two renunciates, disciples who had taken lifelong vows. They were there to move us disciples along, to help facilitate the process. On his left sat a woman renunciate, a longtime member of the community who had taken deeper vows of commitment, dressed in her white sari with her shell mala around her neck, in quiet, focused devotion. To his right sat a male renunciate. They sat without personality, without affect, simply focusing on their task of keeping the double line of community members, which wound around the hall, snaking forward toward the altar. They were there in the service of others. Others of us, disciples like me, waited to get in the growing vandana line until later. We were scattered about the room in order to soak up the energy and the beautiful ambiance of the evening.

213

People sometimes brought an offering to the guru during this process, a token, a symbol of their love for him. These gifts lay at his feet and littered the carpet around his chair. The varied gifts included: several coconuts (symbols of renouncing the mind), bouquets of roses, a potted plant, a pudgy teddy bear with a bright turquoise bow, handwritten signs, apples, bananas, several rings, a huge black raven feather, anonymous and intricately wrapped gift boxes, letters and notes to him, and so on. It was like an explosion of presents at a wild and generous birthday party that had gone haywire.

He sat amidst the growing excitement as the chanting escalated in deep, amused stillness. He wore his usual brown velour-like robe. Unlike us women, in our white saris, flowers in our hair, and the guys, our brothers, in their white Indian punjavas, pajama-like outfits, he was dressed as usual. No need on his part to get decked out, I thought. That was his constant energetic state, decked out. His long black hair framed his face. His features were handsome, almost chiseled, with stunning, high cheekbones dominating his face. His dark eyes were pools of flickering energy. He sat cross-legged and shoeless. His skin was a rich brown. He was handsome, wildly charismatic, and I loved him. I loved what his community offered me. I loved beginning to feel an authentic part of something, both in my study groups as well as in my seva, or work group. I loved the whole community thing. And this evening was a wild encapsulation of my favorite ashram elements: chanting, the guru, the entire community together celebrating, and the energy that was unleashed through our collective focus.

Arpana and I decided we would be vandana partners, and walk up to the altar together later in the evening. She was a dear friend from my seva. She was small and compact, and had wonderfully black curly hair that generously adorned her head, a strong Boston accent, and the kindest, warmest smile. She came up to my shoulder, yet I could never match her energy. Whether it was work related, recreationally related, cleaning related, or simply talking or just hanging out related, she was a focused, effective dynamo of a loving woman. And she was my best friend.

I saw her on the other side of the rise with her eyes closed, dancing wildly to the wondrous, heart-opening, body-moving music.

I am that I am.

I am,

That I am.

I am that I am,

I am

That

I

Am.

The chanting was profoundly engaging. There was no real way to explain it to my mind—it just opened me up, quieted my mind, and reconnected me to myself. When I first joined the community, I found myself tentative and self-conscious about the chanting and dancing. I felt awkward, a fish out of water, still not very comfortable dancing without the false support of alcohol and drugs. But slowly I realized, in my own timing and in my own way, that nobody was looking at me, nobody cared about how I showed up. The chanting and the music of devotion was an internal experience for each and every one of us. There was no right or wrong way to do it, a concept that boggled my mind. Having spent so much effort attempting to get life right, it was quite liberating to find myself beginning to sway to the music just a little, to slowly find my own response to it. The gift of chanting was cultivating relationship to the goodness, to the spirit inside of each of us. I was beginning to understand that. It became one of my favorite practices in the ashram.

I found myself leaving the realm of conscious thought and immersing myself into the well of feelings, of movement, of breath, of sensation. No limiting thoughts took me away from the moment. I was able to, if even just briefly, have a direct experience of myself in the moment: heat rising in my face, sari constricting my legs and hips, heart busily and quickly thumping, palms sweaty, moisture gathering around my lower back where the sari was gathered. I noticed my breath like the soft sounding of the ocean, rhythmic and low. Thought would intersperse the spaciousness, bringing me back into the sights and the sounds of the room. I would slide between the two spheres—directly experiencing the moment in my body, and indirectly filtering the moment through the thoughts in my mind. It was all good, all heart-warming, a great quest in presence, a remarkable adventure in living differently.

I felt tears in my eyes. How did I get here? How did such loving, such out-of-the-box experiences become my day-to-day world? *What grace has it been that has put me here tonight,* I thought, *to laugh, to cry, to celebrate, to feel, to rejoice, to remember who I really am?* By keeping sober, I realized, by just not picking up a joint or a bottle one day at a time, I had been given all this. More tears welled up.

I saw Yannish. She was the coordinator of household, the department in which I worked. She was very tall, long-limbed, with amazingly alabaster skin. She moved quite fluidly in her sari, unlike me. I remembered how very kind and relational she had been with me when I had some seva adjustment struggles. The shift to physical labor from teaching was strange and difficult for me, for awhile. I was initially tremendously bored, cleaning where they was no dirt, vacuuming rugs that seemed perfectly spotless, scrubbing unsoiled toilets. It seemed like such a waste of time to my pragmatic mind. Yannish took time with me, helping me understand that it was service we were performing. It was action as devotion that we were practicing, a way to connect with ourselves and the moment. Meditation in motion, she patiently explained to me. The results were not the point, she taught me. She genuinely guided me through the adjustment by teaching me, not by making me wrong. It was a remarkable and healing experience. Tonight Yannish seemed to be completely and deeply present with herself, which touched me deeply, for some inexplicable reason.

And in the recognizing, the re-recognizing of her goodness, something very strange happened. I received a deep, internal message, a communication from something that was much greater than my mind. It was a communication that filled all of me.

It said to me: "Your life will have a happy ending. No matter what might happen, if you don't pick up a drink or a drug, your life will have…a happy ending."

It was cellular. It was internal. Its knowing radiated up my spine, filling my head, my scalp, my arms, my legs, my belly. I was filled with its truth. There was no disputing it. I knew it now and forever to be the truth of my life. Unlike my experience on Disappearing Sands Beach, this message brought me warmth and tears, connection and openness. It beckoned me into the moment, rather than pushing me away from it. It was as if time stopped, the twirling and whirling suspended, as I dropped down into this reservoir of indisputable knowing.

Then the moment shifted, changed. Sounds came pouring back into me and around me. I laughed to myself, "Phew, that was amazing." It was a stunning and profound life experience—its echoes continued to wash over me. I saw Arpana nodding toward me. It was time for us to head toward the vandana line, to await our turn in receiving the guru's blessing.

The line was long and slow-moving, but it was engaging and fun to continue the moving, the dancing, the internal praying, the external and internal connecting. I inched my way slowly along the line. *No sprinting for this spiritual seeker*, I thought. *Not tonight.* I had some worry about my capacity to kneel with the restrictions of my sari. I whispered my concerns to Arpana. She shrugged it off and whispered back, "Don't even go toward that thought. Of course you will be able to kneel. Don't torture yourself. No need to deny yourself the gift of this moment." I did pretty well waiting without too much projection.

We were getting closer. Four couples ahead of us, three. My nerves screamed with excitement. Pretty soon, us. *Next! We're next.*

Finally it was our turn. Without thought, I hobbled toward his chair and kind of thrust myself forward, catching myself on my forearms and palms. Somehow from that position I managed a pseudo-kneel. Aware of Arpana next to me, my forehead on the ground just in front of his feet, my hands held onto to his foot, as others had coached me to do. I felt the smoothness, the coolness of his skin. My world got silent again. For a long, infinite moment the silence and stillness seemed to ricochet back upon itself. I felt his hand on my back, warm and alive, giving me quite the vigorous thump. It echoed, bounced inside of me.

Time to rise now, a confusing, and strange movement being called for. I could have stayed there forever.

Somehow I managed to make my way up to sitting, swinging legs and trunk and self out of the way of the waiting couple, and from there, inched myself to standing. The rest of the night unfolded in a frenzy of dancing, chanting, celebration, and deep festivity. After prayers and arti, the beautiful ceremony of offering light back to the Source, the hall dropped down into a hushed silence. Gurudev made his way out the back door of the stage area. We scattered apart, each finding our own way.

I wandered aimlessly throughout the large, emptying room, still alive with vibration, my head spinning, my heart enlivened. As impossible as it seemed, the movement and the activity of the evening had actually tightened the sari around me even more closely. I hobbled with even more difficulty toward the door. My bedroom was only half a hallway away, where I lived collectively with forty-eight other women in the big sisters' dorm. I tried to walk as inconspicuously as possible, so as not to draw too much attention to myself. This was only partly effective. By the end of my effortful journey, I had to hop forward in order to keep moving. Entering the silence of the big dorm, I hopped somewhat spastically and wildly toward my bunk, flailing and using my arms for winged balance, attempting to be as spiritually appropriate as might be possible considering the circumstances. Once there, exhausted and relieved, I began unraveling myself from this length of sweaty material. *Free at last,* I thought, as my exhausted flesh relaxed and released. *I am liberated from my cocoon,* I reflected, as it sagged on the floor beneath me in a perspired, twisted mess of material.

No matter what, I am promised a happy ending.

I smiled.

But sure as shooting, it wasn't over yet.

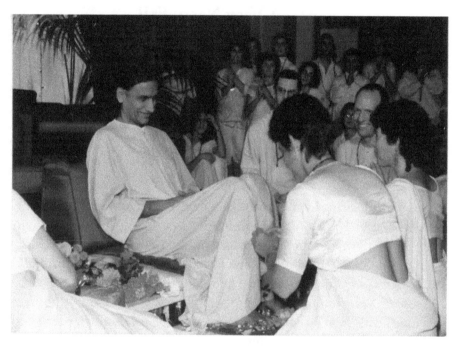

"I managed a pseudo-kneel..."
(center left, with exposed midriff)

31. A Very Nasty Fall
1994 – 1995

"What? I don't believe you. That's ridiculous and impossible," I sputtered, spitting a bit in excited disbelief at my dear friend, Terri.

She stared back at me, deadly serious, a look on her face that I had not seen before in all the years I had known her. Something was going on that I couldn't understand at all.

She sat in still silence in my windowless office. I was the director of resident health care at Kripalu, an administrative job rooted in contradiction. My job was to both support and represent the ashram members needing health care, while holding the line organizationally to limit that very care. It was a frustrating and uncomfortable role. I was relatively young in ashram years to hold such a position. It was stressful, but it put me in touch with more insider information, like the piece of news Terri—a psych nurse who worked in my department, focusing on therapy and the mental/emotional health of the residents—was offering me on this gorgeous, shiny October afternoon. It was pretty dark in my office, both from the lack of light and from Terri's intense disclosure.

"What the heck? Come on, you're kidding me, right? Terri, come on, what's going on here?" I continued prodding her silence, willing her into words. I felt my agitated disbelief accelerating.

"They'll be meeting tomorrow. It will be announced to the permanent and senior residents. M. came forth to report the abuse. There are other women that have reported allegations also. It's all ready to explode, Aruni," she said in a hushed, muted voice. "You must do your best to

220

not tell anyone before tomorrow. Do your best. Okay? And get ready. It's going to be quite the ride around here."

Oh, shit. This was so intense, I didn't even know how to react. "I'll do my best," was all I could say to her. I had no clue what that might even mean. She left my room and I sat in darkness, my tiny desk lamp emitting hardly a ray of light.

It was inconceivable. The guru, our teacher, the rallying force of the community, was being accused of sexual misconduct. Holy shit. My mind raced around from thought to thought, unable to land on any. It didn't compute, didn't make sense. I didn't even know how to think about it. I loved him so much, in a love that was of growth, of opening, of trusting. I marked my days upon the seeing of him. How could he—could he? The woman who came forth was an impeccable, beyond-credible, and respected member of the permanent community. What happened here? This was insane, seemingly impossible to comprehend.

The day was hell and endless, my mind churning, my stomach aching. I went for a walk mid-afternoon down Hawthorn Road. The glorious Berkshire Hills sparkled in the late autumn sunlight. The leaves were off the trees now after an unbelievable display of reds and yellows and goldens. The mountains and the fields seemed opened and vast, the hills undulating and rolling in new, fresh space. I loved the land here. It was my companion, my friend, my soft conduit to a sense of God that I never could access in the City. I loved, too, the grimy, gritty city streets, but they became adversarial and harsh to me the more I walked upon them. The longer I lived in the Berkshires, the more I fell softly into its arms of beauty and open space.

I took a deep breath. The cool, crisp air helped calm me a bit.

I struggled through the long, endless afternoon, had a tasteless dinner alone in my room, and climbed into bed ridiculously early, purposefully avoiding everybody. *Oh, God*, I thought. *What will happen? How can this be happening?* I tossed and turned wildly, praying for a senseless sleep to overtake me. There was a knock on my door.

"Hello? Where are you?" It was Ras, my dear friend. She walked in. The door cracked light into my darkened room and hurt my eyes. I had been crying, senseless tears of fear, of the unknown. "Whatever are you doing in bed at 7:05 p.m.?" she said. I couldn't help but laugh and roll over toward her. "How very unlikely."

She sat on the bed with a soft thump. She was tiny and her weight was almost imperceptible. But her presence of light and warmth filled the room. I whimpered in response to the safety it brought with it.

"I have something awful to tell you." It just rolled out of my mouth; I couldn't remain silent. She sat on the bed next to my knees.

"Awful, it's awful." I sniffled in her direction.

"Is it Eric? Is he HIV+? Is that it?" She jumped right to the worst-case personal-relational scenario. Eric, my dear friend whom I had met at AA, had been an ashram member for several years now. Interesting Ras thought of that first.

"Nope, worse. Much bigger and worse," I answered.

"Aruni, nothing could be worse than that," she said, with that Ras-seriousness I could almost touch. I couldn't see her face but I knew the expression behind that voice—focused, determined, face wiped of emotion.

"It's Gurudev. He's sexually abused several women, disciples—a while ago, but still—and it's all going to explode, and there's a big meeting tomorrow and…" I started sobbing.

She said without hesitation, "Oh, is that all? We'll get through that okay." Her response was remarkable, and spoke worlds to the power of denial, the mind's need to soften the blows of reality. I took some solace there amidst the workings of her denial that night. I would later learn how we all, in our different and specific ways, would dance into the pain of betrayal, dance around it, deny it, reject it, and then dive back again into the brutal disappointment that the coming days would deliver to us.

I wasn't officially invited to the announcement meeting, since I was a younger resident. I just simply went into the Main Chapel, thinking my role made it essential for me to hear the full news. There was a hushed strangeness in the air. Everyone knew something big was bubbling, waiting for full explosion. I sat next to and almost on-top-of Eric, also a gate-crasher. We fiercely held hands, steeling ourselves against the words of the senior resident, Pryasham, who was sitting in the front of the room. His voice was somber, deep, and expressionless.

"There have been allegations of sexual misconduct made against Gurudev," he began.

A random sob broke through the silence, startling him into a loss of rhythm and frightening the breath out of me. I jumped a little. He regrouped and continued.

"Gurudev has been asked by the Board of Trustees to offer his rebuttal." He continued along with some legalese explanation of the process. My hearing faded in and out, as if someone was tinkering with the volume of some inner speaker system I didn't know I had. I couldn't quite land on his words. I would get the meaning of one phrase almost digested, and then another phrase would land, the first meaning scurrying away from me, now completely unattainable. The new phrase offered another vast territory of incomprehension. It was exhausting and futile to try to listen, but I tried so hard. I just didn't know what else to do.

The rest of the meeting blurred into an explosion of disbelief from the people around me. There were sobs, screams, emotional words. I seemed unable to grasp one moment fully, and then another flooded on top of me. Everything seemed to be happening too fast, yet it all seemed like slow-motion, too. We were moving and talking and feeling in the quagmire of smothering quicksand.

One resident, a thin, intense older man named Giam, someone I never warmed to at all, rushed up on the platform stage where Pryasham sat. Pryasham flinched as the other man approached, seemingly unable to move. Giam grabbed the large picture of Gurudev that sat on his empty chair, and started slamming it into the chair, shattering the glass. It was a scene of incomprehensible rage that brought terror to my heart. I didn't know how to feel about it. The cognitive dissonance of the moment was overwhelming; I loved the man in the picture deeply, and yet the disclosures enraged me. My own authentic responses were slippery and ever-changing. I was lost at emotional sea, the waves of conflicting feelings washing over me.

I held Eric's hand so tightly that my knuckles ached. Somehow the pain grounded me, landed me, defined me somewhere in the chaos.

The meeting ended with sobs and disbelief and fury and pain. It was a nightmare. It just didn't end, but continued to unravel and reveal more betrayal.

The next days and then the next only got worse. With each new disclosure, the trauma repeated itself. Just when I felt somewhat emotionally level, something else would be revealed. Just as I relaxed for a moment, I would encounter a friend in deep pain, and I would reenter my own reactions in attempts of supporting the other person. It was as if everyone's father died. There was nowhere to turn for solace. We were all in it together and kept triggering each other inadvertently.

After a few days of attempting to rally and offer some emotional healing work to ourselves, we realized the absurdity of that and looked for outside professional help. Counselors from a trauma center held groups for us to begin the slow process of healing. They were kind, gentle, and very professional. Sitting in the room that day, numbed and exhausted, I heard the definition of trauma that they spoke. Its meaning lived in me as they explained it. As I sat in a fog of pain and listened, the words they spoke jived with my inner experience, giving form and meaning to my experience. They said:

Trauma exists when a situation occurs that changes everything.

Afterward all is different.

That was it. All was different. Closing my eyes, I confronted Gurudev, his image, his energy, sitting on his chair, leading chanting. I wanted him out of me. I squeezed my eyes tightly shut, bringing bands of colors and shapes dancing and moving behind my eyelids.

"It will take five years," the woman psychologist leading the group said to us. "It will take five years to integrate the spiritual betrayal that you are experiencing."

Five years. Her words were nails in the coffin of my life as I knew it. And it would take five years. It would take every moment of what it would take to heal. The changes were just beginning: banishment of the guru by the Board of Trustees, loss of the vowed order, the literal end of the ashram, my decision to stay in the unknown of the Kripalu experiment, my transition from volunteer to employee, watching three quarters of my friends and ashram mates leave the Berkshires, jockeying for the few jobs that were left, finding housing outside the building, shame and embarrassment in telling family, depression, lack of energy, and exhausting despair.

Yet inside each of those experiences lived seeds waiting to be planted, seeds of my own opening, my own development, my own maturation. I would become a senior faculty member, something that never would have happened under the old system due to the amount of teachers with more seniority. I would come into a leadership position in the new Kripalu. With the old system collapsed, we slogged through, re-creating the new. With our old lives literally shattered, we suddenly had the choices we didn't know before that we lacked. We would find our way. Eric and I kept going to meetings. We kept talking about what we felt and needed. Time passed.

It would change and then it would change again.

The greater the trauma, the more wide open the door of healing and new possibilities.

Life slammed me wide open.

I was available now for the next level of my growth.

32. Finally
1992 – 1993

As she walked down the long, narrow ashram hall toward me, I felt my heart quicken, my face flush with heat. *Stay calm*, I coached myself. *Relax.* It was 5:25 a.m., the December Berkshire morning dark and thick without promise of light. We were meeting to carpool in one of the ashram's fleet of eighty cars—no-frills, bottom-of-the-line Toyota Tercels—to the pool for morning swim. There was a core group of anywhere from two to ten residents who regularly swam in the mornings. This morning, to my glee and elated terror, it was only R. and I. We would be alone for the ten-minute ride to and from the pool. Oh! My throbbing heart might give me away. I breathed in deeply in an attempt to quiet it.

Her face lit up as soon as she saw me. She strode with a deliberate, graceful force. Bundled in her red parka, scarves swaddling her face, ready to encounter the zero temperatures, she was elflike goddess embodied. R. lived inside her body proudly and strongly—she was physically home in her flesh. The mere sight of her cascaded bubbly joy throughout my body. She was small, just a few slivers above five feet, but she never appeared small to me. Because of an energetic strength, a ferocity of spirit that lived much larger than her petite frame, she never was anything but a powerful energetic force to be reckoned with. She filled up the space around her. Her eyes crinkled up and smiled at me again. "Here we go," she said, and my heart melted even more. Her Southern accent was charming, engaging, amusing, and never failed to deeply tickle my soul. She was about my age, but had been an ashram resident for five years longer than I had, making her a more experienced senior resident. She was a senior faculty member, using her PhD psychology training to deepen the Kripalu programs she offered.

I was thoroughly and wholly smitten, in body, mind, and spirit.

We had become friends on the morning swim carpools. Of course I had seen her from afar for years. She would sit during ashram activities with a straight back, focused, serious, attentive. She was a committed practitioner of the yogic lifestyle. Unlike many of the more senior residents, she never missed activities or events. She fully participated in the yoga classes and in all the celebrations. I was so drawn to her obvious and deep commitment to the lifestyle and the practices. She was authentic, here at the ashram for the purpose of serving others and serving the evolution of her soul. She was the real deal.

I had had other ashram crushes over the past three and a half years, attractions that came over me like tidal waves and kept me submerged for a few weeks at a time. They came and they went. The attractions were always with women I didn't know, that ancient pattern of "from afar I love you" still running me. This was different. R. and I were good and close friends. We went for walks, we swam, we biked. The feelings that soared through my body at the thought of her, the solace and fun she brought me, the openhearted happiness I felt while near her were all because of who she was in relationship to me. It was different from the other crushes. It was based in the reality of our relationship.

And it wasn't. Because of bramacharyia, the principle of moderation of energy, we were a celibate community. Although there was a couples' track with relationship training and mentoring for senior residents, there was no provision for lesbian and gay couples to participate. And, to my further dismay, R. was not a lesbian! She had been in a long-term heterosexual relationship before her ashram days. But on a deep, core level, I knew what I was feeling, and I knew her response to me to be true. We were falling in love—except she had the luxury of not knowing it.

In the hallway, I mumbled a small, quiet hello. Hopefully I appeared tired rather than tongue-tied, smitten, and silly-minded. We made our way out the door, into the icy Berkshire air. My nostrils breathed into the cold morning and ached instantly. It was darker than dark. We fumbled our way across the slippery parking lot and found the car that was designated for us pool folk. We both scraped our respective sides of the windshield free from the prior evening's collection of ice and snow, and climbed into the frosty car. As usual, I drove. Being the Northerner, I justified it, assuming I simply had more winter driving experience. Perhaps it was the illusion of control I longed for as I daily reached for the wheel.

We made our way cautiously down Hawthorne Road. I slowly picked our way across the wintry path, riding the curves slowly and cautiously, attempting to both focus on auto safety while also savoring this alone time with my beloved. My un-realizing beloved. She began recounting her dreams of the night before:

"There were lots of us sitting in a circle together. I lived with someone, a lover, in a beautiful house, with dark lovely wood and a warm fireplace," she told me.

Just listening to her was a soothing balm for my soul. Her words flowed over me, bringing with them such tactile excitement. She simply touched me deeply. The subject matter was profoundly and frighteningly evocative for me. I tried to breathe, but my breath was short and caught in my chest.

"And my lover, my partner, sat right across the circle from me," she said, getting more excited, which always accentuated her West Virginia accent. "I couldn't quite make out the person's features, which were right out of my sight."

My heart was rapping, tapping, pounding, typing out furiously its own completion to her story.

"But the one thing I could see," she said, excitedly, "This person was wearing a baseball cap. That was all I could see," she finished triumphantly.

My mouth dropped open. A baseball cap! I sat in the car next to her, shepherding her down the road, wearing, as usual, my white ripped Mets baseball cap, a souvenir from my New York days. I always wore it in the mornings—it just simply started the day right. Dumbfounded, my head swiveled toward her on its own volition. She sat there, wrapped in the remnants of her lingering dreams, a sleepy look on her face. *Here I am*, I shouted inside my head. *I am the one wearing the baseball cap! I am fucking sitting next to you right now!* But it was not the time for that. That time would come.

Several of my dear ashram friends offered me remarkable support and focus through the process. Dear, dear Arpana was my relationship coach. My practice became one of profound surrender: feel the feelings of attraction, feel them in my body, let them come and wash over me, let them go, and release attachment to the results. That was the practice. If feelings do not lie, let them inform me. But draw the line at picking out linens for our marriage bed. It was an active 24-7 discipline. I was continually being swept with feelings, and then struggling with letting go.

Winter became spring, which blossomed into a hot, steamy country summer, alive with bugs and bees and humid afternoons. R. and I continued to deepen our friendship. I continued to practice.

Step One: Inform the Woman.

All of my support staff agreed I was ready. It was September first. R. and I sat on the top of a picnic bench in early evening facing the glorious Stockbridge Bowl, its water glistening beneath a growing moon. I prayed for strength, for clarity.

My voice shook, "R., I have something to say."

She turned her gaze from the lake to me quizzically. "Sure—what?"

"I want you to know…"—dear God, was I really doing this?— "…that I am attracted to you."

A look of horrified disbelief clouded her face. "Oh," she said, accent thickening with growing emotion. "I would never…I would never."

I would never. A knife to my heart. She would never. I trembled. I died. I shook. We recovered the evening and unfathomably, it continued in a collegial, cordial friendship-y tone. I limped back, wounded, to Arpana's room, throwing myself on her floor. Oye. Was this defeat? I decided not.

Step Two: Craft Plan B.

I decided, with Arpana's input and sanction, that I would continue my practice of exploring the feelings and letting go of the results. I would outlive the feelings, if they were invalid, through my commitment to staying present with them. Or I, on Easter Sunday, which was April third—seven months and two days from that night—would return to R. again, with any new information for her. I got out my date book and, in ink, in the little space under Easter Sunday, April third, I wrote: *"If there is something left to say, speak it today."*

Autumn descended on the Berkshires in a glorious flush of color. The maples in the hills around us exploded, faded, and reappeared in a variety of heart-stopping hues: reds, yellows, oranges, goldens. The season lifted me up with its beauty and deepened my commitment to truth. Let it come, let it go. Feel what is present, give it to God. R. and I continued to be deeper and deeper friends. My declaration of attraction did not deter her from being fully open and committed to our friendship. We continued our walk-and-talks, our early swims.

Winter landed, embracing us in her frigid, exquisite arms. That year, she hugged us close. Much snow fell, encouraging snow-shoeing, tobogganing, and long, long walks together. With R., with my friends, I found that my relationship to myself, to God, and to my unaware beloved profoundly unfolded.

I prayed for the strength to feel. I prayed for the willingness to let go. I prayed for the courage to speak my truth. I prayed for the willingness to be present, no matter the outcome. I had never felt so intimate, so close to a power greater than myself. My prayer life carried me through, day after day, moment after moment. The feelings were overwhelming, glorious, sensual, sexual, intimate, heart-opening, body-opening, devotional.

I continued to trust R.'s responses to me. In spite of her "I would never" comment, fondly referred to as the anti-mantra by myself and Arpana, I knew something authentic was building between us.

Spring came early, miracle of miracles. The dark, long, grey winter released us slowly from her frigid arms, sending the harbingers of bird songs to awaken our hearts. The light in the day shifted, extended, bent toward light and love and length. To my horror and glee, April was approaching.

"Can I do it?" I asked Coach Arpana, yet again sitting on the floor of her tiny cell-like room.

Her answer was consistent, day after day: "Aruni, trust yourself. Trust the process."

Step Three: Speak Your Truth.

R. and I scheduled an Easter Sunday early morning walk. I awoke early, anxious and delirious with hopeful dread. My calendar said, *"If there is something left to say, speak it today."*

There was something to say. And this was the day in which I would say it, God help me.

I opened the door to my also-teeny cell room which had formerly belonged to a monk. There stood an Easter basket, a present from R. I held its little wicker frame close to my heart, weeping into its fake bright green grass, crying all over the tiny plump chocolate bunny. For this Jewish-girl-turned-Hindu-nun, it was my first official Easter basket.

231

"Are you a harbinger of good outcome?" I asked the little sightless brown rabbit. There was no response. I decided that meant nothing. I shakily dressed, put on my boots, praying, "Take right action, release the results," over and over again.

R. and I met at the front door of the building. We walked to the duck pond, the glorious morning slowly waking up, as we small-talked our way in the early light. I swore to myself and Coach Arpana that I would not return to the building until I had spoken my truth. R. and I ambled toward the duck pond. Once there, I realized my time was half over. I had to speak.

We turned to return. This terrified me. I began contextualizing. "Something I have to say…" — blah blah — "I've waited a long time to say it…" This went on for a few minutes. She looked blankly at me. What the fuck was I talking about? I stopped walking.

"R.," I looked deeply into her eyes. She looked puzzled. I plunged. "I am in love with you."

Deep silence held us close. She looked at me with disbelief, and then a wave of even deeper disbelief flooded her face. In that moment, the sun rose in front of us. With incredulity, R. put her hands over her stomach and said to me breathlessly, "The sun just rose in my stomach, too."

We found a bench above the property, sat and talked and talked and talked. We made our way back to my room, with shy first-dateness, inviting each other in. I fumbled like a teenager with the blinds—we were still very illegal—and reached toward her. I found her. As I pulled her close to me, she pulled me into her. As I sought out her lips, her lips were also searching for mine. As my hands made their way to her neck, to her arms, to her soft, soft stomach, her hands made her way toward mine. We fell into each other with a mutuality of knowing, a mutuality of passion that was forever new to me. We tumbled with bashful laughter toward the bed, and rolled our way toward bliss.

We had found each other amidst the wackiness of this spiritual community, the very community that forbade our loving. In spite of it all, and because of it all, we were found. We were found by love.

Step Four: Surrender.

PART FIVE: SURRENDERING

33. Mom
January 6, 2000 – Present

I never really knew her. It was as if she were in the background of my life, until now, my middle years. My dad's warm love was my foreground. But in January of 2000, my father died and it all changed.

My mother's entire life, up to that point, was in devoted service to him. Her job on the planet was to get him through, to help him take his many pills, to work next to him in his little grocery store, to ease his pain, to assuage his fears. Yes, she was available to me and to L., my sister, in a non-emotional, distant yet loving kind of way. But her primary purpose was the ultimate support of her soul mate and husband: my father, Sidney. Theirs was a truelove story—from their teens to their eighties, they held fast to each other, warmed by each other's love. Now he was, inconceivably, gone.

Who would she be without him? Would she even be?

R. and I sat with her at my sister's Formica kitchen table on the sixth of January, the day after his funeral. It was cold outside in New Jersey, especially cold for her Florida blood, I imagined. She sat there, tiny and distant, bundled in a dark grey sweater, looking out my sister's windows. The windows faced the swimming pool, snow lacing its cover, the pool hardly a memory in the January chill. My mother's eyes seemed unfocused and lost, her beautiful face drawn and tired. She had failed him—he had died. She had literally kept him alive, nursed him, kept him from the hospital which so terrified him. But now it was over. Her eyes came into focus. She looked at me, then at R., and quietly said to no one, "What will I have for breakfast now?"

She literally didn't know the answer. Breakfast was about him, his needs, his desires. She would eat around his needs. Her needs would be met secondarily, as all ours were, in relationship to his giant, needy heart. Everything was about him. It's a good thing my father was such a dear, otherwise he would have been a real shit. He was the sweetest, softest, dearest narcissist one might conjure up. We all rotated in orbit around him happily, eager to be in his kind and gentle sphere. Tillie, my mom, quiet and cool to his warm exuberance, was the major constellation in his solar system. And now she was system-less, lost in space. From the distance of cold earth I watched her, this stranger, my mother.

I shivered in the cold. I was exhausted and deeply frightened. My dearest daddy, the source of such love and warmth, was gone, with so many problems left behind him—their debt, their unsold condo in Florida, his car that wasn't starting, my mom's future. What would happen? How, at the age of eighty, would she create a life of her own? That didn't even seem like an option in my world at the moment, sitting at the kitchen table with an aching heart, my eyes tired from crying, my feet cold from the unknown conflicting forces of grief. The tentacles of fear dulled me. I was ineffectual and quiet with her, so deep was my lack of clarity.

The first few months after my dad's death were a blur of pain and anxiety. Shift began slowly for her. Remarkably, my parents' Florida condo, which she could not afford, sold quickly after he died. Strangely it had been on the market for many months without buyer interest; his death seemed to move the process forward. Mom would move to New Jersey in April to be near L. and her family, into a senior housing unit my sister had found for both my parents. Now it would be for Mom alone. Hers was now a solo trip.

My mom's first uncharacteristic action after my father was gone was her handling of the car. My dad's unreliable Mazda was stranding her everywhere she drove. After he died, Mom went back to her job as a crossing guard, a job they had once done together to attempt to manage their monthly debt payments—debts L. and I didn't understand fully until my dad was gone. Now she was getting stuck there daily, a good thirty minutes away from home. She was on a first name basis with

238

the AAA serviceman. The car had to go, the anxiety it was causing her overshadowing the benefits of the job. Somehow my mom managed to find a garage that would give her $1,000 in cash for the car. Uncharacteristically and with growing anxiety, she did not inform them of its faulty starting mechanism.

Wracked with indecision and concern about selling a "lemon," she decided to take the risk, sell it, and give up her crossing guard job. The morning of the sale, the car did not start. She had the car jumped, drove to the station with baited breath, sold the car, signed the papers, put the cash in her bra, hoped for the best, and walked fiercely two and a half miles to the Publix supermarket to call a friend for a ride home.

When I heard of her walking down the hot Florida highway with the cash in her bra at the age of eighty, I was taken aback. Mom? It was brave and plucky, braver and more plucky than I knew her to be. Her actions began to wake me up from my own grief-tinged stupor.

It was as if my mother were a photographic negative, coming into focus, coming into form and being before my eyes as the chemicals drew the image forward. As life drew her forward, she responded. With great effort of heart and will and mind and body, she and L. packed up the condo, shipped essentials on a truck to New Jersey, and got rid of the rest. Without leaving a forwarding address or telling her friends the details of her move in an attempt to thwart off the creditors, they flew out of the Fort Lauderdale airport one final time, without looking back.

In spite of the odds stacked against her, odds of finance and resource and energy, she forged a home for herself in New Jersey. Using her things from Florida and buying a few new pieces of furniture, she wove together a lovely, comfortable place for herself. With a view of the ocean, her apartment felt familiar, so very tidy and tasteful, our same childhood pictures on the wall. It smelled familiar, too.

"You know, Nan," she said to me one afternoon that spring, "this is the first time I've lived alone since Daddy came back from the War."

We together figured that was about fifty-five years ago. After fifty-five years, she was willing to go it alone.

She became a voracious reader. The community she lived in offered bus trips to the Asbury Park Library. She went regularly. "Daddy never liked it very much when I would read," she said casually one day. Her words sent a chill up my spine. My spouse and partner, R., another ravenous reader, would regularly chide me for interrupting her reading. Truthfully, I didn't like it when she read. *Holy mackerel,* I thought. *I don't want to be like that.* It was behavior I decided to change in myself.

My mother started an arts and crafts club. Together with some other women residents of her building, they knit hats and booties, poodle dogs and scarves, and sold them, making money to benefit their housing association. She was in charge of an ongoing project to knit hats for the Ronald McDonald House. I took her there once, with bags full of hats. The Ronald McDonald House manager, a woman named Joan, called her "Tillie." They knew each other on a first-name basis.

I called her every day. That first year, we talked more than we had talked most of my life. Not that we exchanged much information during those calls. What I received was a sense of giving to her, and a receiving of her attention and care. Our calls were like touchstones, anchored with questions like, "What did you read today?" or "Did you get the rain?" or "How was the JCC club this morning?" She became speed dial #3 on my cell phone, instant, direct, available. Calling her became the cornerstone of my day.

I tried for regular, monthly weekend visits. We would shop in the supermarket, do errands, play Scrabble or gin rummy. She regularly and unabashedly beat me, without apology or concern. I created a Scrabble rule—as you put a word down, you had to make it into a sentence. I hoped this would stimulate more conversation from my reticent mom. Her sentences were so hysterically simple, always slightly mocking my attempts to engage her in words. If her word was "ironing" her sentence might be, "This is an ironing." Her brusqueness made me laugh. Words were just not important to her. Presence was.

L.'s role was management of the daily grind, which she took on with an effort and a push that was monumental. She drove mom from doctor to doctor, from grocery store to grocery store. She stressed over the details. My role was the from-afar emotional support. I relaxed over the bigger picture, letting mom be, listening, taking her in. It took me a long time to recognize how both L.'s and my roles made up a complete package for my mom's new life, as it was a new context for our evolving relationship with her.

Mom visited us the next summer in the Berkshires. R. and I took her to Tanglewood, the outdoor music festival, one night. It was something she had always wanted to do, she told us, shedding a few tears, as we searched for a parking spot. It rained a bit. We bundled and dressed in slickers and jackets. She adored the music and the experience, and was quite the trooper, bundled in layers of rainproof wear.

Sitting in our little house after the concert, having some tea, a horrid black flying thing swooped down from the rafters past my cheek. "Help," R. screamed. "It's a bat!" The three of us, strong brave women all, giggled and screamed and screeched, and locked ourselves into the bathroom, hysterical with excited mock horror. We roared, called my brother-in-law in New Jersey for advice. It was wonderfully hysterical. There is a priceless picture of mom, head bat-proofed in a silly baseball cap and bathrobe, huge giddy grin on her face, holding a broom in bat-self-defense. I never remembered laughing with her like that in all our years. It was not too late for us to share laughter.

In those years of her life, she morphed into who she really was: interesting, smart, reticent, well-read, supportive, beautiful, classy, crusty, non-warm-and-fuzzy, contained, prone to crankiness, family-orientated, beyond loyal. She was an awesome gift to my adulthood, beyond my wildest dreams. She carried my life along with me, held up details and concerns, offered suggestions and ideas. As she came forth, I, the adult, emerged alongside of her. She valued my opinion, and asked for it. Together we enjoyed our time together, in this, the ending of her life.

Diagnosed with lymphoma in the summer of 2005, her last year was a hard and frightening one for us all. Having just received her in my life, letting go of her seemed an impossibility. I was not ready. But let her go I would, in her time, and with so many lessons as gifts to my heart.

She got thinner and thinner. She hated the transfusions and blood work she needed to keep the disease at bay. Her veins were difficult to draw from. She was cranky with the nurses, overwhelming to L. It got harder and harder.

She entered the hospice unit of the hospital in September of 2006. L. and I stood next to the family doctor in her hospital room as he explained the move to hospice. "Tillie," he said, "it's the best place for you and for the family now. You will get the care you need there."

She cried, held the sheet to her face to muffle her sobs, turning her face from us, and said, "Oye, shiva before the wedding." My niece was getting married in a few weeks. Mom's greatest fear was that we would have to sit shiva, the Jewish ritual of mourning, before the wedding. She cried and cried, looking shriveled in the stark white hospital bed. I stood, helpless, hopeless, praying to know how to be present. The pain was riveting, engaging, overwhelming. And yet I somehow knew in that moment that I was equipped to be present with it.

I used the basic tools I had learned in recovery and on the yoga mat. Breathe, relax. Feel what is happening. Watch it. Allow it to be as it is. There is nothing wrong here. There is nothing here I have to do—nothing here that I can change. Being present with her is all that she needs, all that is needed. It is everything. I went to an AA meeting every day I was in New Jersey. Those strangers at that meeting became the loving container of support for me in this profound transition.

She outlived Hospice #1. Her room was at the end of a long hallway. As I walked down the hall, from each room came the death throttle, each of its inhabitants fighting to let go of life. From my mom's room came the sound of Oprah.

"Nan, can you get me a crossword puzzle that's better than this one?" she asked from her hospice bed, holding up the completed Asbury Park Press newspaper puzzle. She got kicked out of Hospice #1 after her allotted weeks were up. She was remarkably alive and relatively well.

My niece, Caryn, got married mid-month. Mom was not there, but a few miles away in the hospice bed. That was a difficult and painful day. She saw Caryn in her wedding gown and watched a video of the ceremony that night. Her heart was broken. But she did not die—she outlived the wedding.

She outlived the Jewish holidays. She outlived the newlywed's return from the honeymoon, enjoying pictures of their time away.

We got her into Hospice #2. Things then changed. Over the next weeks she got quieter and smaller. Her internal bleeding got out of control. I spent days with her, then would drive home, up the damned New Jersey Parkway From Hell, physically and emotionally emptied. It was horrible to be away from her, but so difficult to be away from R., my home, and my work. Finally, recognizing the end was upon us, I surrendered and stayed in New Jersey.

Those last days with her were precious, painful, exquisite, excruciating. She gave me the gift of allowing me to be with her when she died. L. had left earlier, exhausted and spent. It almost felt as if Mom would never go. I, in grief and exhaustion, swung wildly between wanting her to just simply die, and never wanting her to leave. The last thing she had said to me, holding my hand tightly, eyes hugely open and childlike as I read to her from the only book I had with me, was, "Please don't go."

She wasn't talking now, not for the past few days. She was actively dying and I was committed to staying with her. I would be riveted and present and then flip into exhaustion, terror, denial. It was profound, that roller-coaster of life, each minute long and hollow with the unknown.

I had a mini-crisis that afternoon, thinking I was losing it and could not manage. I went for a walk outside the hospice center. It was a warm October morning. There was a little stream running next to the building. I watched a branch float down with the current. I prayed again to relax. I prayed to let her be. I prayed to let her go. I prayed to be of service.

Back in her room, her breathing was quieter now. I relaxed into the present. I prayed with her, saying the Sh'Ma, the cornerstone of Jewish prayer, over and over. I read to her from her journal, one of her six spiral notebooks filled with journal entries and letters to my dad. I sang. I held her hand. Time stopped. Time drained from the moment. I could have stayed there forever. But she couldn't. A little after 8:00 p.m., she pursed up her lips and took a big gulp. "Oh, shit. Is this it? I thought. "Mom?" Then she took another huge breath. "Oh, good," I thought, "she's okay." And then she stopped breathing. The room was filled with an incredible depth of silence, a softness of spirit that fully filled me. She was gone and yet she was so here. My heart stopped with hers, and then chose to begin again, to beat again, to live again my life without her.

My heart aches now that she is gone. Speed dial #3 is empty and irreplaceable. The first year without her was time-warped, thinned of support, horribly hollow. The second year brought some accustomed ease. Now, as I round out toward her second anniversary of dying, I claim myself as her daughter.

Strong and crusty, I, too, am beyond capable.

My mother is my ultimate hero. At the age of eighty, she chose life and embraced it fully. She redirected her life force away from her Sidney, and directed that attention and energy toward herself. She created a world of beauty around her. She reached out, made friends, got involved. She read, she wrote, she knitted, she cried, she mourned, she lived. She chose life.

From my mom I learned that it is never too late to realign. It is never too late to choose yourself, to recommit to your needs and your truths.

From my mom I saw my power to stay present, to grow up with her, to laugh with her, to sit at her side as she died. I saw my capacity to show up as an adult, to assume her role of strong, able woman.

As she brought me into this world, so did I sit with her and witness her leaving it. I will never be without the intimacy and profound presence of those last moments we shared.

I am my mother's daughter. I am strong. I am competent. I am organized and I am clear. I take from her life meaning for my own. I take from her dying my commitment to live more fully. I learn from her absence that love and relationship is all that is ever important. I live through her absence the thinning of my world, the narrowing of my support.

I miss her with an achy heart that defies words. I want her here now to remind me, in her silence, that life is manageable, that all is truly possible. I believe that she is in me, that her values and beliefs and attitudes are my own. I believe that she guides me and protects me and loves me, all from a very far yet nearby distance.

I am and will always be my mother's daughter.

"Mom was quite the trooper at Tanglewood, bundled in layers of rainproof wear."

Mom, in "bat-self-defense."

34. Buzz the Extraordinaire
1990 – Present

She came to me in a dream. I dreamt she sat on my shoulder, a cockatiel, just like one of the series of parakeets that shared my childhood world. "Hi," she said, "I'm ready for you now." I awoke in my little ashram bed, shaking my head. *A bird?* I thought. *How absurd. I'm too busy, practicing and living this spiritual lifestyle.* Although small caged pets and birds were allowed in the ashram, this was a ridiculous proposal. I got up and threw myself into the hectic, engaging, rich day of a devoted disciple.

A few weeks later I sat in meditation in front of the simple wooden altar in my room, quieting my mind, opening my heart. She returned again to me, sitting on my shoulder and said quite clearly to me, "Okay, now it is time." My eyes jolted open. *Holy shit!* I thought. *This is spooky. There is something real going on here.*

And real she was, as she sat there, a tiny cockatiel inside the palm of my hand in the pet store. She had orange rouge circles on her little face, most of which was covered by her enormous, out-of-proportion beak. *Rouge for life,* I thought. *You go, girl.*

"I think I'll call her Bud," I said to Arpana, my bird-shopping support system.

"Um, Aruni," Arpana said slowly, "there may be some strange and lingering associations with that name…like Budweiser beer. And all beer, maybe." She offered a gentle suggestion. "How about Buzz?"

And Buzz she was. Buzz the Bird, my first animal companion since sobriety, since my awakening awareness in the ashram. Buzz was too young to come home with me, still being hand-fed in the pet store. I visited her there several times a week until she was ready to leave, bonding and falling more deeply into a smitten mother-love that I had never before experienced. Eric came once and we had a pseudo-professional photo shoot for tiny Buzz, who did not seem to be growing at all, and who did not mind the many shots Eric took of her one bit. She was distinguished from her sister/brother/community of cockatiels in their communal cage by the stunning circle of yellow around her head. And by her little id tag on her skinny ankle: W 153.

Buzz Futuronsky, W 153, was now ready to become a member of the Kripalu ashram.

Eric and I drove an ashram car out to the pet store to bring her home. It was a steaming Berkshire summer day. She was in a tiny plastic travel container on my lap, her cage and supplies in the back seat, as Eric drove us home. She cost $99.99, for animal and supplies. I was a nervous-Nellie mother, urging Eric's maneuvering of the car around intersections, steeling Buzz and her container into safety through my focused will. The hot temperatures worried me. My role was to keep her safe. I had a plan and we would keep to it. I had an idea about how this transport would run, goddamn it, and it would happen, with highly oiled military-like precision.

Except it didn't. On Route 7, a few minutes away from home, the car behind us slammed into our bumper, as we slammed into the car in front of us. It wasn't bad—by accident standards a mere fender bender—but it was a catastrophe for a newly emerging bird-mom. I had a baby bird on my lap that needed calm, serenity, and safety in her transition.

Eric managed the other drivers and the policeman. Buzz and I sat in the sun in the increasing temperatures. *This is dangerous, this is unsafe,* I thought, my childhood fearful response to life overtaking me. "Excuse me, officer?" I hung out the window. He turned toward me. "I have a baby bird here. Help, please."

So Buzz and I sat in the backseat of the police cruiser, air condition full-on, while Eric, the police, and the other drivers continued with the seemingly endless paperwork. I looked around at the crime-fighting paraphernalia—shotgun locked to the dash, handcuffs, radio, police helmet, and so on.

"It's not always like this," I assured Buzz, who seemed quite content in her tiny container. I wrapped my body around her transport cage. Now it was freezing, putting her at risk at the other end of the temperature spectrum. What was a mom to do? How might I continue to keep her safe?

Eventually we made it home. This first Buzz-Lesson, *Aruni, You Are Not in Control,* continued to play out for us throughout the many rich years of our life together.

During those first days, she made her way into her big-girl cage, without her siblings and community members. She looked out at me with huge eyes, probably wondering what the heck was happening. "Don't ask me," I answered her silent question. "I'm really not so sure myself."

She took her place among us ashram members. She went to seva, my work assignment, with me daily, sitting on my shoulder, making her way down the quieter hallways with me as her tree. I carried her cage everywhere we went, so she would feel grounded and close to water and food at all times. In hindsight, I wonder who I was really trying to comfort—myself or Buzz? Which one of us needed the nearness to food and drink at all times?

Second Buzz-Lesson: *Aruni, I Am Your Mirror. See How You Respond To Me and See Yourself.*

When I went out to AA meetings at night, I would obsess at great length about open vs. closed bedroom windows. How many meetings did I find myself sitting at and suddenly think, "Oh, my God. It's too cold for her. What have I done?" The rest of the meeting and ride home would be a trial of concentration. Do not obsess about open window. Listen to meeting. Do not obsess.

250

She became, despite her obsessive mother, life's most remarkable bird. She went to many meetings at work on my shoulder, where we would chant *om*—Buzz loved that sounding and would fully participate. We would check in and plan the work of the day. She would wander away from me, find someone she liked, hang on their lap or shoulder, make herself at home. In spite of me, she was profoundly comfortable in the world. She was really her own person/bird in fullness. She was much, much braver than I. She lived and worked in an ashram, had 350 people who knew her, and had an admiring always-changing pool of pet-deprived Kripalu guests wanting animal contact.

When I began teaching and had photos taken of myself for the Kripalu catalogue, Eric, the photographer, okayed the plan: Buzz and I would be a photo team. She sat on my shoulder, one of many professional photo shoots she participated in during her life, with an aplomb and calmness that I did not feel. She sat on my shoulder in that picture for years of Kripalu catalogues.

She was, quite frankly, famous. She had a large world view.

Buzz-Lesson Three: *Life Is Safe and Glorious.*

She spoke two words, "pretty" and "bird," but she said them in a variety of inflection and emphasis that gave those two simple words a wide range of meaning. She was an excellent communicator. You could always tell what she needed, what she wanted, and what was happening in her world. She was able to express it fully.

When R. entered my life, Buzz adored her fully and uncompromisingly. Sometimes it appeared that I was a mere bridge between wherever Buzz was and where R. sat. Together they would sit, whistling and humming together, my tiny yet profound non-traditional family emerging.

Fourth Buzz-Lesson: *Aruni, You Are Profoundly Loved.*

One day before Thanksgiving, in an attempt to cut her flight feathers to keep her safe, I hit a blood feather, causing a blood bath. Buzzie stretched her wing and blood splattered against the wall. My heart

251

stopped. I scooped her up, ran her to a car, jacked up the heater, and flew to the vet. He cauterized the feather, shook his head quietly and said, "I don't know if she'll make it. Keep her warm and see how she does." *Oh my God.* I drove home, tears blinding me. *What have I done?*

I borrowed space heaters for my room, covered her cage in layers, apologized and prayed, and left her alone. I attempted unsuccessfully to sleep on R's floor that night, without respite from my terrified grief.

I found myself on the floor of the bathroom in the middle of the night, hands clenched in prayer, feverishly seeking words. 12 Steps taught me to pray only for God's will for me and the power to carry that out. But I had a preference that night. For the first time in my prayer life, my preference emerged as valid and essential. I prayed: "Dear God, please keep Buzzie alive, if it be Your will. And give me the courage to be present with whatever You give me."

Buzzie-Lesson Five: *Preference Is Inevitable And Sacred. It Has An Essential Role In Life. Ask For What You Want, Aruni.*

In the grey morning, I made my way toward my/our room and opened the door, hit in the face with steamy temperatures. I cautiously made my way toward the many layered bird cage, opening one layer at a time with baited breath. There sat Buzzie the Bird, alive and well, ready to celebrate Thanksgiving with me and with my newly expanded, maturing prayer life.

She met the guru once on the back stairs. He, in his velour robe, said in delighted English-Indian, "Oh, what a cute birdie." She was thoroughly unimpressed.

When R. and I moved from the building after the fall of the ashram, Buzz made the transition to commuter life pretty effortlessly. On Monday mornings, I would warm up the car, drive it parallel to the backdoor, wrap Buzzie's same travel case in layers of down and fleece, dash her out into the car, and drive to Kripalu singing some of our favorite songs together:

If it wasn't for my
Buzzie Birdie,
I would not be Mommy,
Mommy.
Loving and beloved Buzzie.

The ritual would be repeated once we arrived at Kripalu and she would find her way to her office cage. There she lived throughout the week, attending meetings, doing paperwork with me, flicking paperclips, eating confidential messages, doing her do. We were inseparable office mates. On Fridays she would commute home again, ready to enjoy the best the weekend had to offer her: rice, videos, corn chips, people with delicious hair, and sunshine.

Buzzie Lesson Number Six: *Work With Somebody You Really Like.*

She worked at Kripalu for fourteen years. Kripalu got busier, more upscale and "professionalized" at the end of her career. She almost got fired, due to some incessant and exuberant chirping. But she had the class to retire before she was fired. She spent the last year of her life in our home, hunkered down in our bedroom, her cage by the window, softly chirping along with the outdoor birdies. She deserved this quiet retirement. R. and I agreed to heat that portion of the house, to keep her safe and warm, a costly yet appropriate decision.

And the end, of course, came sooner than I wanted. Seeing her lying on the bottom of her cage, my beautifully feathered teacher and healer lying lifeless, broke my heart and then splintered it in a dozen aching fragments. Our house was emptied and silent without her 3-ounce hugeness of spirit.

Moving her and burying her was so very challenging. Picking up her gloriously beautiful body out of the cage was terrifying and overwhelming, yet it was my job to do. As her caregiver and companion, it was mine. I obsessed and fretted over finding an appropriate container for her. An old, used Tupperware that had held tomatoes and beans was not appropriate. Thankfully, R. had a spotless, perfectly sized container from India that had carried herbs. It was meant for Buzzie. I prayed for courage as I reached into the cage. In death she was extraordinarily beautiful, not unlike my mother. Her body weight and feel was odd, dense, difficult. I wrapped her in Lucy the Dog's favorite pink bandana. Into the container she went, my glorious friend.

We buried her in the corner of our yard nearest the bedroom, next to the window she looked out with such glee. She was diagonal from Tillie's bush, which we had planted the year before, to keep Mom blossoming. We prayed and sang and cried and chanted *om*, her favorite sound. I found a lovely old wrought iron angel garden figure, with wings, her hands cupped around her heart. Buzzie rests beneath that today.

She was gone now. The final words she told our animal communicator after her death were, "Oh, tell them to not be sad. My wings never worked so good."

I was touched by a bird, taught by a bird, loved by a bird, grown by a bird.

I was healed by a bird.

Buzzie and Me

35. My (Several) Marriages
1995 & 2004

In the explosion of blood and guts and broken dreams that the fall of the ashram left behind, there was also a new moment of freedom. Yes, gone was the vowed community with all its gifts, and gone was the guru with all his richness. But gone, too, were the restrictions, the limitations, the authoritarian hierarchy that had determined our lives. Within the profound loss of our lives as we knew them lived the seeds of new beginnings. Change, both terrifying and heady, was in the air.

R. and I were now free to explore relationship. There were no longer any organizational obstacles to moving forward in our commitment to each other. As we slowly began integrating the trauma of the guru's fall and shift into our new, hired roles, we continued along with our relationship mentoring. We worked well with our mentor, with many lessons unfolding for us both. Using powerful conscious communication techniques, I was learning to let R. be where she was emotionally. My job was not to change her or fix her, but to support her. I noticed the times that I tried to talk her out of her feelings were usually the times I was uncomfortable with what she was feeling. I was slowly beginning to see that relationship was about more than being comfortable or getting my needs met.

But the impetus to move forward in commitment didn't actually come from us. One bright, sunny winter day, Moose—longtime resident, major sweetheart-guy, and administrator of housing—came to me with an excited twinkle in his eyes. "Aruni," he said, "I have an idea. I'm reordering housing assignments. If you and R. were married, you could get that great suite of rooms on the third floor."

As he said those words, I knew the truth. I knew *my* truth. I would propose to R. We would be "married" in the eyes of the remaining Kripalu community. I wasn't able to see my next step until he put words to it.

Moose and I high-fived. He was our dear, 200-pound bundle of Cupid energy.

I was off to plan my romantic proposal. I didn't take too long to think about it, knowing myself well—the planning phase would become the obsessing phase. The decision was so obvious, so right. I knew if I thought about it for very long, I would agitate myself needlessly.

I found R. that evening, quietly reading in her tiny ashram single room. Down on one knee I fell. She looked at me curiously. "Dearest," my voice cracked. "Dearest." I tried to settle down. "Will you marry me?" I blurted. No fancy words, just out with the truth.

Her jaw dropped noticeably. "Oh," she said, accent picking up. "Oh," with more emphasis.

Does that mean yes or no? I wondered. *Where does "oh" fall in the chart of acceptance/rejection?* More silence, some squirming on her part. My knee was starting to ache.

"Do you have an answer?" I blurted. She was shifting positions, looking around. Was her face flushed, or was it my face that was flushed?

"Well," she said, drawing out the sounds, West Virginia strongly alive in her voice. "I'm not saying no."

I'm not saying no! It was a far leap from her ancient anti-mantra of yesteryear, "I would never." She seemed slightly giggly now, fidgeting around her bed. My knee was killing me. I guessed it was time to move.

We continued along, talking about my proposal, discussing it in our mentoring sessions, considering the pros and cons. And eventually, over time, the "I'm not saying no" transformed itself into the affirmative. We were getting married. We would have a commitment ceremony at Kripalu on June third. We had the winter and spring to plan.

I was bubbly, silly, excited, terrified, horrified, elated—it was all true.

Although the vowed order was officially ending and most people were in major transition, a large percentage of the 350 former ashram members were still at Kripalu. R. and I drew on community support in an awesome and out-of-the-box way, and received an abundance of dear, heart-centered support in the creation of our celebration day.

Sata worked on creating invitations for us. Our mentor, Devi, would conduct the service that we created. Sushana helped us brainstorm, using a technique called a mind map to generate awareness of our desires and needs. Eric would take pictures and make the toast. The Kripalu baker was creating a fabulous cake. Specific people were in charge of flowers, décor, the chuppa. It took a village; we still had a village upon which to draw.

Besides community support, our families were delighted. R.'s sister and family, with their Quaker-Unitarian roots and their open-minded world view, were completely eager to celebrate her new life. They would make the trip from Wisconsin, as well as her Gestalt group, friends for decades, who were also making the pilgrimage up. My sister and her family would come, my dad and mom not able to travel from Florida. My family was so relieved that there was some stability, some maturity in my world. They instantly liked R. My childhood friend Gladys was coming from Baltimore, my dear friend Andrea from New York.

Somehow, the day arrived. There was quite the flutter around the community. For all of the Kripalu years, no lesbian or gay couple had been "officially" sanctioned. R. and I were fortunate enough to walk through the open doors that other lesbian and gay disciples in the past had knocked upon, bumped into, railed against. For a series of strange coincidental reasons, the door opened for us. Our wedding was a deep healing for the community at large. The day was much bigger than just us.

That morning we dressed with giddy anxiousness in our new suite of rooms—well, two rooms and a bath, quite the Kripalu score. I had energized the shopping-for-dresses-campaign. R. wore a fabulous flapper-looking short dress, in blacks and browns. My dress was long, flowing, ivory—perfect. And, with the gods shining upon us, both were on sale.

It was a humid June day with storm clouds beading the horizon, which dashed our plans for an outside, lakeside event. We had reserved a lovely room at Fox Hollow, owned by Kripalu at that point in time. Folks were decorating and setting up. We, the brides, were freed of responsibility.

I remember walking into the building, almost lightheaded with excitement, seeing friends and attendees, waving to all. I remember Eric with his camera snapping at us, saying, "Here come the brides, here come the brides." I remember seeing L. and her family drive up, right as we did. I remember walking in, and being ushered off to a room to wait. I remember the general air of celebration—palpable, delicious on my lips.

We spent a few anxious long minutes in the waiting room, nerves jangled. I had to pee, then didn't, then did again. Finally the time had arrived—one of our ushers was waving us frantically toward the open door. I looked at R. We shrugged at each other, and headed toward it.

We walked into the celebration room, with entry music played by one of our friends on the keyboard. It was one of my favorite old Chris Williamson songs, from my women-music days:

Filling up
And spilling over
It's an endless waterfall,

> *Filling up*
> *And spilling over,*
> *Over all....*

The plan was: we would walk in together and then separate, R. to the right, me to the left, and then we would proceed down the stairs into the room. As we entered the room, we were met with an absolute barrage of love, applause, whistling, excitement, and warm affection. The crowd roared and got on their feet, stomping and loving us. R. and I both stopped in our tracks, overwhelmed and filled up. We just stood there and drank it in. At some point, after a few long minutes of this, we looked at each other, and continued down our individual stairways.

It was a healing for all Kripalu that day—Kripalu of the past, Kripalu of the present and of the future.

The ceremony was lovely, funny, deep, perfect. I relaxed into it with surprising ease, and was able to savor and be present for it. I never remember feeling such love and support. Buzzie's feather was on the altar, blessing us.

I remember our vows, which we had written on a mountaintop in South Berkshire County one long hiking afternoon, one segment saying:

> R: *I commit to be with you in such a way that old relationship*
> *hurts and wounds can be healed. I not only to not re-*
> *wounding you, but to being part your healing process.*

> Aruni: *I commit to be with you in whatever you are experiencing*
> *without trying to change you*

I thought to myself at several junctures of the day, "This is the best day of my life." And then I felt somewhat embarrassed by that shallow conclusion. How could my wedding be the best day? Wasn't that terribly gushy and superficially romantic? Shouldn't it be some personal achievement, some professional event, something individuated?

No. This was the day I felt the most loved, the most seen, the most held. This was the best day of my life.

Wedding #2—To the Same Person—April 21, 2004

Through a profoundly difficult political process, the legislature of the state of Massachusetts, where we just happened to be legal residents, declared it illegal to deprive same-sex couples of the legal right to marriage. I had watched the clouds of this political debate on the horizon for months with fascination and crossed fingers. As same-sex marriage became more of a legal possibility, I had another opportunity to propose to R., to demonstrate to her my commitment and love, to legally sanctify our family, and to bring healing to the child inside of me.

"R., would you marry me legally now?"

Who could fathom that possibility? Who could ever imagine that I would have the legal right to ask that question, to request what people all over the planet forever have asked of each other? If the child in me, the wounded, terrified little girl who wanted to kiss the other girls, who wanted to run away with Mary Travers, could only have heard that question, how much pain, how much trauma might have been eased from her body?

Interesting discussions unfolded between us. R. never wanted or needed the formal institution of marriage in her life. She at first agreed to get married, to support my healing process. Then her decision evolved into a realization that it was a statement she wanted to make; that all people, all love, is sacred and honorable, and obviously deserved legal merit.

I called our town hall, to alert them that we would be coming for a license. They were polite, quiet, the town manager coming out to shake our hands. They took a Polaroid of us. The paper reported that "two gay couples" in Richmond filed for a marriage license. We never did find out about couple number two.

We had a small ceremony with a justice of the peace and three of our friends present under Anne and Tom's gazebo. The day was gloriously blue and sunny; my stomach was aflutter. Unfortunately the "gay-friendly" justice of the peace kept pronouncing R.'s name wrong, the only wrench in the otherwise stunning afternoon.

When the justice of the peace said, "…recognized in the eyes of the Commonwealth of Massachusetts," a flood of nameless feelings surged through me. However anti-establishment and marginal I had painted myself to be, there was a profound validity in these words. There was profound validity in this action.

In this moment, there was profound healing.

We had a gathering of friends that evening and received much love and support.

We sent our announcement and picture to the *Sunday Berkshire Eagle* before the ceremony, without much forethought. As the Sunday of our publication approached, I found myself more and more anxious. What about drive-by shootings? Anti-gay mobs? Hate crimes? I talked myself into a bit of a frenzy.

The newspaper came out and there we were, on the page, official, women, married. We were next to an ancient couple celebrating their 60th anniversary. I smiled, wondering the talk amongst their family members about the couple on their left.

But we received only love. People in my AA meetings applauded when I walked in. Folks in R.'s gym class were profuse in their support. A young woman we did not know approached us while shopping to offer her congratulations. There were no hate crimes, no antagonism for us in Berkshire County—only love, support, and seeing.

To be seen in our loving, to be offered what has been offered to all, to be equalized in the eyes of the state, to be witnessed as two women committed to each other—this has been remarkable, miraculous, ordinary, and astounding. It has offered me the banality of a miracle, the extraordinary rolled into a common and ordinary moment of transformation.

I live today in the comfort and support of a marriage that would be illegal in much of the world. I am so very blessed.

Our Kripalu wedding day

36. The Later Day Saints
2002 – Present

Yet again, it began in a dream. Only this time around, it wasn't my dream, it was R.'s. She kept having a recurring dream of kissing a puppy's belly. This was strange, since there were no puppies in our life. She would wake, startled and disoriented, shake her head and say, "Damn, another puppy belly showed up last night."

Having had my share of animals-appearing-in-dreams-and-then-manifesting-themselves, I was quiet. *A puppy!* My heart soared at the thought. But I was deathly allergic to dogs, and surely Buzz the Bird, our dearest companion, was deathly vulnerable to doggies. It seemed an impossibility.

This energetic stalemate continued along for months. At some point, we began investigating breeds of hypoallergenic dogs. What a concept! A dog you could kiss, cuddle with, run with, and play with, all without triggering my allergies. How could this be? But we were still spinning our wheels. Poodles? Too cunning. I didn't want a dog that was smarter than I was. Wheaton Terriers? Too silly, hard to train, too strong a prey drive. Prey drive? Prey? That would mean Buzzie Futuronsky. She could not be prey to anybody. Portuguese Water Dogs? We made the mistake of going to a dog show where they were being shown, all gussied up and hair teased. It soured us on the possibility of a non-teased, non-gussied Water Dog. We were frozen in indecision.

For all of Buzz's life, we worked with an effective animal communicator, a woman who psychically attunes to animals' thought pictures and exchanges thoughts with them. This process had been very powerful, helpful, and fun with Buzz. When "discussing" the possibility of a new member of our family with Buzz, our little bird was eager and willing. "Just let me train the dog," was her only request.

What? That was too much for me. Let a bird train a dog? Ensuring Buzzie's safety was my purpose on the planet. But surely considering a breed that had a weak prey drive—oh, I couldn't even say those words—was essential to protecting our 3-ounce spiritual bird-teacher's life. We continued the never-ending investigation.

Very matter-of-factly, at a party one evening, a dog trainer friend happened to mention, "Oh, I thought of you both just the other day. I have an interesting new breed of dog in one of my classes. A Goldendoodle. A bred offspring of a Golden Retriever and a Standard Poodle. She's hypoallergenic and adorable."

Something clicked inside my world. A Goldendoodle. I adored Golden Retrievers, but knew I could not live through their dander and shedding. Hummm. We rushed home to explore the Doodle-Thing on line. Sure enough, there they were: cuter than cute, smart like a Poodle (the literature promised), yet sweet and loving like a Golden. I sat, mesmerized, hypnotized by the official website. R. looked cautiously over my shoulder, agreeing to their cuteness. The site described their prey drive as low and specific to each dog. That was not helpful. But something was unfolding here. Magic was in the air in our family.

I looked up breeders. There were several fancy ones, their websites replete with music, dog family trees, applications, required forms for purchasing, and long waits. I didn't want to wait until "Choo Choo and Bridget have their litter at Christmas." Damn it all, I was an addict. Okay, a recovering addict...but nevertheless, I wanted what I wanted. After months and months of processing, I wanted a Doodle, and I wanted her *now*.

I found a small, non-flashy website, the Mullners of Wisconsin. They were humble farm folks who bred Doodles and had two little girls ready to go. TWO LITTLE GIRLS READY TO GO! Oh, shit. We called and spoke to the Mullners. They were sweet, easy, no muss, no fuss. They emailed out a picture of the two remaining girl pups.

R. and I sat glued to the computer screen. There, before our eyes, sat two precious beings of fur and fuzz and blondness. Which one? I couldn't abide the decision. It seemed easier to not choose, and not have a dog. R. had an insight. "Call Dawn." Our communicator. But it was impossible to get an instant appointment with her. Oh, well. I called anyway. Miracle of miracles, she had a slot open in the morning.

R. and I continued to stare, measure, weigh, intuit, and sense these two puppies, staring endlessly at their pictures. Finally morning came, and our call with Dawn.

"Okay," Dawn said, as she looked at the picture we'd sent. "The one on the right will be bigger, more shy, perhaps more cuddly. She would be okay enough with Buzz."

Yes, I thought, *and the other? Hurry up, the other.* There was a strange sense of urgency rumbling in my belly.

"And the other," Dawn giggled. "She's a character. She'll be the life of the party, the energetic one. Everyone in the park will be drawn to her and want to love her up. She'll be a handful. Smaller. Less cuddly. She would be fine with Buzz, easy to train in that realm. Oh, wait a second. She's telling me something." Silence. R. and I sat spellbound, glued to the two receivers.

"Oh," Dawn said. "The puppy says, 'They've already contacted me. I'm going there to those people.'"

And that was our Lucy Kay Doodle. We had already contacted her. Well, we had been spending a whole lot of time and effort focusing on their picture, and R. had spent much focus on the little girl on the left. We agreed to purchase her, sent a check, and prepared for the arrival of our first born. She flew from Wisconsin, a terrifying concept to me. Little did I know, she was one strong, determined little puppy.

On the day of her arrival, I had a heady winter flu, along with its accompanying crankiness and longing for silence and/or death. As we left for the airport, I felt crappy as only one with a flu can feel Upon arrival, we found out that Lucy (not yet named—a long list of options awaited her) was delayed in Cincinnati. Delayed in Cincinnati? Our dog was delayed in Cincinnati by herself? Inconceivable. We had four hours to kill. Not enough time to go home, but too much time on one's hands—let alone one sick person's hands—to stand an airport. I lay on a bench in the Albany Mall, a few miles from the airport, wearing sunglasses, hat pulled over my aching ears, trying to soften the glare on my eyes and praying for sleep, while R. restlessly window-shopped, awaiting our new arrival.

Finally she was there, self-assured, fuzzy, interested, our 12-pound ball of blond and white fur, looking "just like herself," as R. said. One look named her "Lucy. Lucy Kay Doodle." My headache disappeared in one swooning look. And the rest is history. Our expanding family headed home to the Berkshires.

The next morning I lay in bed, feverish with flu and new puppyhood. R. and Lucy were walking. I was talking to my mom on the phone, sharing my delight of motherhood, when I heard furious footsteps in the front room. *What the heck is that,* I wondered? In came R., her wrist hanging at an odd, abnormal angle, dog in arms.

"I broke my wrist," she announced, without fanfare. In her new motherhood exuberance, she slipped on the ice and had a serious tumble.

Dog into the crate, the people went to the hospital. Sure enough, R.'s right wrist was broken. She, mother #1, Dr. R., psychologist and primo behaviorist and trainer, was out for the count on the couch with Percocet. I saw myself as the sous chef of training, the one willing to follow the directions of the head trainer. But when it came to spearheading the training? I felt utterly inept and unwilling.

The little dog looked up at me with huge eyes.

Lucy Doodle Lesson #1—*So Much For Plans. Deal With Life As It Is.*

We decided to call Dawn, concerned that Lucy would be freaked out by the accident and feel guilty. When asked about the fall, twelve-week-old Lucy Kay Doodle, said, "What? It wasn't my fault. She just fell."

Lucy Doodle Lesson #2—*Know Your Responsibility and Assume It Fully. Don't Waste Time With The Rest.*

She was outrageously wild as a puppy, unable to walk on a leash without chewing it, dancing with it, hopping with it, yanking on it, shadowboxing with it. She had her own mind, her own idea of the moment. She was terrified of Buzz, who hissed her into place. Lucy would back slowly out of a room if Buzzie were there. Buzz, on the other hand, grew more and more fascinated by the puppy, and wanted her close; as such, a strange dynamic emerged.

R. with her cast, and me holding on for dear life to the wild beast, we somehow plodded through those early months together.

We went to every dog training class in Berkshire County, each one repeated twice. Lucy barked while the teacher talked, took the other participants' toys, peed at crucial intersections of the lesson, refused to cooperate, and rolled on her back in glee rather than concentration. She just wanted to party. She was the "worst" dog. My heart sank. I thought that meant I was the worst mother of a dog. The classes were mortifying for me, humiliating and embarrassing.

Lucy Doodle Lesson #3—*Get Over Yourself. I Am Not You.*

Everyone told me—she's a puppy, she'll get it. I dreaded the classes, but did so love her. She was wild, adorable, her growth patterns fascinating. She'd run down the hall in the morning, with brand new enlarging body parts. "Where did that tail come from?" R. inquired one morning. She looked like a fullback now.

She learned to swim that summer, taught by a dog friend named Baloo. She loved jumping into the ponds to fetch sticks. It was her life. She was good off-leash...good-ish. We were committed to her daily off-leash times. "If she's a dog, she is going to live the life of a dog," R. said. I silently thought she should be more contained at home, barricaded into the illusion of safety.

Lucy Doodle Lesson #4—*Life Is Really, Really Fun. If You Are Not Enjoying Yourself, What is Your Problem?*

I thought it was my job to keep her from stimulation, and I tried so valiantly to create the illusion of control for myself. She and I had difficulty in off-leash situations. There were a few times when, alone with me, she chose to ignore my commands and continue her partying. It was terrifying—she wouldn't come back to me. I had deep dread of being alone with her off-leash. R. and I decided that Lucy and I needed to go to the "bad-dog trainer," the trainer who dealt with the juvenile delinquent doggies of Berkshire County.

Lucy and I met Lois-the-Bad-Dog-Trainer on Main Street of Great Barrington. Lucy and I were diagnosed. Lois decided I needed to take Lucy toward stimulation, rather than try to shelter her from it. Strangely, the lesson seemed to be more about me than the dog. "Don't try to protect her," Lois said. "Your assignment: Take her into town every day. Walk up and down the street and let her encounter stimulation. Let her get accustomed to it. You can't control her environment."

Lucy Doodle Lesson #5—*Life Is Safe. Relax and Enjoy.*

Sometime around two-years-old, I saw a flicker of understanding in her eyes. We were at another dreadful training class, and she was supposedly learning how to "stay," an ongoing lesson in futility. I looked in her eyes, and I saw her trying. I saw a flicker of dog-willingness. It was a cornerstone of a moment. Her behavior began to slowly improve.

Over time, she has become somewhat well-behaved. She tries to listen, does her best to come back to us, and will mostly respond to our commands—except when she doesn't.

Lucy Doodle Lesson #6—*Change Takes Time. Have Patience and Tolerance For The Process.*

Over time, she and Buzzie fell in love. Well, Buzzie fell into deeper love while Lucy fell into some level of tolerance. They would hang out with relative ease together. Buzzie really wanted to preen Lucy. Lucy held the line at that request—no preening by a dumb bird, even if she *is* my sister.

And the years passed, with lessons and love and licks and laughs. Worries and concerns and accidents and blood and mess, too, were part of our dog lives, but all worth it. All so, so worth it

Lucy Doodle Lesson #9763—*It's All Good, It's All Sacred, It's All Inevitable. You Can't Have One Without the Other.*

After Buzzie's death, our house was hollow with emptiness. Three months passed, and we agreed to rescue another Doodle, operating under the urban legend that "two dogs are not so much more work than one." Zac Doodle dropped from the sky, a tall, dark, handsome Lab-Doodle, with a silver muzzle, bedroom eyes, and eyelashes from here to eternity. We were his third home and he was cautious, quiet, and well-behaved. On Christmas Eve, his name expanded—looking like a nice Jewish man who would marry his pregnant girlfriend, we renamed him Zac Joseph Doodle.

Over this year he has relaxed, opened, gotten ridiculously silly, dropped the good boy thing, and recovered his inner puppyhood. Emotionally, Zac is mine—his history of trauma, his cautious heart, his skirting the outsides of life. I identify. Lucy Kay is so R.'s daughter—self-assured from the start.

Zac Joseph Doodle Lesson #Forever—*It's Never Too Late To Have A Happy Puppyhood. Love Heals All. It Works For People, Too.*

There is quite a lot of excitement in our house, from the people-knees on down.

It doesn't get much better than this.

"There she was, fuzzy, interested, our twelve-pound ball of blond and white fur."
Lucy Kay Doodle

"Buzz and Lucy would hang out with relative ease. But Lucy held the line at preening—no preening by a dumb bird, even if she is my sister."

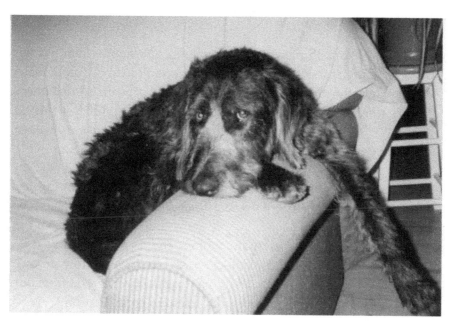

"Love heals all."
Zac Joseph Doodle

37. Growing Into My Sister's Love
1948 – Present

A memory: it is 5:35 p.m. on a dark winter's afternoon. I am a child. My sister and I stand in our kitchen, preparing to help my mom make dinner when she arrives home from a hard day of work at my father's grocery store. He will be home at 6:00 to eat, nap, and then return to the store at 7:00. Time is of the essence now. It is a time of great silence and great stress, a time of hushed rushing, a time of constriction.

Our mother now stands in the middle of the kitchen, wearing her winter coat and her anxieties wrapped closely around her. She hugs to her chest a bag of groceries, hastily gathered, I am certain, from the shelves of the store at the last minutes of her endless shift. I would have to learn, many years later, the skill of wisely buying food from grocery stores, so entrenched was I in the automatic gathering of food from our store's shelves, mindlessly and without financial consideration.

There is a great pause. We three stand on the precipice of dinner prep, a crisis of nerves for me, the youngest. From the stillness of memory we launch into our respective tasks, L. lining the broiler pan, mom prepping the chops to be cooked, and me, fumbling as usual, with the silverware. Setting the table. My nightly job. It unnerves me, as I hold four forks, four spoons, four dinner knives in my hands. Time is ticking. The air in my lungs is constricted, the air around me silent and thick with potential error. I lay down one setting at a time, fork on top of napkin, knife and spoon to the left of the big white plates, one at a time, carefully, cautiously.

"Nan," my mother's voice interrupts my concentration and I imperceptibly jump. "Finish that up now. Make the salad while L. puts the vegetables on."

Make the salad. *Oh my God. What does make the salad entail?* In this moment, I am without a clue. I fumble with the lettuce head she thrusts toward me, attempt to hold it under the faucet. It becomes leaky, heavy with water, which I try to splash off against the white porcelain sink. Holding the lettuce in front of me, trying to conceal its leaking, I carry it over to the salad bowl, where I begin plucking off leaves, one at a time. I feel sweaty, doomed, and in a vice of ill-preparedness. How to not be discovered as incompetent?

"Here." My mom's voice, now stern, grabs my attention. "Give me that." She takes the lettuce from me and hands it to my competent, bossy older sister. "L., *you* do it."

The memory fades. I come into the present.

My sister is four years older than I, a dynamic that the family system professionals might explain as an emotional set-up. It always seemed to me that L. had the capacity to navigate in the places in which I was the most vulnerable. When we were kids, she seemed to have our mother's attention, seemed to know how to function in our mother's world, seemed to know how to best support her, while I was clueless. Let it be known that this is only my perception, filtered through all of the childhood wounding, all the family of origin issues that have both kept me stuck and set me free. But the differences in our capacities shamed and hurt me. I thought I should be doing it all better, that perhaps I should be more like her, my sister.

She and I didn't talk much during our early lives. I spent a lot of time in my room, fantasizing and imagining my other world, the world in which I could do what I want, touch girls, play guitar, be a hero. At other times I would ride my bike alone in the park, or go to a movie with my friend, Gladys. My sister and I lived very separate lives.

As we grew, L. had breasts and boyfriends, while I had neither. Socializing at the Jewish Community Club on Sunday afternoons terrified me. I couldn't find the words or the ways to relate, to be with other kids. The boys were ominously other-worldly for me. I knew I needed to know how to travel down those roads, but I couldn't. Deep down inside of me, I didn't even want to, sacrilege of sacrileges. And L. did function in that world, always with a boyfriend, always on a date. It always looked right to see her in that world. It was a world I had no admittance to. It seemed to me that L. had it right and I didn't.

When I became a freshman in high school, she was a senior. We didn't have much interaction throughout high school. I imagined that L. was ashamed of me, of my stuttering, of my non-feminine way of being. I imagined, too, that she resented my parents' attention to me—I was the youngest, threateningly sick in infancy and babyhood, with a speech impediment. L. was off and running; I was stuck in the starting gate. I wanted to be out there, too, in an ambivalent kind of way. Yet I imagined she wanted some of the appearance of comfort that I received from being stuck where I was.

When she went to college, I had three years alone with my parents. I remember no change of focus, no differences in my life. My parents continued to work just as hard. I had the luxury of a driver's license, which gave my one-and-only friend, Gladys, and I some freedom to get pizza and drive to the movies.

Another memory: it is 1966. I stand at eighteen years old in front of my parents' house on Arthur Avenue. My sister's new college boyfriend, Rog, who would become her husband and my brother-in-law, stands before me. I am seeing him for the first time. He wears khaki jeans, brown penny loafers, a blue button-down shirt, and a college varsity jacket. He is handsome, cool, mysterious, unknown, male, unreachable. In this instant I know I can never have what my sister has—I have no access to this heterosexual world. I feel emptied, sad, lost, envious, confused. Longing. I feel longing. For something that is yet unnamed.

When I went to college, our dynamic began to change. For a variety of reasons, I went to the same college where L. was a senior. She had married Rog that summer. They lived a few miles away from my freshman dorm room, and their home became a bit of a safe haven. I occasionally borrowed Rog's old car, Big Grey, the same car I would later buy and drive on my illicit D.C. protest. They would invite me over for a meal when I was hungry for real food, not cafeteria-style food. When I had recurring sore throats, I would sleep on the cot in their living room. I pledged a sorority in which my sister's friends were members. Knowing L.'s friends probably got me into that particular, cool sorority. Our relationship was getting better, a bit more peered.

When my sister gave birth to her first daughter in February of 1970, I was a senior and living just a few miles away. I remember just shortly after Baby Marcy came home, L. had some medical emergency. She called me for help. I rushed over, and spent a few profoundly touching and intimate hours alone with Marcy. I remember being terrified, but holding her, sitting in the rocking chair and singing over and over:

Ahh, ahh, baby.

Marcy is a lady.

Daddy is a gentleman.

And Marcy is a lady.

I again felt that deep and tragic truth: what L. had I could never, never attain. None of this was, of course, logical. Being gay did not have to prevent me from having a child. Nor did I even want access to that world. It was, however, the only world that I saw. My feelings were deeper than any logic.

During the next years of my life, I struggled in my relationship with L. Her two great daughters always occupied a major niche in the depths of my heart. Being an aunt was wonderful for me—love them, adore them, leave them. I remember one time having a silly, fun time with my nieces. They were both teenagers. L. got mad at us for fooling around and yelled at us to stop. I remember feeling young, as if I were another one of my sister's children. It angered me, but I kept silent, locked in my childlike role.

When I told my sister I was an addict and entering recovery, she said to me, "No, you're not." I did not have the strength, the patience, the ability to share my reality with her. I pulled away and made her wrong, rather than to stay present with her, to take responsibility for my truth and my reality.

The four years separating my sister and I were significant ones. I was a child of the sixties and she was not. I was exposed to alternative ideas and, because I was gay, I had to find non-conventional ways to live. L. lived in the convention that I left. That was uncomfortable, annoying, and sometimes painful to confront.

My sister organized the circumstances around my father's dying. She and my mom were with him when he died. She was a driving force in moving my mom to New Jersey, putting in the planning, the grunt work, the money, the effort. Although I was certainly involved in my mother's aging, I felt sidelined by these old dynamics, and marginalized in my involvement.

With Mom in New Jersey assuming a new life for herself, I found myself around my sister and her family more. I still found it hard to move from being the child, to not sink beneath what I labeled my sister's judgment of me, to have a voice that was respected and heard. Throughout my mom's illness, the tension between L. and I grew. We had very different ways of responding, of coping, very different gifts to offer the situation. I always felt L. wanted more involvement from me. I knew in my heart that even if I were with Mom 24/7, it would not be enough for my sister. So I did what I could to be a supportive force in my mother's world, and I prayed to let that be enough.

I prayed to release my sister from my judgment. I prayed to let her be. I prayed to keep the focus on myself. Yet I never felt much of a shift in my internal relationship with her. It was very painful to feel so stuck for so long—to have awareness and to not be able to change it.

My mother's world in New Jersey was like my sister's, defined by an upper middle class Jewish world view. She trusted those models. It would not have been possible for my mom to live in the Berkshires with R. and me, even though that was my fantasy. The more alternative model of living that I might have offered her was not what my mom knew or needed. It would not have worked for her. I knew that, but the dynamic still created unconscious tension.

We are different and we are alike, my sister and I. We share a love of and commitment to family. We both have large hearts and a deep love of animals. We have different values concerning the externals. L. is more committed to the form of things, the style, the look. Because of my history, I have had to learn to embrace the essence of things. My sister would be appalled at the funkiness of my house. But to my heart it feels safe, tender, and home.

We share the same anxiety, the same compulsive patterns and responses to life, the same need to control and take charge. I have been given specific tools to work with these challenges. My sister has not had a need to find tools for change. For me it has been: change or die. This is not the case for L. It's a slippery slope of possible judgment for me. My sister is a well-polished mirror to my inner self, showing me my own potential behaviors.

As my mother's illness grew worse, the tension between L. and I increased. We were functional enough together to be there for my mom. Yet I know my mom was brokenhearted that L. and I always "bickered." She said to me one day on the phone, "I just wish you girls would get along. You are very different, I know. But still, you are sisters."

Mom would be relieved and delighted. Since her death, the balance between my sister and I has drastically changed. There is no major project for us to manage together, no focal point of our process. We are both devastated by the loss of our parents, and without the struggle over our mom, we have found ways to relate to each other. It is quite the miracle.

We talk often on the phone, catching up on the details of each other's day. This means so much to me. Both of us are attempting to fill in the void where our mom would be in our lives. Looking to each other is a surprising gift. I've had wonderful times with L. and her family without Mom, times that are just easier, more fluid.

There is nothing left for us to fight about in our post-parental world, nothing substantial left to stress over. She has a life blessed with children, with grandchildren, with resources. My life is rich and abundant in other ways. I have a fabulous family life, too, but of a different configuration: two wives and two dogs we are.

Certainly one of the gifts of my mother's dying is my capacity to have a more equal relationship with my sister. How odd is life that in such loss, there can be renewal and rebirth. I never would have imagined that without the internal competition for our mother's love, we would be freed to find love in each other. Without having to manage our mother's life, we are becoming able to look toward each other's lives with eyes more opened.

It is my responsibility to soften around our differences, to look to the essence of my sister's life and not get stuck on its form.

It is my responsibility to think the best of her, to do my best to communicate my reality and my truths, and to respect her process.

Today I am able to do these things.

Surrendering into my sister's differences, I am freed.

38. That's Why They Call It Work
Present Day

I sit on the teaching bench. The guests sit in front of me, each in their individual state of delight or grief, hope or hopelessness. In general, they look quite fuzzy, relaxed, and released, with just a few pockets of discouragement still alive. We are on the final night of a three-day intensive program that I teach called *The Inner Quest Intensive* at Kripalu. I have been teaching this program several times a year since 1996. Staff members lounge around the outskirts of the group. They are my colleagues and friends, people I respect and hold dear to my heart.

I pick up the mike. "Okay," I say into it, my voice still raring to go even after this long weekend. With mock seriousness, I cough to capture their attention. "And now I'm going to read to you a profound, deep spiritual tome. I request that you pay close attention, and prepare yourself for a book of ancient meaning and depth." The guests respond en masse, some sitting more upright, some guiltily putting down the chocolate chip cookies they have been given after three days of a light, sugar-free diet. Some smiles fade from faces. Some forced attention is donned.

I pull out the book hidden behind me.

"*The Monster at the End of This Book*," I read, "starring loveable, furry old Grover."

There are snickers of relief, chuckles, and guffaws. A collective sigh of reprieve can be felt in the large, spacious room.

I shift my weight, holding the book's pages out to them, and begin this most precious routine:

"The Monster At the End of This Book—WHAT DID YOU SAY? On the first page, what did that say? Did that say there will be a MONSTER at the end of this book? IT DID? Oh, I am so, so scared of Mon--sters!!!!"

I am Grover. There is no effort, there is no stress. I am a clear and open channel of loveable, furry old Grover. I encourage the guests, Rocky-Horror-Picture-Show-like, to respond with certain collective sounds and movements to different cues in the story. When I say "monster," they look horrified, hold their heads and make a scary face with accompanying noises of mock terror. When I, as Grover, attempt to hammer the pages of the book together to prevent further page turning, they make hammering and sawing sounds. It is hysterical, touching, and so freeing for us all.

At the book's end, I deliver the fabulous punch-line: "Well, look at that," Grover says. "This is the end of the book, and the only one here is ME. I, loveable, furry old GROVER, I am the Monster at the end of this book. And you were so SCARED!"

The guests' faces soften. This "teaching" perfectly parallels the yogic model of healing in which we have been working all weekend. The "monsters," the places we run from in ourselves, are the very doorways to healing. Emotional wounds live in the body, held in the tissues, causing imbalance and disease. Life will bring us exactly the people, the places, and the things to trigger those "monsters," those very blocks, for our purification, for our wholeness. Life comes to heal us. The program teaches the yogic skills necessary to be present in the moment, even and especially present with those monstrous parts of ourselves from which we run—our fear, our self-doubt, our judgment, our anger. Breath, awareness, and right action are all tools that we practice.

The guests, all forty-seven of them, sigh and come back into silence to prepare for our transition to bed. Social silence, talking only as is necessary, is one of many elements of the program that help promote the development of conscious awareness, the capacity to notice and not judge, and realign with right action.

I am a teacher, a facilitator of consciousness and transformation. I am a holder of sacred space. I allow each one of us—participants, staff, and myself—to be exactly where we are emotionally, physically, mentally, and spiritually. Transformation happens by being present with life as it is. My work is to support people in both being present with and creating right action for change. My work is to pray with people, to allow their prayers to come forth.

I am remarkably good at this, and, strangely enough, this is remarkably easy for me.

This, my work, is effortless, without force or push. It is the easiest place in my world in which I might be. Give me forty people in emotional challenge—give me a crowd of people wanting and seeking truth. For reasons I do not logically understand, I am fully equipped to allow it to be, to not give up before the miracle of change happens. I am relaxed and present. Life for me gets hard when I put down the microphone, when I go home. Trying to select a video to watch, negotiating with R.—those are the intensive things in my life. Teaching, facilitating, and coaching are arenas that are void of self-consciousness for me. I am simply present and able, plugged in like nowhere else in my world.

It's not all Grover and silliness, although the laughter and the humor have the profound capacity to release and relax people, to bring organic bonding and connection to a room full of strangers. I teach. I coach individuals. I am at my best when I am using the individual's or the group's experience and wisdom to move the process forward. I am at my worst when I think I have to logically explain a cognitive process.

I have led thousands of groups of people over the years of my Kripalu teaching. My favorite format was called the Sharing Circle, which we held daily, first thing in the morning, for many years. In this experience, a group of strangers, guests at Kripalu, would gather, be given simple guidelines, be led in a meditation and centering, and then would share, without giving or receiving feedback, their particular experience of the moment. Inevitably it worked as a profound connector, allowing people to deeply relate to others in a non-habitual, non-social, non-threatening way. For me, it was a powerful way to deeply learn one of our core teachings: there is nothing wrong with this moment. My job was not to change anybody or anything. There was nothing there to fix. My job was simply to allow these people to be where they were

Here is a Sharing Circle memory. The guests dribble into the room. The backjacks are in a circle, with a few candles in its center. The eight guests are cautious, quiet, not relating to each other. I welcome them, introduce myself. They begin to peek, open their eyes, look around.

"For an opening introduction, let's simply go around and introduce ourselves. Please tell us your first name and where you are from. Also tell us a favorite childhood food. Idiosyncratic food combinations are welcomed," I say, and am met with laughter.

I begin, describing my favorite childhood food as the chicken-roll-on-a-hard-roll-with-mayo-and-pepper, made by my daddy in the store.

Mary, to my left, an older, tired looking woman with thinning hair, looks cautious and defensive. She launches quietly in, and begins to describe her love of her grandmother's special holiday-only oatmeal. Her eyes sparkle by the end of the story. Fred, to her right, a lanky, tall middle-aged guy, recounts his love of Oreo cookies and his specific, slightly obsessive-compulsive milk-dunking ritual. The circle continues around. By the time we get to Janie, a round woman at the other end of the circle wearing a high-end maroon yoga top, a childhood devotee of s'mores, there is a collective breath of relaxation and connection in the room.

I lead the opening meditation. "In your own way, allow your eyes to close. Looking inside, begin to scan your body without judgment— just notice. Direct your breath and your awareness to any places of sensation in your body. Nothing needs to be different. Relax, and let the sensations of breath carry you inside, each breath taking you more deeply home. Notice your internal world. What is happening in this moment? If a microphone could make its way into your belly, what needs to be said? What do you need to say to be present in this moment?" We complete our centering by chanting *om* together.

We are open for sharing. I go first, hopefully modeling appropriate length and depth, claiming my place amongst them, as AA says, "one among many, a worker among workers." I am not separate from this experience, yet I hold it, I allow it to unfold.

I speak of my sadness at the loss of summer, the impact the change of season has had on my energy, my heart, my openness. I finish. I pass and instruct the guests to take a deep breath with me. "A collective breath, a breath of mercy, is a profound way to respond, perhaps more powerful than words," I offer. We look toward Mary. She tears up, swallows her feelings, trying to control them. Then she tears up again. She begins her story.

"It's been two and a half months. I watched him die, my husband of fifty-one years. I can't quite find myself yet," she explains to us strangers, and continues to elaborate on her grieving process, her widowhood, her new aloneness in the world. She speaks in a way she would not to her family, not to her children whom she is protecting, not to her friends who share their own grief. Without feedback, she is able to download energetically and spiritually, to release that which she has been keeping pent up inside. It is precious to share in her aching heart, to witness her words, words that break her silence. We take a breath with her at her completion.

Fred goes next, obviously moved and conflicted. He blurts out, "My wife left me on Christmas Day. I had no clue it was coming. I'm a wreck." His story tumbles out, his silent heartbreak finding words, his loss now witnessed and held in the hearts of us perfect strangers.

We take a breath at his completion.

We are a circle of grieving. In most circles, an organic theme seems to emerge. Today, ours is loss. Around the circle we go, revealing and releasing our hiding, our cautious silence turned into openness, a flow of energy. Into the awareness and the witnessing of others, we are no longer alone.

We end with another centering: "Returning back to yourself. Feel yourself sitting in this moment. Feel the air on your hands, your face. Imagine you can send a beam of light, a prayer of hope around this circle, wrapping up each one of us in your prayerfulness. Imagine that as you offer this prayer, you receive it many times. Let's together pray for patience and tolerance for the process. Let's pray for the willingness to do the next best thing. And let's pray for peace. Peace for ourselves, peace for each other. Peace for all living beings here, and there, and everywhere. Let's share in the sound of *om* together."

We have ended. A few folks mingle, a few slip out, grateful for their anonymity. In general, connection was made. Bridges were built, from heart to heart, from experience to experience.

This is the work that I do.

It wasn't always this good. In the years after the end of the ashram, I was organically carried to a position of upper management and leadership at Kripalu. With the more senior members of the community gone, I had an opportunity to move up. This image of myself "as a big knocker," as my father would say, mattered to me. It defined me, and kept me captive. I was unconsciously impressed with it, and had a quiet and secret ambition for more of the illusion of authority and power. It felt good and right to be in leadership.

For many years, my main work at Kripalu was running a department called Ongoing Programs, which included the daily classes like yoga and dance, the workshops, the hikes, and the administration and implementation of them all. I taught when I could, always loving it, always thriving within it, but my head was stuck in the budget, in the staff meetings I had to run and the politics that dominated the organization's culture.

With the newest set of upper management changes several years back, the writing was on the wall. I was now the old guard, defined by the new administration as one of the dinosaurs who were committed to the ways things used to be, and who lacked the aptitude to move the organization in the direction it needed to go. As much as I tried to prevent it from happening, I eventually was removed from my management role, had a vile salary reduction, and found myself dropped into despair. I had to confront that haunting question: Is it now time to leave Kripalu? Is my work here complete?

I was dizzied by shame, embarrassment, and fear. Although I logically knew it would work out fine, no matter my decision to go or to stay, my feeling world was awash with waves of conflicting emotions. It was a long spell, months that were grey and dense with feelings and indecision. I felt so much shame. Yet my new job description was radically amazing. I would only teach and coach. All the parts of my old job that were challenging for me—the juggling of the political, the many stressful meetings, the budget—were released. I was being offered a chance to do what I loved best.

I outlived my feelings. It wasn't easy and it wasn't immediate, but I saw them through. I decided to stay. And these last years have been rich with meaning, expansive in time, alive with contact with people, and bubbling with self-growth. I have had the time and the inspiration to create a CD of my guided meditations, one of my passions, something that never would have happened if I were still managing.

Beyond my wildest dreams, I have been put in the perfect role to utilize my gifts. I am not fully out of the woods of my ego in this regard. If I am tired, if I am upset, if I worry about finances, I can pick up a thread of resentment and once again feel marginalized or discounted. But if I keep my spiritual connection vibrant, I relax into the perfection of my job.

Dharma is a Sanskrit word that means purpose, life path, contribution to the planet, doing that which we are meant to do. I ponder this concept today, as I acknowledge my professional journey.

From teaching nouns and verbs in Malcolm X Shabazz High School, to fighting with the vacuum cord in the household department, to running the Kripalu kitchen, to administrating the resident health department, to running Retreat and Renewal: like stepping stones, I have been taken forward toward my truth, toward my dharma. It's not over yet, yet I am so profoundly blessed. Blessed I am, too, to add the title "writer" to this eclectic listing.

The words of a Leonard Cohen song resonate in my head:

"You chose this journey
Long before
You stepped upon
The highway."

39. Faith, Unfolding
The Present

Quite frankly, I find life quite a lot to deal with. Reality is radically relentless, and continues to bestow upon me (without my consent) wave upon wave of new life events, perfectly tailored for my growth and evolution. Left to my own devices on this ride of a lifetime, I would focus on the negative, think the worst about myself and life around me, sink beneath the waves of my own destructive thoughts, and interpret my sensations and feelings harmfully. I am surely my own worst enemy in this regard. Yet I continue to cobble together a faith that works, a faith that, unfolding, gives me a context for life events; that tells me that this moment is not a disaster yet again coming "to get me"; that I am protected and cared for, no matter the external circumstances.

This faith, this perspective, this context for my life is very much a work in progress, and I am most imperfect in my practice of it. Yet without it I would not have made it this far. Without it, I would be fully and tragically lost. That's not to say that today I am necessarily always found. But I am certainly more comfortable being occasionally adrift. I spend a good portion of my time floating along the waves of my life contentedly and with open-hearted gratitude. This is truly remarkable, and occurs only when I am able to soften around reality and accept it as it is. My developing muscle of faith makes this possible.

The spiritual practices that build this daily container of faith are a combination of 12 Step philosophy and the ancient art of living yoga, spiced with delicious seasonings from a renewed connection to Reform Judaism, the religion of my upbringing. These three pillars of my belief flow perfectly together without contradiction, without conflict, seamlessly supporting each other, beautifully representing the same eternal truths: life is safe, there is nothing wrong here, and I am not alone.

12 step principles got me sober when I first stumbled into the rooms of AA and keep me sober today. They carry in them simplicity of practice, a daily immersion into truths that diffuse my addictive personality and open me to the possibility of transformation. They also carry in them a way of living, a path of right relationship with reality that impacts and improves the quality of my life in all its arenas.

The first three steps of the 12 Step program tell me that I am powerless over the addictive substances in my life, as I am powerless over life circumstances. It tells me that there is a power greater than myself that I can look to and with which I can come into relationship, a source that can bring to me more power than my meager ego and crazy mind can ever muster. And it teaches me that my responsibility is to continually make a decision to return to that relationship, the awareness of that which is greater than myself. That is my work, to come into alignment with this passive and all-powerful grace.

For the last five years of my twenty years of active drinking and drugging, I tried to control my intake. I lived by a set of self-inflicted, shifting, and ever-changing rules and regulations: no *x* drug until after work, no *y* drug until Friday night, no *z* alcoholic intake until a special occasion. I attempted to control, to be powerful over the screeching locomotive of my cravings. It never worked. My boundaries always evaporated in an unconscious instant of desire. I could not stop drinking and drugging, even as I began to become aware that the substances were no longer working and that my life was not pretty. I was a mess and I was beginning to see that. Nevertheless, I couldn't change it myself. Even Albert Einstein, that famous spiritual practitioner, says that the mind that creates the problem cannot be the sole solution to that problem.

I'm learning to practice creating "conscious contact," to imagine, to assume, to pretend, to begin to believe that there is a benevolent force around me, protecting me and caring for me. This completely reframes my original life doctrine of, "I fall upon the thorns of life, I bleed," which I inked upon the inside of my high school binder. That philosophy morphed itself into a slightly more mature perspective of, "Life sucks and then you die," which I lived by for many, many years. I no longer believe that today.

Creating conscious contact does not have to look like a mystical, wrapping-my-leg-around-my-neck-on-the-yoga-mat experience. It can be: hugging a doggie, mowing a lawn, soaking in a hot tub, walking in the woods, calling a dear friend, driving down a stunning country road, or asking for help during a scary moment. Anything that quiets my mind, anything that reminds me that I am not alone, anything that takes me away from my fear and toward relaxation—I believe that is conscious contact.

AA taught me not to pick up that first drink, and to substitute that action with anything positive. It taught me that it was the first drink that got me drunk, a very confusing concept in the beginning. I always thought it was the fourth drink that did me in, that numbers one, two, and three were good to go. And it taught me the brilliant concept of "just for today." It is just one day in which I have to practice all of this. It is not for forever, not about tomorrow, not focused on next Wednesday afternoon. Today and only today becomes my focus. I can handle today—it is manageable. Next Wednesday afternoon gets overwhelming and frightening.

These principles apply to all my life. They tell me that life is not coming to hurt me, not coming to take something away from me. Life comes to heal me, to grow me, and if I don't pick up, I will receive more than I can imagine in return. This is my sober experience. No matter how terrifying, how overwhelming the situation—the ending of the Kripalu community, the collapse of my professional world as it knew it, the dying of my mother—not picking up a drink or a drug, staying in awareness that something else is running the show, and outliving my trauma-induced feelings of loss, grief, and terror always brings me into a better, more appropriate expression of my life.

This I know to be true.

The Big Book of AA, its official literature, says that "either God is everything or God is nothing." To me this translates as that catchy witticism, "It's all good." That for me is a much more comfortable platform to stand on than my original strategy for life, "Why the fuck does this always happen to me?" The Big Book also tells me that I get to practice this, and that "I will not always feel inspired." I love that! I'm allowed to do it imperfectly, as long as I don't drink or drug. The rest is practice, the cultivation of conscious awareness of the moment.

Everything I need exists in a 12 Step meeting. If all I did was to attend them, my life would continue to unfold with brilliance and grace.

And yet, I have been given much, much more. I think of the Hebrew concept of "dayanu," meaning, it is enough. Dayanu, my 12 Step support, would have been enough for a fabulous and free life. Yet I have been given yogic philosophy to flesh out the concept of "right relationship" with reality. It makes my life richer and anchored in the body.

When I speak of yoga, I am describing much more than simply the hatha yoga practice, the yoga of postures. Yoga is a six-thousand-year-old art of living, with many limbs of teaching, practice, and philosophy. Its philosophy focuses on direct experience of the moment in the body. Its core teaching is the practice of being present with what is.

My relationship to hatha yoga, yoga on the mat, has always been one of ambivalence and inconsistency. I practice not seeing myself as a hypocrite and shithead yogi because of this, but I work to include body-centered activities that return me to an awareness of my body. And I continue exploring my blocks regarding my on-the-mat practice. But yogic philosophy, the off-the-mat practice, has made my daily life so much richer.

Yoga is about living in direct experience with life as it is happening through the feelings in the body, rather than interpreting it through the filter of the mind. It is about quieting the mind and allowing the body to be present with what is. One of its core practices, cultivating awareness of the moment, has been a rallying point for me. The yogis teach us that wounding and trauma live in the body. Life in its perfection triggers these traumas, for our healing, for the release of the tightly held energy blocks. Even the very feelings I have been denying and running from are doorways home, doorways to more energy, more grace, more freedom.

The moment is safe, the moment is holy. As I notice what is happening, be it my dying mother's last breath or a squabble with my boss, I am given a choice of response. I no longer have to be victim to my own wild and erratic responses. Instead of putting all of my life energy toward attempting to control life around me and the feelings inside of me—both pretty damn futile activities—the paradigm shifts. It becomes less important what happens than what my response to the external event is. I am learning to relax around what happens, to feel it, to practice letting it go. Life comes, life goes. The Bible tells us, "It came to pass." It does not tell us that it came to stay. This muscle of flexibility and release is one I continually explore, sometimes more effectively than other times. But I practice.

Yoga tells us that allowing imperfection to be is the doorway to perfection; that befriending the fear is the pathway to faith; that accepting ourselves as we are is the doorway to right action and change. It is a generous, spacious, inviting perspective. For all of the years I drove myself, for all of the years that, wracked with shame, I tried to do my life "right" and failed, I now get to relax. Now I can relax, see my fear, know it is as inevitable and sacred as my faith, and know that I can't have one without the other.

For me, the body-centered perspective of yoga perfectly anchors the 12 Step principles into a daily, workable system for living. If it's happening, it's okay. It's about passionately living my life, going for what I want and believe, and letting go of the results of my actions. Passionate non-attachment is a profound gift to me today.

Yet something was still missing. A year or so after the explosion of the ashram, although I attended my 12 Step meetings consistently throughout those years as I have on a regular basis since 1986, I began to miss a practice of devotion. To me, devotion implies the opening of my heart, the relaxing of my mind, the reconnection to my spirit, the regaining of a perspective. So I did some temple-hopping, to see if Judaism held any relevancy for me.

The first several synagogues felt either stodgy or contrived, too Hebrew-orientated (a language I did not know), too heady or too formal. And then I wandered my way to Hevreh of Southern Berkshire, a reform temple about twenty-five minutes from my home. Being extremely cautious about "religious community," having been there and done that, I peeked into the experience with great hesitancy, but also with a great longing.

Walking into the building, I could hear the melody of a prayer being sung. Its familiarity, its ancient resonance in my being, brought tears to my eyes. Something in my heart opened, and has not yet shut. Sitting in that congregation over the years has reunited me with the melody, the ritual, the feeling that already lives in my cellular self. I am a Jew—it is that simple. To sit in the presence of Jewish ritual, made relevant and interesting by a profoundly skillful rabbi, has been the spiritual icing on the cake. Rabbi Deborah Zecher is a funny, brilliant, relational woman who has held Hevreh in loving arms and heart for many years, and brings a perspective, social conscience, and commitment to "mending the world"—something that I so need.

I started to go to Friday evening Shabbat services. R., my non-Jewish Southern belle who never knew a Jew until graduate school, fell in love with the warmth of the prayers, the rhythm of the music, and the depth of the liturgy, alongside of me. Thanks to transliteration, the English spelling out of the Hebrew, I no longer feel different since I can't read Hebrew. I manage well enough. We attend most holiday services, and attempt to go to Shabbat services. It releases the week's struggles and renews connection to heart, a good and essential thing.

When my father died, I used the Jewish rituals of mourning with a half-hearted involvement. Because of my fear of the unknowns, my grieving process was muffled and disjointed. But when my mom died, being simply more present and more alive to the circumstances, the pain was riveting, overwhelming, breathtaking. I needed something to help me through. I made commitment to 90-and-90, 90 AA meetings in 90 days. That really began to weave the days together, helping me to relax in the container of support AA offered me.

But it was the Jewish ritual of mourning that literally carried me through. The prayer of grieving, the Kaddish, is said regularly for the first year after a death. I found the prayer overwhelming and had great fear about learning it, since it was in obscure Aramaic, an archaic language. In telling our assistant rabbi, Andy Klein, about my fears, he smiled and reached into his desk. He handed me a CD with his voice slowly repeating Jewish prayers, for Hebrew-phobic folks just like me; I really wasn't unique. Every morning for that year I drove to work and said Kaddish in my car with Rabbi Andy. We had our own minyan, our own congregation, our own sacred and intimate gathering of two. And I learned the prayer. On Friday nights at Shabbat service, I would stand and speak my mother's name aloud along with the other recent mourners. Then the rest of the congregation would stand and join us.

It is a fascinating prayer, its literal meaning "holy." It is a doxology, a listing of God's holy attributes:

> *"Blessed,*
>
> *praised and honored,*
>
> *extolled and glorified,*
>
> *adored and exalted."*

Its sounds and rhythms comforted me. Its ritual of standing and speaking my mother's name grounded me. Its literal meaning, the praising of God, turned me away from loss and death, back to love and living. It profoundly impacted me, and carried me through that first year. After the first year, the prayer is recited in unison with the congregation, but the name of the lost one is only repeated during a few holidays and on the *yyahrzeit*, the anniversary of the death. I took my place as a Jewish mourner and was given a way back to life.

Speaking my mother's name aloud; having this architecture of time, from Friday to Friday, built into the timeless emptiness of my days; having a structure in which to mourn—all were profound gifts to me from Judaism. It worked. Time passed. The pain changed. The loss is integrating into my life.

I am beyond blessed, and have all angles covered. My 12 Step program, the art of living the yogic paradigm, the deliciousness of my Jewish core—dayanu. Any of the three would be enough. When put together, I am abundantly able to practice living simply and authentically in a complex and confusing world.

So here I sit, on the hinge of turning sixty. I could easily flip into fear of the unknown, and I sometimes do. Economic insecurity, the financial impossibility of retirement, the dangerous insanity of the world at large, the shapeless form my aging might take without an offspring to bring me bananas and take me to the urologist, the inevitable physical changes and breakdowns I will be given—all these and more are areas of potentially looming terror. But truthfully, just for today, I am fine.

I know, one day at a time, if I do my best, if I show up, the quality of my life is not dependent on any external factor.

Just for today, I know that if I don't pick up a drink or a drug, I will continue to heal.

Just for today, I know that whatever life brings me, I will have the capacity to muddle through it.

Just for today, I know that I am indeed safely held in the arms of something much vaster than myself.

Just for today.

Epilogue
Recovering My Voice
Just For Today

It seemed as if I had been traveling forever.

When I began this book some months ago, I wrote that as the first sentence of the first chapter. I remember thinking then, "Hum. I wonder if that sentence would work, too, as the first sentence of the final chapter?" And as I sit here on this rainy, dark September morning, the two Doodles conked out on their couch, this last chapter lies invisible and silent upon my blank computer page. Yes, it seems as if I have been traveling forever. It is an appropriate sentiment to open the curtain onto these final pages.

I face my sixtieth birthday this coming winter. Birthdays and aging in general have not been too difficult for me. At forty, I was jubilant. At forty-five, I was empowered. At fifty, I was "woman, hear me roar." At fifty-five, although quieted down a bit, I celebrated. However, the last few years have heralded in a new era of aging, replete with some significant body changes—eyes that grow fuzzy and blurry, feet that don't fit into shoes all that well. Combined with the general craziness of the world and concerns of financial insecurity, the number "sixty" has rattled me. Yes, of course, I know it is the new forty. And yes, I know, too, I look "really young" and am "relatively healthy and fit." Yet the echo of this upcoming decade has continued to haunt me.

In muttering and moaning my aging issues to my dearest friend, Audrey, this summer, her response, consistent with her kind strength and capacity to hold me accountable, ran something like this:

Me:"Holy shit, sixty."

Aud:"And?"

Me:"Holy shit, sixty."

Aud:"So what do you want to do?

Me:"What do you mean?"

Aud:"What do you want to do that you haven't done yet?"

Me;"Oh, you mean like *The Bucket List*, that horrible movie?"

Aud:"Yes."

Me;"Write a book. I always wanted to write a book."

Aud:"So write the damn book already."

And in that instant, the time had arrived. I knew it from inside, out. The ultimate birthday present for myself, the gift that I always wanted to receive, my own focused commitment to write, had come of age. For my fortieth birthday present, I gave myself a year at Kripalu. And for my sixtieth birthday present, I gave myself the permission, the focus, the time, the willingness to confront the blank pages of my life, and to invite the words to emerge.

I've learned from the process, the structure of the writing itself. It has been: effortless, nerve-wracking, beyond insightful, revealing, funny, amusing, humbling, heart-squeezing, bigger-than-valuable, and, most importantly, possible. The process has been possible. One word informed the next, one chapter revealed its following companion. That which during my entire life was impossible, became real, became possible. I have been given yet another major lesson in patience and tolerance. I insist on believing that every moment in my life before my sitting down at my computer made me ready for that opening sentence.

Every single moment, even and perhaps especially the painful ones, made me ready to say:

It seemed as if I had been traveling forever.

At how many junctures in my life, at how many moments, did I chafe at the process, the timing? In how many moments did I want what wasn't happening, did I push and pull myself toward what I thought *should* be happening? I have heard it said that we live within God's timetable and we need to cooperate and work within it. We do the footwork, we do the rowing. But ultimately something greater than ourselves directs the boat. Ultimately there needs to be a divine intervention to make manifest that which is meant to be.

This I know to be true.

I have learned so much from the content, these stories, my remembered adventures of my life. Although these are stories I've told my entire life, writing them down, weaving them together and inviting the themes to emerge, has been astounding. The theme of voice, although not surprising, snuck up on me. I was peering anxiously at these pages, thinking "journey." Journey is the core theme here. The images of traveling, being on the road, excited me and interested me. Yet remembering the child that I was, silent and speechless, growing into the stuttering, terrified little girl, riveted my attention, and it suddenly hit me: that *is* my journey. Yes! From silence to stuttering to the gift of voice, that is the sparkling gem hidden in all these words. Clearly the deepest trauma unfolds into the greatest gift, with the presence of consciousness and healing. The greatest block in my life, my inability to speak, has become my most profound gift to offer others. The most blocked of obstacles becomes the greatest channel for energy, healing, and God.

This I know to be true.

I have become a talker. I talk to store clerks, waitresses, people in elevators, children in grocery stores, bank tellers. Strangers are easier and much more powerful an experience for me than people I know, since I am too attached to outcome and more self-conscious with familiar folks. My father was one of life's finest schmoozers, something that, as a kid, tended to embarrass me. Yet, always his daughter, I seem to be following in his verbal footsteps. Sometimes I almost embarrass myself, but it is so rich, so good, and so worth it to be verbally out there. I learn so much, receive so much, from these random and sacred interactions. They call forth the goodness, the god-ness in these "strangers." The spiritual principle of the Sanskrit greeting, *Jai Bhagwan, I honor the spirit in you*, operates automatically in me. May the God in me unite with the God in you. Talking has become my bridge. I practically cannot help myself. This spiritual practice is a place in my life in which I receive great solace, great pleasure, and great beauty. I must believe that as I offer that out, so do I receive it. Quite a leap from little Nan, sitting in her desk in school, feverishly counting the kids between her and the terror of having to recite her line of "The Highwayman."

This I know to be true.

And, taken to another level, the gift of voice operates profoundly in my teaching and coaching work. My greatest strength is verbally navigating in the void of the unknown. Without sounding too New Age-ish, if I am relaxed and in a relatively fit spiritual condition—which for me means attending to exercise, right nutrition, healthy sleep patterns, inspiration, and connection with others—words are simply available to me. They do not come to me via a thought process. Yes, of course, I come into a teaching session with a sense of the core teachings that serve as objectives, and with the structure through which I want to explore those concepts. But then I dive off a platform, leaving conscious thought behind me, and I splash into the waters of a very cooling and reliable intuition. I have words. In teaching, in coaching, I have words that work, that touch, that pray, that soothe, that confront, that integrate, that relax, that heal. This is not because of my own doing. This is just simply so. Thinking about the stuttering trauma that once engulfed me, this outcome, so many years later, astonishes me.

This I know to be true.

I do not believe that there has been an extraneous moment or experience in my life. I believe that each and all of my life events have brought me to this perfect moment. Hearing myself in these pages reliving the depths of confusion around my sexual identity, the horrors and self-hatred that ran me during my active addiction, the self-consciousness, the perfectionism, the lack of self-esteem that almost killed me again and again, has been immensely humbling. And today I believe that each of those hideous moments of pain and disconnection was essential to my development. More than that, today I believe that each and every one of those moments is sacred.

This I know to be true.

The concept of non-duality teaches us that God or divine force is in everything. The fear and the faith, the hopelessness and the hope, the darkness and the light are all equally sacred and inevitable—you cannot have one without the other. The traditional philosophy of Tantric Yoga teaches us that God is available here, in this human moment. Goodness and grace are not up ahead, not some day, not the end result of doing enough yoga, enough prayer or meditation. Now. God is here now. In the stuttering child. In the terrified little girl who wanted her Zorro sword. In the lost and frightened addict on the beach under the full moon, screaming out her loneliness. It is all Grace disguised as human experience.

This I know to be true.

The Big Book of Alcoholics Anonymous says that "God is either everything or God is nothing."

Surely God was in my mother's final breath.

This I know to be true.

The Sh'Ma, the cornerstone of Jewish liturgy, says, "Hear oh, Israel, the Lord our God, the Lord is One." It is all Grace.

This I know to be true.

The Tao Te Ching so beautifully says:

> *"Being and non-being create each other.*
> *Difficult and easy support each other.*
> *Long and short define each other.*
> *High and low depend on each other.*
> *Before and after follow each other."*

And I say:

I have traveled long. I am both tired and renewed, hopeless and filled with possibility. I am that young, terrified child. I am a sober and centered adult. I am frightened and alone. I am inspired and ultimately connected.

It's all true. It's all sacred. It's all inevitable.

Today I pray for the willingness to let life be exactly as it is.

Today I pray for patience and tolerance for the process of change.

Today I pray for loving kindness and offer, with ultimate humility, this prayer:

May you be healthy.

May you be happy.

May you ride the waves of your life.

May you live in peace, no matter what you're given.

Our evolving family

Home at last.

Photo Credits

Page 141.   MXS amphitheater
                   By Dina Kageler

Page 152.   Seneca Peace Camp
                   By Catherine Allport

Page 161.   MXS Kids
                   By Dina Kageler

Page 280.   Buzzie and Me
                   By Adam Mastoon

Page 289.   R. & A.—Kripalu Wedding
                   By Adam Mastoon

Page 337.   Our Evolving Family
                   By Adam Mastoon

All other photos are from the author's family album.
Author Photo (back cover)
by Adam Mastoon
Cover designed by Derek Hansen.

CPSIA information can be obtained
at www.ICGtesting.com
Printed in the USA
FFHW021419090119
50112515-54977FF